THE MORTGAGING OF CHURCH PROPERTY

THE CATHOLIC UNIVERSITY OF AMERICA
CANON LAW STUDIES
No. 169

THE MORTGAGING OF CHURCH PROPERTY

A HISTORICAL SYNOPSIS AND COMMENTARY

BY

REV. JOSEPH BERNARD STENGER, J.C.L.
Priest of the Diocese of Belleville

A DISSERTATION

Submitted to the Faculty of Canon Law of the Catholic University of America in Partial Fulfillment of the Requirements for the Degree of Doctor of Canon Law

THE CATHOLIC UNIVERSITY OF AMERICA PRESS
WASHINGTON, D. C.
1942

NIHIL OBSTAT:
HIERONYMUS D. HANNAN, A.M., LL.B., S.T.D., J.C.D.
Censor Deputatus
Washingtonii, D. C., die I Iunii, 1942.

IMPRIMATUR:
✠HENRICUS ALTHOFF, D.D.
Episcopus Bellevillensis
Bellevillii, Ill., die X Iunii, 1942.

Copyright 1942
by
THE CATHOLIC UNIVERSITY OF AMERICA PRESS

MURRAY & HEISTER, WASHINGTON, D. C.
Printed in the United States of America

9

To

His Excellency

The Most Reverend Henry Althoff, D.D.

Bishop of Belleville

TABLE OF CONTENTS

PART ONE

PRELIMINARY NOTIONS AND HISTORICAL SYNOPSIS

PART TWO

CANONICAL COMMENTARY

FOREWORD

THE word mortgage in its present-day connotation has been born and reborn. Great voids are found in history wherein the term was not used at all. Often when it was used its meaning was not clear. To exhaust adequately the possibilities of the subject of this dissertation it would be necessary to study the financial condition of the Church in all periods of history to see its bearing on the presence or absence of mortgages on Church property, and to study the civil law of the nations where the property was situated to see whether there existed any differences between the national or racial concept and the ecclesiastical idea of the term. Time and space do not permit such an exhaustive treatment, though undoubtedly much of interest lies behind the ecclesiastical legal enactments relative to mortgaging. The historical part of this dissertation is therefore limited with a definite purpose in mind, namely, to prepare the way for a proper treatment of the present-day legislation.

Because the first laws regarding the subject were made by the Roman Emperors and because the Church for centuries used "mortgage" in the Roman law sense, a chapter will be devoted to this foundation of succeeding concepts.

The writer has no intention of comprehensively treating the American mortgage law, but because mortgage is a concept of civil law and because the Code canonizes the civil law of the present day in the matter of contracts, a chapter will trace the mortgage idea through early French, English, and American law with an explanation of the different theories of modern mortgages in the United States.

There often arise certain questions the importance of which cannot be denied. In order to find the variable or invariable answer of history and the answer of modern legislation, this monograph will restrict its study to the canonical laws in history and in the Code regarding the following questions: Was and is mortgaging a species of alienation? What solemnities were and are required for the contracting of mortgages on Church property?

Did and do penalties for illegal alienation apply also to mortgaging? Because of the divergent opinions before the Code and in view of the absence of an altogether satisfactory definition of the concept of alienation as the Code treats of it, space seemingly out of proportion to a treatise on mortgaging had to be allotted to the definition and projection of the idea of alienation. Because in many points of law relating to these questions the legislation has been changed by the Code, the treatment of the historical and modern legislation will be separated. A chapter will be devoted to each question in both the historical synopsis and the canonical commentary. Chapters III and VII deal with the first question; IV and VIII, with the second; and V and IX, with the third.

The writer wishes to express his deep appreciation to His Excellency, the Most Reverend Henry Althoff, D.D., Bishop of Belleville, for the opportunity of advanced study and for his many kindnesses in the preparation and publication of this dissertation. To him and to all those, especially the members of the Faculty of the School of Canon Law, who assisted in its preparation, the writer is sincerely grateful.

PART ONE

PRELIMINARY NOTIONS AND HISTORICAL SYNOPSIS

CHAPTER I

Preliminary Notions

In Canon law, as in Roman law, the word for mortgage is *hypotheca.* Though the origin of the word is disputed, the name seems to indicate that it was borrowed from the Greeks, and it is easy to see why it might have evolved from ὑπο, under, and τιθέναι, to put.[1] Whenever the word *hypotheca* appears in historical documents it will be translated as meaning mortgage even though its use at the time may not have had the same purpose of signification that American law now has. Until 1918 the Church had always used mortgage in the sense of the Roman law of Justinian's time.[2] Naturally the complexity and divergencies of State laws not based upon Roman law must have caused the administrators of Church property many difficulties. In trying to determine the extent of their ability to act and the method of procedure to be followed in their desire to observe the Canons, they wanted at the same time to be law-abiding citizens of their respective localities.

An indication of what was to come was given when the Sacred Congregation of the Propagation of the Faith ordered the Bishops and religious Superiors in the United States to make their last wills and testaments according to the laws of the State

---

1 For the discussion as to its origin, cf. Manigk in Pauly-Wissowa-Kroll, *Real-Encyclopadie der classischen Altertumswissenschaft* (Stuttgart, 1914), Vol. 9i, col. 343. Cf. also Merlinus, *De Pignoribus et Hypothecis Tractatus Absolutissimus* (Venetiis, 1649), lib. I, tit. I, q. 2, n. 1. Hereafter cited *De Pignoribus.*

2 Cf. Schmalzgrueber, *Jus Ecclesiasticum Universum* (5 vols. in 12, Romae, 1843–1845), lib. III, tit. 21, nn. 2 and 3 (hereafter cited Schmalzgrueber); Wernz-Vidal, *Ius Canonicum* (7 tom. in 8 vols., Romae: Apud Aedes Universitatis Gregorianiae, 1927–1938. Tom. IV, Vol. II, 1935; Tom. VII, 1937), Tom. IV, Vol. II, n. 844; Cocchi, *Commentarium in Codicem Iuris Canonici* (8 vols., Taurinorum Augustae: Marietti, 1931–1940. Vol. I, 5. ed., 1938; Vol. II, 4. ed., 1937; Vol. III, 3. ed., 1931; Vol. IV, 3. ed., 1932; Vol. V, 5. ed., 1932; Vol. VI, 3. ed., 1933; Vol. VII, 3. ed., 1940; Vol. VIII, 4. ed., 1938), VI, n. 211 (hereafter cited *Commentarium*).

in which they lived, to this end that Church property might be conveyed to their successors in the proper legal manner.[3] From this provision it was only a logical step to issue canon 1529 which orders the state laws of any particular territory to be used in the drafting of any contract, provided there is no contravention of the Divine law or of other canonical enactments. Therefore, since 1918 the term *hypotheca* of Canon law[4] must be understood in the light of State law, and in this monograph it is limited to the laws in force in the United States.

In American law there is a primary distinction into mortgages of real property, and mortgages of personal property. The latter are called chattel mortgages.[5] The former can be subdivided into legal and equitable mortgages.

A legal mortgage, both in title theory states and in the more numerous lien theory states,[6] is made in the form of a deed of conveyance by the mortgagor to the mortgagee with a defeasance clause, i.e., an agreement making the conveyance null and void upon payment of the debt. In lien theory states this conveyance of the legal title results only in creating a lien at law. In some statutory states no conveyance is used but the mortgagor simply "mortgages" his property to the mortgagee.[7] The result is the same in all the states in that only a legal lien is created.

Equitable mortgages are those in which money is loaned or credit is given by A to B, with A relying on the security of B's property, which B had pledged in a way which leaves him with-

---

[3] S. C. de Prop. Fide, decr. 15 dec. 1840—*Collectanea S. Congregationis de Propaganda Fide* (2 vols., Romae: Typographia Polyglotta S. C. de Propaganda Fide, 1907), n. 916. Hereafter cited *Coll. S. C. P. F.* Cf. also *Acta et Decreta Concilii Plenarii Baltimorensis Tertii, A. D. MDCCCLXXXIV* (Baltimorae: Typis Joannis Murphy et Sociorum, 1886), n. 270, concerning contracts generally.

[4] C. 1538. This is the only canon of the Code in which the word appears.

[5] *The College Law Dictionary* (Rochester, New York: The Lawyers Co-operative Publishing Company, 1931), s. v. "chattel mortgage"; cf. also 5 R. C. L. 383.

[6] Cf. *infra*, Chapter VI, p. 69, for explanation of title, lien, statutory and Common Law states.

[7] Cal. Civ. Code (Deering, 1925) #2498—quoted in Walsh, *A Treatise on Mortgages* (Chicago: Callaghan and Company, 1934), p. 33, note 112. Hereafter cited *On Mortgages.*

out the protection given a mortgage at law, viz., a legal mortgage. This type of mortgage dates back to the fifteenth century and seems to have been construed as a result of error in drafting what should otherwise have been legal mortgages. Absolute conveyances made to secure loans were unenforceable as mortgages at law because they lacked a defeasance clause. In this type of mortgage the borrower has a mere equity and no right at law. The grantee, A, on the other hand, has a legal title in both lien and common law states alike, though equity intervenes to relieve the grantor, B, from forfeiting his property should the grantee refuse to reconvey (the title) when the debt is paid or an offer to pay is made. This establishing of the transfer of title as a mere mortgage is done by parol evidence, since evidence of error, fraud, and other bases for equitable adjustment rarely appear in the written document. The parol evidence rule was never intended as a barrier to proof of such facts. The real danger of equitable mortgages lies in the fact that even in lien states the holder of the title at law might convey the legal title to an innocent purchaser for value without notice, and thereby cut off the mortgagor's purely equitable right of redemption. In trying to determine whether any certain transaction is a sale for a price or an equitable mortgage the most important factor is the *quid pro quo.* A mortgage loan is rarely above sixty percent of the fair value of the mortgaged property, and thus if the amount paid is far less than the fair value of the property there is good evidence that the contract was a mortgage and not a sale. Other evidences of a mortgage are retention of possession by the borrower after the loan is made, subsequent payment of taxes by the borrower, and payment of interest by the borrower.[8]

Other types of equitable mortgages are those arising from an *offering* of property as security for a loan made, or credit actually given (not a promise to loan or give credit), in reliance upon such security. This type includes: written documents which seemingly evidence the offering of property as security for a loan but which for some reason do not produce the desired effect, viz., a legal mortgage; written contracts to give a mortgage; unwritten contracts to give a mortgage; written contracts or contracts

[8] Walsh, *op. cit.*, pp. 34–40.

proven by parol evidence that the property shall be security for the loan.[9]

Hence it can be seen that, while in the latter cases an equitable mortgage is construed without any conveyance, the difference between the legal and equitable mortgages when a conveyance is given is that in the former the conveyance contains a defeasance clause, while in the latter the conveyance is absolute in form or contains a privilege of repurchase. If the conveyance of title and a written defeasance are executed and delivered separately, but as part of the same transaction, the two instruments are understood to be complementary and effect a legal mortgage.[10] We can therefore define a legal mortgage as a transfer of title or other interest in land (property) to secure the performance of some obligation, the conveyance of which is to become void on the due performance thereof.[11]

The real property considered herein is limited as to its kind, namely Church property. But even here qualification is necessary because Canon 1497 defines ecclesiastical property as comprising both corporeal, whether movable or immovable, and incorporeal goods. Corporeal goods are those which can be recognized by the senses, as a house, money, a field, etc., while incorporeal goods are those which have not this quality of being sensible but must be recognized directly by the intellect, as rights, obligations, actions, etc. The corporeal property is divided further into movable and immovable goods, the former being those which can be transferred from place to place without jeopardizing or destroying their integrity, as money, furniture, utensils, etc., and the latter being those which would suffer this loss in the transfer,

---

[9] *Op. cit.*, p. 52.

[10] *Op. cit.*, p. 72.

[11] R. C. L. 243. Any interest in land which may be the subject of sale, grant, or assignment may be mortgaged—Tiffany, *A Treatise on the Modern Law of Real Property and Other Interests in Land* (2 vols. in 1, Chicago, 1912), p. 1170. Hereafter cited *Real Property*. The conveyance of an estate or property by way of pledge for the security of a debt, and to become void on payment of it—*The Cyclopedic Law Dictionary*, s. v. "mortgage." That kind of pledge in which the possession of the thing pledged remains with the debtor; the obligation resting on mere contract.—4 Kent. Comm. 136 s. v. "hypotheca."

as a plot of ground, a building, etc.[12] The distinction between movable and immovable property is considered, for practical purposes, in American law, as the distinction between personal property and real property.

By "ecclesiastical" is meant that property belonging either to the Universal Church or to any other moral person having a juridical existence within the Church,[13] as individual dioceses, parishes, hospitals, orphan asylums, seminaries, and other institutes destined for religious or charitable purposes.[14]

The moral persons spoken of are those who have received a canonical juristic personality as a result of an ecclesiastical act of administration. Since no canonical moral personality can exist which does not derive its authority from the Church, their creation is reserved to the ecclesiastical authorities, and requires a formal decree of erection. Hence it is the property of these formally created ecclesiastical juristic personalities only which has the nature of ecclesiastical property. The goods of organizations of Catholic people, with either previous or subsequent ecclesiastical approval alone, are not ecclesiastical goods and do not therefore fall under the laws of the Code.[15] Property of an

---

[12] Cocchi, *Commentarium*, III, n. 169. Cf. also Doheny, *Church Property: Modes of Acquisition*, The Catholic University of America Canon Law Studies, No. 41 (Washington, D. C.: The Catholic University of America, 1927), p. 31 (hereafter cited *Church Property*); Lesne, *Histoire de la Propriété Ecclésiastique en France*, Tome III *L'inventaire de la Propriété. Églises et trésors des Églises du commencement du VIIIe a la fin du XIe siècle* (Lille: Facultés Catholiques, 1936), pp. 85–131; Santi, *Praelectiones Juris Canonici juxta ordinem Decretalium Gregorii IX* (2 vols., Rathisbonae, Neo Eboraci, Cincinnati, 1886), lib. III, tit. 21, nn. 4 and 5. Hereafter cited Santi.

[13] Canons 1497, §1, 1498; Pirhing, *Jus Canonicum Nova Methodo Explicatum* (5 vols. in 4, Dilingae, 1674–1678), lib. III, tit. 13, n. 1 (hereafter cited Pirhing); *Periodica de re Canonica et Morali utili Praesertim Religiosis et Missionariis* (editio altera, Bruges, 1905–), IV (1913), 326. Hereafter cited *Periodica*.

[14] Can. 1489, §1; c. 2, *de religiosis domibus*, III, 2, in *Clem;* Wernz, *Ius Decretalium* (2. ed., 6 vols., Romae et Prati, 1905–1913), III, n. 155.

[15] Can. 100. Cf. also Brown, *The Canonical Juristic Personality with Special Reference to its Status in the United States of America*, The Catholic University of America Canon Law Studies, No. 39 (Washington, D. C., 1927), pp. 92–94. Hereafter cited *Juristic Personality*. (For a list of what Ecclesiastical Superiors can erect what moral personalities, see

institution not separately canonically erected but attached to an existing ecclesiastical moral person is considered ecclesiastical.[16]

What properties can be mortgaged? The answer is implicitly contained in the answer to the question, "What properties can be alienated?" Since the Code withdraws no property from that which can be alienated through the observance of the proper form,[17] it would seem any property is mortgageable even though it be blessed or consecrated.

The idea, therefore, that a consecrated church must remain debt free is unfounded in the general law.[18] The Code regards ecclesiastical property that is consecrated as *bona sacra.*[19] This envisions the possibility of a sacred thing being in the ownership of private individuals.[20] There is no reason to exclude a church.

If it is admitted that a church can be private property, it follows that it can be mortgaged.[21] Too, the Code legislates against increasing the sale or exchange price of a sacred object, because of its added consecration or blessing,[22] and there is no reason to exclude a church from the sacred objects here protected. If it can be sold, a church can therefore also be mortgaged. A case is reported in which a parish priest of Lausanne, Switzerland, with his Ordinary supporting the petition, asked the S. Congregation of the Council for permission to mortgage a parochial church. After an initial refusal the permission was granted on June 15, 1918, as a special favor with the provision that care be taken to avoid any detrimental results from the transaction. It can be noted that this permission was granted almost a month after the

---

Brown, *op. cit.*, pp. 92–93.) An example of non-ecclesiastical goods is the property of St. Vincent de Paul Societies—Bouscaren, *The Canon Law Digest* (2 vols. and Supplement—1941, Milwaukee; Bruce, 1934–1941), I, 714. Hereafter cited Bouscaren.

[16] Cf. Hannan, "The Local Ordinary's Guardianship of Church Property,"—*The Jurist,* I (1941), 317–328, esp. p. 325.

[17] C. 1530 speaks of movable and immovable properties while C. 1532 §1, 1° merely decrees special solemnities for a portion of these which might also be precious.

[18] Bishops could issue particular laws to this effect.

[19] C. 1497, §2.

[20] Cf. C. 1510, §1.

[21] Cf. Nevin, in *The Australasian Catholic Record* (Manly, 1923–), X (1933), 349. Hereafter cited *ACR.*

[22] C. 1539, §1.

Code went into effect (May 19, 1918). If there were anything intrinsically illegal or wrong in such a contract, the Holy See would not have permitted the mortgage even in this one case.[23] There is a provision in the Code that if it is foreseen, previous to the consecration, that a church is going to be given over to a usage other than spiritual, the Ordinary is not to consecrate it.[24] But this prohibition affects also its blessing. If, therefore, the idea that a consecrated church cannot be mortgaged has this same canon for its foundation, it would mean that even a blessed church would have to remain debt free. Both these conclusions are unjustified. The only licit parallel would be this: that if the debt to be imposed on a consecrated or blessed church is so great that it is prudently foreseen the church will be turned over to profane usage as a result of the debt, the debt could not be contracted. This would be against all sound business principles besides, since a mortgage should ordinarily not be greater than sixty percent of the actual value of the building. Moreover, in permitting the mortgage to be contracted, the Ordinary before giving permission must know how and within what time the debt will be removed. Naturally, if there is no possible means of removing the debt it should not be contracted.

Once a church is consecrated, however, it is a different problem. If all the requisites demanded by Canon law and prudent business judgment are fulfilled, the church will never be lost except in most rare situations. A prudent judgment previous to mortgaging it that the church will not be lost is altogether different from a prudent judgment prior to consecrating it that the church will be lost. The former permits its mortgaging while the latter would prevent its consecration. If, with the former, circumstances occur which could not be foreseen and cause the building to pass out of the hands of the Church, Canon law provides for the method. The consecration of a church is lost through being reduced to profane usage by the Ordinary of the

---

[23] Cf. Nevin, *ibid.*, p. 350.

[24] C. 1165, §2. There is a widespread belief among the clergy that a church cannot be consecrated so long as there is a debt on it, but the origin of this opinion cannot be traced, nor is there any foundation for it in the Code.—Cf. Nevin, *ACR,* XV (1938), 260; C. 1165, §§2–4.

place.[25] This reduction is brought about whenever by official decree the Bishop permits the sale, donation, rent, or exchange of a sacred place. The provision that it must be used for a dignified purpose must always be present. The Bishop can permit the *execratio* when the church can no longer be used for divine worship or when all means *ad eam reficiendam* are lacking.[26] In other words, a grave cause is necessary, but any grave cause will suffice.[27] This method of *execratio* is an innovation by the Code from the previous legislation that permitted only the razing of the consecrated church,[28] and is probably not as yet sufficiently recognized.

In this method of *execratio* the church passes out of possession of the ecclesiastical moral person. In a mortgage possession is retained and hence no *execratio* would result until such a time as the mortgage might be foreclosed, and the *decretum execrationis* would only then be necessary. The *omnes aditus interclusi sint ad eam reficiendam* of canon 1187 would certainly be present if the moral person could not redeem the property in a foreclosure sale.[29]

May a consecrated cemetery be mortgaged? Canon 1207 says that the violation of a cemetery occurs in the same way as does the violation of a church and makes no mention of *execratio*. Violation has no effect on the consecration or even blessing of a

---

[25] C. 1170. When the Code itself provides for the method of transferring a church to the use of the laity it seems odd that Wernz-Vidal should repeat Schmalzgrueber's idea that it cannot be done. "Neque desunt casus, quibus res ecclesiasticae etiam servatis solemnitatibus alienari prohibentur, v.g. si ecclesia in usum laicorum, vel alia bona ecclesiastica cum scandalo in Hebraeum vel haereticum transferantur, . . ."—Wernz-Vidal, Tom. IV, Vol. 2, 226.

[26] C. 1187; cf. also Beste, *Introductio in Codicem* (Collegeville, Minn., 1938), p. 571. Hereafter cited Beste.

[27] Coronata, *Institutiones Iuris Canonici* (5 vols., Taurini Romae: Marietti, 1933–1939. Vols. I et II, 2. ed., 1939; Vol. III, 1933; Vol. IV, 1935; Vol. V, 1936), II, 44. Hereafter cited *Institutiones.*

[28] Vermeersch-Creusen, *Epitome Iuris Canonici* (3 vols., Mechliniac-Romae: H. Dessain, 1934–1937. Vol. I, 6. ed., 1937; Vol. II, 5. ed., 1934; Vol. III, 5. ed., 1936), II, 345. Hereafter cited *Epitome.*

[29] Coronata (*loc. cit.*) maintains that even if no cause existed, or if an error were made in judging the cause, the *execratio* would nevertheless be valid.

church and hence can have none on the consecration or blessing of a cemetery. Violation has the effect of impeding its further use before reconciliation, whereas *execratio* removes the consecration or blessing and requires a new consecration or blessing.[30]

Since the law is therefore silent regarding the *execratio* of a cemetery, we should look for a similar case in the Code and proceed along the same lines.[31] The procedure for the *execratio* of a church as contained in canons 1170 and 1187 could be used therefore in the *execratio* of a cemetery. This would in no way wound the sense of propriety and fitness of things that Catholics and non-Catholics alike enjoy regarding the proper reverence for the last resting places of their loved ones, nor would it be contrary to the mind of the Church, which regards the bodies of the dead as being the disused temples of divinely created souls and as being necessary objects of our reverence when they have been consecrated in the reception of the sacraments.

When a mortgage is given, the creditor receives a title only as clear as is possessed by the debtor. Deeds to lots or separate graves wherein bodies are already placed or will be placed are given by the ecclesiastical moral person to the " owners " of these lots or graves. Sometimes mere burial licenses are given. These deeds do not transfer ownership but, like the burial licenses, give only a private right to burial either in perpetuity or, as is more commonly held, until the bodies of those to be buried have

---

[30] Beste, pp. 562, 564. Coronata is of the opinion that there can be no *execratio* properly speaking in regard to a cemetery, because it is only blessed solemnly or simply in accordance with the directions of canon 1205, §1.—*Institutiones,* II, 93. Beste, on the other hand, holds that a place is constituted a *locus sacer* when it receives a constitutive blessing, which blessing can be of two kinds: the solemn, which is properly called consecration, and the simple (or less solemn), which is more correctly called a blessing. Consecration and blessing have this in common that they remove a place from profane hands and determine it for a sacred use, but they differ in their effect in that the consecration makes them more stably and irrevocably destined for sacred use than does the blessing; and they differ also in the manner of being constituted sacred since the consecration is effected by the use of chrism and the prescribed formula, while the blessing is effected by the use of holy water and the prescribed prayers.—Beste, pp. 552, 553. But in either case the cemetery is a *locus sacer* with the question as to its mortgageability and the solution remaining the same.

[31] C. 20.

reached the stage of thorough disintegration.[32] These previous grants of right to burial adhere to the cemetery and hence the conveyance in a mortgage would be subject to these rights. In case of foreclosure, this would prevent the conversion to other uses until such a time as no more living people intended to use their rights to burial and the bodies of those actually interred had disintegrated.

Since it has been shown that consecrated churches and cemeteries can be mortgaged, which are possibly the only kinds of property wherein a doubt would be raised, we will treat the contractual conveyance of *any* real property belonging to a juridical moral ecclesiastical person with the purpose of securing a debt and to become void on the payment thereof.

---

[32] Beste, p. 587.

CHAPTER II

ROMAN LAW

ARTICLE I. GENERAL PROVISIONS OF CIVIL LAW

THE Roman law mortgage (*hypotheca*) played an important rôle in our modern securing of property. That a creditor today has security for his loans is not a creation of recent times but can be traced almost directly to the legal genius of the Romans, who created and developed the pawn, lien, and mortgage.[1]

Originally, the nature of this security had been called *Fiducia*. In *Fiducia, dominium* and possession were passed, with an added agreement that they would be returned when the debt was paid.[2]

The next form of securing debts was by way of *Pignus*. Herein the possession of the property was given to the creditor,[3] but the ownership (*dominium*) was retained by the debtor,[4] who recovered or forfeited his property on the date due. Only if a pact (*pactum de vendendo*) supplementing the agreement was made, could the creditor sell the property on default.

The third stage in the evolution of pledges as security for loans produced the *Hypotheca*, recognized and enforced as a simple agreement (*Pactum Hypothecae*), whereby a certain amount or all of a debtor's property should be the security for his debt.[5] The great advantage of *hypotheca* lay in the fact that

---

[1] Sherman, *Roman Law in the Modern World* (3. ed., 3 vols., New Haven, 1922), II, 612 (hereafter cited *Roman Law*). "And the tendency of American Law is to regard a mortgage, although cast in the form of a conveyance of property, as a mere lien—as a pledge or security of a certain property for a debt . . . facts reveal the assimilation of the Anglo-American mortgage along the lines of the Roman *hypotheca*."—Sherman, *op. cit.*, 616.

[2] Gaius, II, 59.

[3] D. (41.3), 16; "Proprie pignus dicimus quod ad creditorem transit, hypothecam, cum non transit nec possessio ad creditorem."—D. (13.7), 9, 2.

[4] "Pignus manente proprietate debitoris solam possessionem transfert ad creditorem; . . ."—D. (13.7), 35, 1.

[5] I. (4.6), 7; D. (20.1), 4.

dominium and possession were retained by the debtor.[6] The property hypothecated was liable to sale if the debt was not paid.[7] At times, all of a debtor's property was obligated to the payment of the debt, viz., by a General mortgage,[8] while at other times only a specific portion or piece of property was agreed on as security, i.e., by a Special mortgage.[9] The latter gave the creditor a " real " right (*jus in re aliena*), in contradistinction to a " personal " right or an obligation, which was transferred in the former. But the debtor retained his " real " rights of ownership called *dominium,*[10] though after mortgaging his property his *dominium* was restricted.[11] The right of the creditor [12] was created by agreement,[13] and was enforceable by the *actio hypothecaria.*

The mortgage was discharged if paid in full before default,[14] and also if after default the debtor paid before two years had elapsed.[15] Should the property really have to be sold at the end of two years, the creditor, selling to regain his loan, had to remit any surplus to the debtor.[16]

The term mortgage will hereafter be used as meaning *hypotheca* and not *pignus* because the Anglo-American modern law

---

[6] I. (4.6), 7; D. (13.7), 9; D. (20.1), 4; cf. also Leage, *Roman Private Law Founded on the 'Institutes' of Gaius and Justinian* (2. ed. by C. H. Ziegler, London: MacMillan and Co., Ltd., 1937), p. 193 (hereafter cited *Roman Private Law*); Burdick, *The Principles of Roman Law and Their Relation to Modern Law* (Rochester: The Lawyers Co-operative Publishing Company, 1938), p. 381.

[7] D. (13.7), 4–5.

[8] D. (20.1), 5; C. (5.13), 1; N. (7.6), 1.

[9] D. (13.7), 1; D. (13.7), 11, 5; D. (20.2), 4; D. (20.6), 8, 7; D. (20.4), 11, 2; C. (8.14), 5; C. (8.14), 7; N. (7.6), 1; N. (120.11).

[10] D. (13.7), 9, 2, quoted above; D. (13.7), 35, 1; C. (4.24), 9.

[11] Regarding the specific rights of the creditor in the event of foreclosure, cf. Sherman, *Roman Law,* II, 620–622.

[12] Regarding the priority of rights among several creditors see C. (8.16), 8, 9, 17; D. (20.4), especially paragraphs (fragments) 11 and 12.

[13] D. (20.1), 4.

[14] D. (20.5), 4; C. (8.27), 6; D. (46.2), 18; D. (13.7), 9, 4–5; D. (13.7), 13, pr.

[15] C. (8.33), 3, 1.

[16] D. (20.4), 20; C. (8.33), 5.

concept of mortgage is practically the same as the *hypotheca* of Roman law.[17]

ARTICLE II. LEGISLATION REGARDING THE MORTGAGING OF CHURCH PROPERTY

Roman law granted religious liberty to the Church by the Edict of Milan in 313,[18] thereby recognizing for the first time the inherent right of the Church to hold and administer property through the medium of corporations and institutions. This safeguarded the vast amount of property, which before was held precariously by giving the Church the right to protect its property by recourse to the proper tribunals of the civil law.

The bishop was considered the administrator of the property within his jurisdiction.[19] But his right, and thus the Church's right, to dispose of this property was first recognized in 470 by the Emperors Leo and Anthemius,[20] and subsequently by Anastasius,[21] and Justinian.[22] In the canonical concept of the term, the right to dispose of church property is the right to alienate.[23]

---

[17] For instance, the California Civil Code defines "pledge" as a deposit of personal property by way of security for the performance of another act; "mortgage" as a contract by which specific property is hypothecated for an act without the necessity of a change of possession—2986, 2920. The Louisiana Civil Code (Art. 3281): in pledge the movables and effects subjected to it are put in possession of the creditor, but the mortgage only subjects to the rights of the creditor the property on which it is imposed, without it being necessary that he should have actual possession.—Sherman, *op. cit.*, 616.

[18] Kirch, *Enchiridion Fontium Historiae Ecclesiasticae Antiquae* (4. ed., Friburgi Brisgoviae: Herder & Co., 1923), nn. 352, 353.

[19] *Breviatio Canonum of Fulgentius Ferrandus* (546), can. 36—Migne, *Patrologiae Cursus Completus, Series Latina* (221 vols., Parisiis, 1844–1864), LXVII, 951 (hereafter cited: *MPL*); *Breviatio Canonum of Cresconius* (690), can. 40—*MPL*, LXXXVIII, 858.

[20] Grashof, "Die Gesetze der Römishen Kaiser über die Veräusserung des kirchlichen Vermögens"—*Archiv für katholisches Kirchenrechts* (Innsbruck, 1857–1861; Mainz, 1862), XXXVI (1876), 204 (hereafter cited: *AKKR*).

[21] C. (1.2), 17.

[22] C. (1.2), 21.

[23] For an extensive treatment of these points, confer the monographs previously prepared at the Catholic University of America: Brown, *Juristic*

It is well to use it in this sense for the purpose of discussion regarding the mortgaging in Roman law.

Throughout the Emperors' legislation on the administration of Church property, one thing is uppermost in their minds—to keep goods that are in the possession of the Church from being permanently lost. Their laws on the mortgaging of Church property are necessarily contained in the enactments which deal, for the most part, with alienation. Yet the former is not on that account to be considered a species of the latter. There is a technical difference between them. Alienation is the handing over of not only rights but also the thing itself—it is the loss of *dominium* or ownership.[24] But a mortgage, as has been seen, transferred no possession and no *dominium*, but only created a *jus in re aliena*. The mortgagor was still master over his property, still enjoyed its use, and, to all intents and purposes, acted as though there were no encumbrance on his property as far as the rest of the world was concerned.

In general, Roman law forbade the alienation of Church property.[25] But in the first laws on the matter, mortgage was not expressly mentioned, though it seemed to have been forbidden not by inclusion but by inference in that all species of alienation were forbidden and then, seemingly as an afterthought, the leg-

---

Personality; Cleary, *Canonical Limitations on the Alienation of Church Property,* The Catholic University of America Canon Law Studies, No. 100 (Washington, D. C.: The Catholic University of America, 1936) (hereafter cited *Alienation*); Doheny, *Church Property;* Hannan, *The Canon Law of Wills,* The Catholic University of America Canon Law Studies, No. 86 (Washington, D. C.: The Catholic University of America, 1934) (hereafter cited *On Wills*).

[24] Alienatio est omnis actus, per quem dominium transfertur."—D. (5.23), 1. Cf. also N. (7.1): "Alienationis vero nomen generalius ideo posuimus, ut prohiberemus et venditionem et donationem et permutationem, et emphyteusin in perpetuum extensam, quae non procul ab alienatione abest." Here the law forbidding alienation also forbade perpetual emphyteusis only because it was similar to alienation on account of the property leaving the possession of the Church forever. N. (7.5) enumerates the penalties for sale, donation, and exchange; N. (7.7), for emphyteusis; and N. (7.6) for pignus (which transfers possession), but there is no penalty mentioned in this decree for hypothecation (wherein possession is retained).

[25] Cf. Cleary, *Alienation,* p. 16, note 12.

islator banned the conveying of any interest (right, no doubt) in Church property.[26]

Quite some time after this (531), Justinian ruled that when alienation is forbidden, it likewise prohibits hypothecation.[27] But only four years later he included particular laws in reference to mortgages in his summary of all Roman law on Church property alienation, and did the same thing in his laws of 544.[28] Some of these provisions are indicated herewith.

In order to contract a General mortgage, it was not necessary to have so great a reason as in making a Special mortgage. For a General mortgage any good cause sufficed, as e. g., necessity, or great utility.[29] For a Special mortgage the cause had to be a real necessity, as e. g., to pay taxes to the State,[30] or to repair the ecclesiastical establishment.[31]

If the mortgage was to last longer than five years, certain formalities had to be observed. The execution of the contract had to have the approval and consent of the bishop (or Archbishop or Patriarch) given in the presence of the ecclesiastical dignitaries and clergy concerned. An oath was taken that there was no intention to defraud the Church of any of its rights, and that no injury would result from the mortgage. If no "Chartularies" (keepers of records) were present, the oath had to be taken in the presence of the Bible.[32]

---

[26] ". . . nec ulli isdem praediis audere cedere."—C. (1.2), 14, pr. (470 A. D.).

[27] "Sancimus, sive lex alienationem inhibuerit sive . . . non solum dominii alienationem vel . . . esse prohibendam, sed etiam . . . hypothecam . . . penitus prohiberi; nisi in his tantummodo casibus, in quibus constitutionum auctoritas . . . qui alienationem interdixit aliquid tale fieri permiserit."—C. (4.51), 7. Here a sharp contrast is drawn between the alienation of *dominium* and *hypotheca,* again showing their difference. In the next legislation on Church property (the law just stated was a purely civil law but dealt with Church property), which followed very shortly, the cases indicated by "in his tantummodo casibus" were provided for by stating the situations under which the exception, "aliquid tale fieri permiserit," would actually be permitted.

[28] N. 7 (in 535); N. 120 (in 544).

[29] N. (7.6), 1.

[30] N. (120.4).

[31] C. (1.2), 17.

[32] N. (120.5). This is similar to the solemnities required by Canons

Because the Emperor realized that there will always be a few, even in high places, who attempt to serve God and Mammon, special efforts were made to forestall fraud and simony in the administration of Church property. To this end he forbade the authorities of religious establishments, their parents, and those related to them by affinity or consanguinity, directly, or through others, to become mortgagees of Church property.[33] The creditor who loaned money to Church authorities had to be sure it was borrowed and used for the benefit of the Church; and should the authorities be his heirs and thus be in a position to inherit any Church property which would pass to him through their defaulting on the mortgage, he was forbidden to become mortgagee.[34]

To circumvent the wiles of any who might nevertheless love to take risks, or make a practice of breaking the laws,[35] fraudulent mortgages were void and all the property of the persons implicated, viz., mortgagors, mortgagees, and accomplices, became the property of the Church at their death.[36]

1530–1532, but instead of the reason being the amount of the mortgage, it was, in Roman law, the length of time the mortgage was to last.

[33] N. (120.5), 1; N. (120.7), 1.

[34] N. (120.6), 3.

[35] N. (7.5).

[36] N. (120.5), 1.

CHAPTER III

Mortgage as Alienation

Article I. Canonical Legislation

The ecclesiastical legislation on mortgaging of Church property is necessarily found in the general laws of the Church regarding alienation as formed in the Councils and decrees of the Popes and in the interpretation of these laws by the Sacred Congregations and authors. Mortgaging is only one instrument used by the administrator of Church property, and the laws were formed to direct this administration in general, with a view to rescinding or preventing any acts that harmed the condition of the Church in her temporalities.

Until 447, the concept of alienation included only the contract of sale.[1] At that time, Pope Leo the Great (440–461) extended it to exchange and donation.[2] The special synod at Rome in 502 under Pope Symmachus brought precision to the law and distinguished between perpetual alienation and giving in usufruct. Though not specifically treating *hypotheca,* it forbade the transfer of any rights.[3]

The "Dionysian Collection" and the so-called "Ancient Statutes of the Church" (Arles) both contained laws effected by Pope Symmachus,[4] and thereby, the same legislation was spread

[1] Cleary, *Alienation,* p. 27. Mortgage was not mentioned by the important Councils of Ancyra (314)—Hardouin, *Acta Conciliorum et Epistolae Decretales ac Constitutiones Summorum Pontificum* (12 vols., Parisiis, 1715), I, 278 (hereafter cited Hardouin); Antioch (341)—Hardouin, I, 604; I Hippo (393)—Hardouin, I, 879; V Carthage (401)—Hardouin, I, 987.

[2] Ep. XVII (ad Epis. Sicil.)—*MPL,* LIV, 705; *Bullarum Diplomatum et Privilegiorum Sanctorum Romanorum Pontificum, Taurinensis Editio* (24 vols. et Appendix, Augustae Taurinorum, Neapoli, 1857–1872), I, 65 (hereafter cited: *Bull. Rom. Taur.*).

[3] Cf. Mansi, *Sacrorum Conciliorum Nova et Amplissima Collectio* (53 vols. in 60, Parisiis, Lipsiae—Arnhem, 1901–1927), VIII, 267, 268 (hereafter cited: Mansi); Cleary, *Alienation,* p. 28.

[4] Cleary, *Alienation,* p. 30.

throughout Italy, Spain, France, England, Ireland, Africa, and the Orient.[5] These collections, too, spoke only of the transfer of rights.

The first specific mention of mortgaging seems to be in the laws made for the Church by the Roman Emperor, Justinian, in 535 and 544 when he forbade alienation and securing the payment of debts by Special mortgages.[6] However, between these two enactments the Third Council of Orleans, 7 May, 538, ruled that small fields and other property are not only not to be alienated but are also not to be obligated by any useless contract.[7]

After this, no more ecclesiastical legislation regarding mortgaging is found for several centuries, and then only in collections of the old laws. As a possible solution for this problem, it might be suggested that the system of Private Churches was disturbing the Church laws on property. This system came with the entry of the Germanic peoples into the Church. In this system, nearly all monasteries and churches except Cathedrals were built on land belonging to private persons. The possession of the soil was the basis of ownership of the church, and the proprietor contracted with a cleric to conduct the divine services. The proprietor also could donate the church and land to another proprietor, provided its religious designation was preserved, because he had full civil rights over the church and its possession. As a

---

[5] Cicognani, *Canon Law* (2. ed., authorized English version by J. O'Hara and F. Brennan, Philadelphia: Dolphin Press, 1935), p. 216; Dionysius died between 526 and 555 (?)—Cicognani, *op. cit.*, p. 215; Van Hove, *Commentarium Lovaniense in Codicem Iuris Canonici*, Vol. I, Tom. I, *Prolegomena* (Mechlinae—Romae; H. Dessain, 1928), p. 107 (hereafter cited: *Prolegomena*). "Statuta Ecclesiae Antiqua" appeared before 503—Cicognani, *op. cit.*, p. 222, n. 41 and note 51; Van Hove, *Prolegomena*, p. 116.

[6] N. (7); N. (120). Before this, alienation but not mortgage was mentioned in the Council of Agde (506)—Mansi, VIII, 323-329; Lesne, *Histoire de la Propriété Ecclésiastique en France*, Vol. I, *Époques Romaine et Mérovingienne* (Lille-Paris, 1910), pp. 290-293; and the IV Council of Orleans (541)—Mansi, IX, 116 and *Monumenta Germaniae Historica* (hereafter cited: *MGH*), *Legum Sectio III*, *Concilia*, Tom. I, *Concilia Aevi Merovingici* (recensivit Fredericus Maassen, Hannoverae, 1893), 87.

[7] "De agellis vero, ceterisque facultatibus ecclesiasticis . . . non alienandis, nec per contractus inutiles obligandis . . . ut nobis per nullos contractus res ecclesiae alienare, aut inutiliter liceat obligare."—Canon 12—Mansi, XI, 16; *MGH*, *Legum Sectio III*, *Concilia*, Tom. I, 77.

whole, the lord of the land could, therefore, sell, exchange, or bestow it to whomsoever he pleased; he could give it as a dowry, or otherwise alienate it; he could devise it, grant it as a fief, or lease it; he could, moreover, mortgage it—anything, provided the Church laws prohibiting secularization were not broken. The proprietary church outlived the Frankish empire. In the Merovingian period the tendency of legislation was to assure, as far as possible, the stability of the proprietary church and its property. Louis the Pious and Lothor I attempted, in the Carolingian period, to abolish the proprietary church but to no effect. In the post-Carolingian times, the system was applied even to bishoprics; from it flowed in great measure the Investiture Contest, the near reduction of the Holy See to the state of a proprietary church during the time of Henry III, and finally the struggle of the Church to throw off these yokes in the "war" of self-defense waged by Pope Gregory VII. It was Gregory's peculiar honor to have recognized with remarkable clarity of vision the dangers of the situation which faced him, but it was as much the intrinsic rightness of the cause as it was due to the personal merits of its first, or any of its later, champions or leaders which finally obtained success for the Church.[8]

In the ninth century there appeared a canon supposedly taken from the Seventh Novel of Justinian.[9] Originally, it did not refer to mortgages, but by the time it appeared in two capitularies of this century it was changed to forbid both alienation of immovable property and obligating it under a title of Special mortgage.[10]

---

[8] Cf. Stutz, "The Proprietary Church as an Element of Mediaeval Germanic Ecclesiastical Law"—Barraclough, *Mediaeval Germany, 911–1250, Essays by German Historians* (Oxford: Basil Blackwell and Mott, Ltd., 1938), Studies in Mediaeval History: No. II, Essays, pp. 35–70 (hereafter cited "The Proprietary Church"); Clercq, *La Législation Religieuse Franque de Clovis à Charlemagne, Étude sur les Actions de Conciles et les Capitulaires les Statuts Diocésains et les Règles Monastiques (507–814)* (Université de Louvain, Recueil de Travaux publiés par les Membres des Conférences d'Histoire et de Philologie, 2e série, 38e fascicule, Louvain: Bureaux du Recueil, Bibliothèque de l'Université, 1936), pp. 97, 303–304. Hereafter cited *La Législation Religieuse Franque*.

[9] N. (7.1).

[10] *Hludowici Pii Capitulari, Capitula e lege Romana Excerpta (826?)*—

After this it was contained in the important systematic collections of the tenth and eleventh centuries, namely those of Regino of Prüm (c. 906), Burchard of Worms (c. 1012), and Ivo of Chartres (1092–1115). With only minor variations in style of composition, it read:

> Nulli liceat alienare rem immobilem Ecclesiae sive domum, sive agrum, sive hortum, sive rusticum mancipium, vel panes civiles, neque creditoribus specialis hypothecae titulo obligare. Alienationis autem verbum contineat conditionem, donationem, permutationem et emphyteoseos perpetuum contractum. Sed omnes omnino sacerdotes ab hujusmodi alienatione abstineant, poenas timentes, quas Leonina constitutio minatur.[11]

For the change in text to the present form, the reader is directed to the chapter on penalties,[12] because the importance of the change has its effect there. Here it remains to be indicated that the wording of this canon (hereafter called *Nulli*) plainly indicated that Special mortgaging was not included in the concept of alienation.

A most interesting point apropos to the inscription given to the canon *Nulli* is that when it appeared in the *Decretum* of Burchard of Worms its inscription read, "*Ex concil. apud Sylvanectim praesente Ludovico rege*, cap. 5." After previous collections had acknowledged its Justinian parentage, Burchard attributed it to this council—"*Sylvanectim.*"[13] It was to carry

---

MGH, *Legum Sectio II, Capitularia Regum Francorum*, Tom. I, (ed. Alfredus Boretius), 310; *Collectio Capitularium Ansegisi* (834), lib. II, c. 29 —*MGH*, *ibid.*, p. 420: also in *MPL*, XCVII, 545.

[11] Regino of Prüm, *De Ecclesiis Disciplinis*, lib. I, can. 360—*MPL*, CXXXII, 261; Burchard of Worms, *Decretum*, lib. III, can. 164—*MPL*, CXL, 706; Ivo of Chartres, *Decretum*, lib. III, can. 183—*MPL*, CLXI, 241. The passage is found also in *Iuliani Epitome Latina Novellarum Justiniani*, edited by Haenel (Lipsiae, 1873). Haenel notes that in the Miraei edition (1561) it read: ". . . neque creditoribus specialis vel generalis hypothecae titulo obligare."—Haenel, *op. cit.*, chap. 32.

[12] *Infra*, p. 59.

[13] He seems to have been the first to inscribe the same council to cc. 1 and 3, X, *de rerum permutatione*, III, 19, causing confusion to later canonists regarding these canons likewise. Ex. gr. Gonzalez, *Commentaria Perpetua in Singulos Textus quinque Librorum Decretalium Gregorii IX* (Maceratae, 1761), lib. III, tit. 19, cap. 1 and 3. Hereafter cited Gonzalez.

this adopted lineage thereafter. In explanation, it might be recalled that Burchard was attempting to impugn the proprietary churches,[14] and consequently, the legislation of secular powers and especially of Roman law. He did not admit the competence of the secular powers. But it was not sufficient to eliminate. He had to supply something which, naturally, would be false. For that reason he borrowed names and even invented names of apocryphal councils.[15] No record of any such council exists. It can, therefore, be concluded with a great measure of surety that for this canon Burchard invented the council of *Sylvanectim* at which a fictitious King Louis presided.

The law was not changed by the Great Decretals, but on the contrary, Pope St. Gregory IX repeated the canon *Nulli* with its distinction of alienation and Special mortgage. He even repeated the inscription: *Ex concilio apud Silvanectim.*[16] In addition, he most firmly forbade the mortgaging of churches on the part of prelates for the purpose of paying the debts of their clerical or lay friends.[17]

Pope Clement V, at the beginning of the fourteenth century, extended and enlarged these laws of Gregory IX. Whereas Gregory legislated regarding immovable goods, Clement included any kind of goods. Whereas the former mentioned only *Ecclesia,* the latter more specifically listed monasteries, priories, churches, and any other place under the administration of reli-

---

[14] Van Hove, *Prolegomena,* p. 151.

[15] Cf. Fournier-LeBras, *Histoire des Collections Canoniques en Occident depuis les Fausses Décrétales jusqu'au Décret de Gratien,* Tom. I: *De la Réforme Carolingienne à la Réforme Grégorienne* (Paris: Recueil Sirey, 1931), 378, 379; Van Hove, *Prolegomena,* p. 151.

[16] C. 5, X, *de rebus ecclesiae alienandis vel non,* III, 13. This inscription puzzled the Decretalists. There had been a council held at " Silvanectense " [Beauvois, France] during the time of Nicholas I (863), to depose Rothaldus, Bishop of Soissons, but they could not find this canon *Nulli* among its acts. They believed that some council of " Silvanectim " had incorporated it from Justinian's law.—Cf. Gonzalez, lib. III, tit. 13, cap. 5.

[17] ". . . inhibemus, ne quis praesumat . . . ecclesiam sibi commissam pro alienis gravare debitis, aut literas alicui seu sigilla concedere, quibus possint ecclesiae obligari."—C. 2, X, *de solutionibus,* III, 23. " Obligari, vel hypothecari, quot inquit glossa est idem:"—Redoanus, *De Alienationibus Rerum Ecclesiarum* (Placentiae, 1589), Q. XII, n. 25 (hereafter cited: *De Alienationibus*).

gious, in his prohibition. The word "mortgage" is not used, but seems to be implied because he speaks in very broad terms in prohibiting any long-term concession of rights in return for money, unless for the purpose of meeting debts. Necessity or utility were required as a motive cause.[18]

The councils of these and succeeding centuries added nothing to the solution of the present problem, for the reason that they were content to repeat the general law of the Church when they considered mortgaging at all.[19]

Evidently many abuses still occurred, so that Pope Paul II, on March 1, 1467, issued the important Constitution *Ambitiosae,* which served as the body of the law on alienation until the promulgation of the Code.[20] Though including mortgages in its prohibition of acts that were unlawful without the Holy See's permission, the purpose of the constitution was to demand that this permission be obtained, and consequently it is difficult to determine whether he definitely intended to class mortgages as a species of alienation or as a thing prohibited in the same way that alienations were banned.

It prohibited the alienation of all ecclesiastical property, every contract by which *dominium* was transferred, every concession, mortgage, and lease for more than three years, except in cases permitted by law:

Ambitiosae, cupiditati, illorum praecipue, qui divinis

[18] "Monasteriorum et aliarum administrationum regularium dispendiis occurrere cupientes, perpetuo prohibemus edicto, ne quis religiosus, monasterio, prioratui, ecclesiae seu administrationi cuivis praesidens, jura, reditus aut possessiones eiusdem, alicui ad vitam eius seu aliud certum tempus, pecunia etiam inde recepta, quovis modo concedat, nisi necessitas aut utilitas monasterii, . . . hoc exposcat, conventus sui, aut, si conventum non habeat, praelati proprii assensu ad hoc nihilominus accedente."—c. 1, *de rebus ecclesiae non alienandis,* III, 4, in Clem. At least insofar as the penalties are concerned, it is directed to religious only.—Pirhing, lib. III, tit. 13, n. 51.

[19] Cf. Council of Avignon, France (1282), can. 3—Mansi, XXIV, 441; Council of Melfi, Italy (1284), can. 7—Mansi, XXIV, 574; Synod of Nîmes, France (1284), n. 4—Mansi, XXIV, 541; National Council of Würzburg, Germany (1287), can. 9—Mansi, XXIV, 854; Council of Buda, Hungary (1279), can. 36 and 50—Mansi, XXIV, 287, 292; Council of Avignon, France (1326), can. 51—Mansi, XXV, 771; Council of Constance (1414-1418), sess. XLIII (Oecumenical), can. 9—Hardouin, VIII, 880.

[20] Cf. Cleary, *Alienation,* p. 51.

et humanis affectati, damnatione postposita, immobilia et pretiosa mobilia Deo dicata, ex quibus ecclesiae, monasteria et pia loca reguntur illustranturque, et eorum ministri sibi alimoniam vindicant, profanis usibus applicare, aut cum maximo illorum ac divini cultus detrimento exquisitis mediis usurpare praesumunt, occurrere cupientes, omnium rerum et bonorum ecclesiasticorum alienationem, omneque pactum, per quod ipsorum dominium transfertur, concessionem, hypothecam, locationem et conductionem ultra triennium, nec non infeudationem vel contractum emphyteuticum, praeterquam in casibus a jure permissis, ac de rebus et bonis in emphyteusim ab antiquo concedi solitis, et tunc ecclesiarum evidenti utilitate, ac de fructibus et bonis, quae servando servari non possunt, pro instantis temporis exigentia, hac perpetuo valitura constitutione praesenti fieri prohibemus, praedecessorum nostrorum constitutionibus, prohibitionibus et decretis allis super hoc editis, quae tenore praesentium innovamus, in suo nihilominus robore permansuris. Si quis autem contra huius nostrae prohibitionis seriem de bonis et rebus eisdem quicquam alienare praesumpserit: alienatio, hypotheca, concessio, locatio, conductio et infeudatio huiusmodi, nullius omnino sint roboris vel momenti, et tam qui alienat, quam is, qui alienatas res et bona praedicta receperit, sententium excommunicationis incurrat. Alienanti vero bona ecclesiarum, monasteriorum locorumque piorum quorumlibet, inconsulto Romano Pontifice, aut contra praesentis constitutionis tenorem, si pontificali vel abbatiali praefulgeat dignitate, ingressus ecclesiae sit penitus interdictus. Et si per sex menses immediate sequentes sub interdicto huiusmodi animo (quod absit) perseveraverit indurato: lapsis mensibus eisdem a regimine et administratione suae ecclesiae vel monasterii, cui praesidet, in spiritualibus et temporalibus sit eo ipso suspensus. Inferiores vero praelati, commendatarii, et aliarum ecclesiarum rectores, beneficia, vel administrationem quomodolibet obtinentes, prioratibus, praeposituris, praepositatibus, dignitatibus, personatibus, administrationibus, officiis, canonicatibus, praebendis, aliisque ecclesiasticis cum cura et sine cura saecularibus et regularibus beneficiis, quorum res et bona alienarunt duntaxat, ipso facto privati existant, illaque absque declaratione aliqua vacare censeantur, possintque per locorum ordinarios, vel alios, ad quos eorum collatio pertinet, personis idoneis (illis exceptis, quae propterea privatae fuerint), libere de jure conferri, nisi alias dispositioni apostolicae sedis sint specialiter aut generaliter reservata; nihilominus alienatae res et bona huiusmodi ad ecclesias, monasteria et loca pia, ad quae ante alienationem huiusmodi pertinebant, libere revertantur.[21]

Does *hypotheca* here mean a mortgage that gives possession? In the beginning of the Constitution it seems to be grouped purposely with other methods of granting possession while retaining *dominium*. Moreover, at the end of the Constitution, it speaks of "*things and goods* [not rights] of this kind being voluntarily *returned* to the institute to which they belonged before the alienation." Does it mean any mortgage, or only one for more than three years? Again the grouping and punctuation would seem to indicate the latter. Does it mean to define mortgage as a species of alienation? The complete text quoted above and especially the following sentence,

> Si quis autem contra huius nostrae prohibitionis seriem de bonis et rebus eisdem quicquam alienare praesumpserit: alienatio, hypotheca, concessio, locatio, conductio et infeudatio huiusmodi nullius omnino sint roboris vel momenti, . . .

seems to indicate a positive response, because a colon (as in the latter) is used to introduce a formal enumeration of particulars. However, the possibility of possession's being transferred and of the loss of *dominium* at default without redemption must be considered because this would have been alienation in a more perfect sense. Transgressors of the laws of the constitution are called alienators (*alienanti*).

This constitution was specifically reaffirmed by Julius III, in 1552 and by Paul IV, in 1555[22] and remained the clearest state-

---

[21] C. un., *de rebus ecclesiae non aliendis,* III, 4, in Extravag. com. In the interpretation of this text, it is perhaps enlightening to know the development of mortgage in the civil law outside of Roman law. As will be seen more fully in a later chapter, in mortgages at this time, possession was passed, generally a term of years was stipulated, and at default the property was immediately and absolutely lost to the mortgagor. This was a very dangerous and harmful contract; cf. Walsh, *On Mortgages,* pp. 1, 2.

[22] Constitution *Dilecti filii,* 23 maii 1552—Redoanus, *De Alienationibus,* p. 578. Constitution *Injunctum Nobis,* 14 iul. 1555—*Codicis Iuris Canonici*

ment of the common Church law,[23] to the time of the Code, many other Popes in general terms having reaffirmed its measures in attempting to stamp out particular abuses.[24]

The Council of Trent spoke in broad terms in trying to prevent the conversion to, and usurpation by, the laity of Church goods and rights.[25]

So far it is shown that only three real enactments regarding mortgage and alienation were made: one, the canon *Nulli,* originating with Justinian and extended to embrace mortgages before 826, and successively copied through the time of Gregory IX; another, the Clementine instruction enlarging the canon *Nulli* to embrace all types of goods and revenues and all types of churches; and the third, the Constitution *Ambitiosae* of Paul II. Succeeding councils, synods, papal decrees and decisions of the Congregations renewed the latter but threw no light on the question of mortgaging's being alienation.[26]

Fontes cura Emi. Petri Card. Gasparri editi (9 vols., Romae [later Civitate Vaticane]: Typis Polyglottis Vaticanis, 1923-1939. Vols. VII-IX ed. cura et studio Emi. Iustiniani Card. Serédi), n. 88 (hereafter cited *Fontes*).

[23] Cf. Constitution of Pius IV, *Motu proprio,* 10 sep. 1560, by which above noted constitution of Paul IV was raised to the condition of common law —in Redoanus, *op. cit.,* p. 581.

[24] Pius V, const. *Admonet nos,* 29 mart. 1567—*Fontes,* n. 120; Gregory XIII, const. *Inter caetera,* 26 maii 1572—*Fontes,* n. 142; Sixtus V, const. *Quanta Apostolicae,* 18 mart. 1586—*Fontes,* n. 158; Gregory XIV, const. *Romanus Pontifex,* 19 dec. 1590—*Fontes,* n. 168; Innocent IX, const. *Quae ab hac,* 4 nov. 1591—*Fontes,* n. 174; Clement VIII, const. *Ad Romani,* 14 febr. 1592—*Fontes,* n. 175; Paul V, const. *Inter caetera,* 30 dec. 1605—*Fontes,* n. 193; Urban VIII, const. *Sacrosancti,* 30 sept. 1624—*Fontes,* n. 203; Innocent X, const. *In supremo,* 15 nov. 1644—*Fontes,* n. 229.

[25] Sess. XXII, *de ref.,* c. 11.

[26] Provincial Council of Gnesen (Poland, 19 May, 1577)—Mansi, XXXVI bis, 716; S. C. C., decr., 7 sept. 1624—*Fontes,* n. 2453; S. C. C., rescr. ad Archiep. *Neapol.,* 7 feb. 1637—*Canones et Decreta Concilii Tridentini ex editione Romana A. MDCCCXXXIV repetiti* (editio Neapolitana, Neapoli, 1859), p. 170; Constitutiones et Canones S. Synodi Montis Libani (Maronite Church, a. 1736)—*Acta et Decreta Sacrorum Conciliorum Recentiorum, Collectio Lacensis* (7 vols., Friburgi Brisgoviae, 1870-1890), II, 353, n. 14 (hereafter cited *Coll. Lac.*); S. C. Ep. et Reg., decr., 18 mart. 1835—Bizzarri, *Collectanea in usum Secretariae Sacrae Congregationis Episcoporum et Regularium* (Romae, 1863), p. 721 (hereafter cited *Coll. S.C. EE. RR.*); S. Cong. de Prop. Fid. instr. ad Patriarch. Armenien., 30 iul., 1867—*Collectanea S. Congregationis de Propaganda Fide* (2 vols., Romae;

ARTICLE II. OPPOSING THEORIES

Therefore, one turns to the Decretalists and authors for interpretation. Six propositions are possible.

(1) Mortgage (without qualification) Is Alienation.

(2) Mortgage (without qualification) Is Not Alienation.

(3) Both General and Special Mortgages Are Alienation.

(4) Both General and Special Mortgages Are Not Alienation.

(5) Special Mortgage Is Alienation (Silent regarding General).

(6) Special Mortgage Is Alienation; General Mortgage Is Not.

Prop. 1. Mortgage (without qualification) Is Alienation.

(a) Commenting on the canon *Nulli* alone, Bernard of Pavia was of this opinion [27] and held that alienation is the transfer of a thing or a right to another, and what cannot be sold cannot be mortgaged,[28] although in listing the contracts that are contained in alienation, he does not mention mortgage.[29]

Cardinal Hostiensis held that the word alienation should be ex-

---

Typographis Polyglotta S. C. de Propaganda Fide 1907), n. 1310 par. 4 and Fontes, n. 4867; S. C. C., 8 iul. 1877—*Acta Sanctae Sedis* (41 vols., Romae, 1865–1908) (hereafter cited: *ASS*), X (1877), 173; II Provincial Council of Quebec, 1854—*Coll. Lac.*, III, 657, par. 2, n. 4; Provincial Synod of the Province of Russia (Greek Uniate Church), 1720—*Coll. Lac.*, II, 59; Concilium Plenarium Americae Latinae (1899)—*Appendix ad Concilium Plenarium Americae Latinae Romae celebratum anno Domini MDCCCXCIX, additis Recentioribus Documentis* (Romae, 1910), n. 2. The Third Plenary Council of Baltimore (1884) received an indult regarding the solemnities of law, which, together with the Council's legislation and the final renewal of the indult (1916), spoke of "mortgaging and other acts which have the appearance of alienation"; nor was a distinction made between General and Special mortgages.—*Acta et Decreta Concilii Plenarii Baltimorensis Tertii A. D. MDCCCLXXXIV*, p. ciii et can. 20, n. 6; S. C. C., 31 iul. 1916—*The Ecclesiastical Review* (Philadelphia, 1889–), LV (1916), 664 (private response). Hereafter cited *AER*.

[27] "alienatio est rei vel iuris in alium translatio."—Bernardus Papiensis, *Summa Decretalium* (ed. Ern. Laspeyres, Ratisbonae, 1860), p. 76.

[28] ". . . quae vendi non possunt nec obligari possunt . . ."—Bernardus Papiensis, *loc. cit.* "Obligari, vel, hypothecari, quod inquit glossa est idem."—Redoanus, *De Alienationibus*, q. XII, n. 25.

[29] "Nomen autem alienationis continetur venditio, donatio, permutatio, pignoratio, et in emphyteusim datio, ususfructus, pensionis vel servitutis constitutio, manumissio . . ."—Bernardus Papiensis, *loc. cit.*

tended even to acts through which *dominium* is not transferred.[30]

(b) After the Constitution *Ambitiosae* was published (1467) this same opinion was sustained by Barbosa in the seventeenth century, and by von Schulte, Santi, Hergenroether, and Hollweck in the nineteenth century.[31] The Sacred Congregation of the Council at the beginning of the nineteenth century seems to have held this opinion, from what can be gathered from the private collection of Pallottini.[32]

Prop. 2. Mortgage (without qualification) Is Not Alienation.

This is concluded from the writings of Sá in the seventeenth century, and Engel in the eighteenth century, wherein definitions of alienation are given without any mention of mortgage.[33]

---

[30] Hostiensis, *Commentaria in Quinque Decretalium Libros* (Venetiis, 1581), lib. III, tit. *de rebus ecclesiae alienandis vel non,* cap. 5, n. 3.

[31] Barbosa, *Pastoralis Solicitudinis, sive De Officio et Potestate Episcopi tripartita* descriptio (Lugduni, 1656), vol. III, pars II, alleg. XIX, n. 85; von Schulte, *Lehrbuch des katholischen Kirchenrechts* (3. ed. Giessen, 1873), p. 590; Santi, *Praelectiones Juris Canonici* (Ratisbonae, Neo Eboraci, Cincinnati, 1866), II, 152, n. 1 and 192, n. 4; Hergenroether, *Lehrbuch des katholischen Kirchenrechts* (Freiburg im Breisgau, 1888), n. 1098; Hollweck, *Die kirchlichen Strafgesetze* (Mainz, 1899), para. 158, note 11.

[32] "Verbo alienationis continetur omnis alienatio, quae transfert dominium, et omnis illa, per quam res obligatur (in *Neapolitana Beneplaciti Apostolici,* 21 sept. 1822)."—Pallottini, *Collectio Omnium Conclusionum et Resolutionum Quae in Causis propositis apud Sacram Congregationem Cardinalium S. Concilii Tridentini Interpretum Prodierunt ab eius institutione anno MDLXIV ad annum MDCCCLX, distinctis titulis alphabetico ordine per materias digesta* (18 vols., Romae, 1868–1895), s. v. "Alienatio," I, n. 1. "Amplia, nomine alienationis intelligitur omnis actus, ex quo directum vel utile alicuius rei dominium, aut illius jus seu ususfructus in alterum transfertur, vel damnum quomodocumque Ecclesiae irrogatur. Hinc, sive Lex alienationem inhibuerit sive Testator hoc fecerit . . . non solum dominii alienationem . . . sed ususfructus dationem, vel hypothecam, vel pignoris nexum penitus prohiberi (in *Camerinen. Fabricae,* 30 iul. 1774)."—*ibid.*, nn. 2, 3. "Profecto verbum alienationis in hoc loco latissime accipitur, quemadmodum ad hoc Caput Nulli de rebus Ecclesiae alienandis vel non adnotat Glossa (in *Neapolitana Beneplaciti Apostolici,* 21 sept. 1882)."—*ibid.*, n. 11. See also *ASS,* XXII (1889), 415.

[33] "Prohibita alienari, possunt pignori dari;"—Sá, *Aphorismi Confessariorum ex variis doctorum Sententiis Collecti* (Lugduni, 1669), p. 374, n. 7. "Pignus dicitur de re mobili, hypotheca de immobili."—Sá, *ibid.*, n. 10. "Nomine alienationis in primis omnes contractus intelligantur, quibus

Redoanus, in the sixteenth century, held that mortgage is not alienation so long as no transfer of possession takes place. He called a mortgage with transfer of possession a real mortgage, and one without this transfer a verbal mortgage. If alienation alone were prohibited, the former type of mortgage therefore would be included in the prohibition.[34] However, regarding what is *de facto* prohibited, excluding the concept of alienation, a Special mortgage is prohibited, but a General mortgage is not.[35]

Prop. 3. Both General and Special Mortgages Are Alienation.

This opinion was held and defended at some length by Schmier in the eighteenth century. He maintained that the distinction between General and Special mortgage was groundless; that though only Special mortgage was mentioned by the canon *Nulli*, the argument from contraries was not licit since the Constitution *Ambitiosae* prohibits mortgage, and it is not a restrictive prohibition but an illustrative one; that though General mortgage does not cause so much harm to the Church as a Special mortgage does, since if it should happen that a foreclosure took place, the movable goods would be sacrificed before the immovables, nevertheless, even if the obligation is to be satisfied completely through the loss only of movables, the fact that the movables are in the *dominium* of the Church does not permit this.[36]

---

dominium utile, vel directum transfertur, ut donatio, venditio, permutatio, feudam, emphyteusis, et similes. Deinde etiam omnes contractus, quibus . . . possessio, aut jus percipiendi fructus ex re Ecclesiastica ad longum tempus transfertur, cujusmodi sunt oppignoratio specialis, usufructus, et elocationes . . ."—Engel, *Collegium Universi Juris Canonici* (ed. 9, cui adjectae sunt annotationes Caspari Barthel, 3 vols., Beneventi, 1760), lib. III, tit. XXI, n. 11.

[34] "Item sub vocabulo alienationis venit . . . hypotheca, realis tamen, non verbalis tantum idest, hypotheca sine traditione."—Redoanus, *De Alienationibus,* q. II, cap. VI, n. 1.

[35] "Melius declara, ut . . . specialis hypotheca est prohibita, generalis vero non; et quod sicut regulariter est prohibita rerum ecclesiae alienatio, ita specialis hypotheca: a pari enim procedunt, quo ad solemnitatem per tex. d. c. nulli."—Redoanus, *op. cit.,* q. II, cap. VI, n. 21.

[36] Schmier, *Jurisprudentia Canonico—Civilis seu Jus Canonicum Universum juxta Quinque Libros Decretalium* (5 vols. in 2, Venetiis, 1754), lib. III, tract. I, par. II, cap. IV, nn. 112–116. Hereafter cited *Jurisprudentia.*

These were necessary conclusions on his part since his definition of alienation included the transfer of any right *in re* or *ad rem.*[37]

Reiffenstuel, the great canonist and moralist of the seventeenth century,[38] supported this opinion without subscribing to it in so many words. He said that alienation included the transfer of a right to another,[39] and in discussing the opinion that would permit a General mortgage without the solemnities required for alienation, he uses the term " to alienate by means of a General mortgage." [40] Referring to the canon *Nulli,* he had previously included Special mortgage as a species of alienation.[41]

Prop. 4. Both General and Special Mortgages Are Not Alienation.[42]

---

[37] Though holding that alienation in the strict sense is the transfer of *dominium,* he continues: " Alienatio lata continet actus et negotia, quibus aliquod jus in re vel *ad rem* ab uno in alium transfertur . . ."—*ibid.,* n. 57. Then he adds: " In praesenti materia latior alienationis acceptio praefertur strictiori ut patet ex cap. *Nulli* et *Ambitiosae,* in quibus locis non solum donatio . . ., et hypotheca prohibetur, . . ."—*ibid.,* n. 58.

[38] Cf. Van Hove, *Prolegomena,* pp. 287 and 302.

[39] " Alienationis nomen in proposito sumitur large, ac prout complectitur omnem actum quo . . . jus in alterum transfertur."—Reiffenstuel, *Jus Canonicum Universum* (4 vols., Romae, 1833), lib. III, tit. 13, n. 3. Hereafter cited Reiffenstuel.

[40] " Possunt tamen eadem bona Ecclesiae . . . per hypothecam Generalem alienare . . ."—Reiffenstuel, lib. III, tit. 21, n. 34.

[41] " Idque patet *ex. c. Nulli, 5 h. t.* ubi dicitur: quod alienationis verbum continet . . . atque etiam (ut ibid. 1 dicitur) specialis hypotheca titulo obligationem."—Reiffenstuel, lib. III, tit. 13, n. 3. Cf. also, *op. cit.,* lib. III, tit. 21, n. 35, where referring to Ambitiosae, he says: ". . . sicut omnium rerum et bonorum Ecclesiasticorum alienatio, ita etiam hypotheca generaliter prohibetur. Nam contra est, quod licet omnium rerum, non tamen omnis, id est, tam Generalis quam Specialis Hypotheca prohibetur: prout consideranti patet."

[42] It can be noted that the supporters of Proposition 2 must be included in the patrons of this proposition because in saying that no mortgage is alienation, they would logically have to hold that neither kind is alienation. The same conclusion could not be drawn for Proposition 3 from the adherents of Proposition 1, because Hostiensis and Papiensis were discussing the canon *Nulli,* which spoke of Special mortgage only and therefore they might possibly not have been considering General mortgage. Those after

Fagnanus, the blind genius of the seventeenth century, whose authority is still appealed to by the Sacred Congregations,[43] held, in commenting on the canon *Nulli* and on the Constitution *Ambitiosae,* that even Special mortgage was not alienation, though prohibited.[44]

Prop. 5. Special Mortgage Is Alienation (Silent regarding General).

Wernz, in his famous "*Ius Decretalium,*" at the turn of the twentieth century,[45] held that alienation should be considered in the wide sense to include the legal acts which transfer a *jus in re.* Again, he says Special mortgage should be adjudged alienation because it is the forerunner of alienation.[46] It is without positive allegation but through inference that he says a General mortgage

---

the time of *Ambitiosae* lay themselves open to wide interpretation by the very fact that in a matter of strict law they made no definite distinction nor definite inclusion before stating a rigorous opinion.

[43] Cf. Cicognani, *Canon Law,* p. 390, n. 2, calling Fagnanus not only the "*Doctor Caecus Oculatissimus*" but also the "*Magnus rigoristarum princeps.*" This is noteworthy and the latter appellation seems somewhat paradoxical in the present instance, since of all the commentators consulted, he holds the most lax opinion. Cf. also Van Hove, *Prolegomena,* p. 286.

[44] "Secundo nota ibi, *Specialis hypothecae,* aliud esse alienare, aliud specialis hypothecae titulo obligare . . ."; Fagnanus, *Jus Canonicum seu Commentaria Absolutissima in Quinque Libros Decretalium* (5 vols., Romae, 1661), Vol. III, de rebus ecclesiae non alienandis, cap. Nulli, n. 29 (hereafter cited *Jus Canonicum*); "Tertio nota in eisdem verbis, specialem hypothecam bonorum Ecclesiae esse prohibitum . . . et ita intelligas Extravag. Ambitiosae, de rebus Eccles. non alienand. ibi hypothecam, scilicet specialem."—Fagnanus, *ibid.,* n. 30. Cf. also *ibid.,* n. 34: ". . . et alienationis appellatione continetur actus, per quem dominium etiam utile transfertur. Et ita alienationis verbum hic latissime accipitur."

[45] Cf. Van Hove, *Prolegomena,* p. 314.

[46] "Alienatio bonorum ecclesiasticorum hoc loco sumitur sensu lato, quatenus actum legitimum, quo in alium transfertur rei dominium (venditio), . . . aut aliud jus in re (hypotheca) . . . Comprehendit illos actus legitimos, quibus bona ecclesiastica . . . aliis juribus in illa concessis periculo amissionis exponuntur aut generatim peioris conditionis fiunt. Porro alienationi adnumerantur . . . actus, qui alienationem, praeparare et inchoare censentur velut . . . hypotheca specialis."—Wernz, *Ius Decretalium,* III, n. 154.

is permitted to be placed on the goods of the Church by prelates.[47]

Prop. 6. Special Mortgage Is Alienation; General Mortgage Is Not.

This principle was held by three authors in the seventeenth century. Merlin, in 1649, writing exclusively on pawns and mortgages, regarded the canon *Nulli* and the Constitution *Ambitiosae* as wishing to include Special mortgage in their concept of alienation, and he reasons that when alienation is prohibited, so also is every act through which the alienation can result.[48]

Turricellius, in 1674, taught that the concept of alienation extends to the transfer of any *jus in re,* and to any undertaking that will result in alienation.[49]

Both conclude that General mortgage is not alienation because it is considered less harmful than the Special, since the former grants only a *jus ad rem,* while the latter grants a *jus in re.*[50]

---

[47] "Quare praelati ecclesiastici, qui non habent liberam potestatem alienandi, absque indulto apostolico nequeant constituere hypothecam specialem super rebus immobilibus Ecclesiae."—Wernz, *op. cit.,* n. 269. He refers to *Nulli* and *Ambitiosae* as his authorities for the statement in his footnote 232.

[48] "Ratio est, quia prohibita alienatione, sicuti prohibetur de bonis Ecclesiae, censetur prohibitus omnis actus per quem pervenitur ad eam . . . et quia sub nomine alienationis saltem late sumpto vocabulo continetur specialis hypotheca . . . sicuti in materia favorabili contineri scribit . . ."—Merlinus, *De Pignoribus,* lib. II, tit. I, q. 85, n. 3. . . . "quando lex, aut statutum pupillis, mulieribus, ac similibus propter concilii imbecillitatem, hoc casu censetur prohibita . . . hypotheca, . . ."—Merlinus, *op. cit.,* lib. II, tit. I, q. 42, n. 68.

[49] "Alienatio rerum Ecclesiae prohibita est. Et alienationis nomen comprehendit omnem actum translativum dominii, tam directi quam utilis, et cuiuslibet juris in re. (Rota dec. 280, n. 7, par. 1, recen.)"—Turricellius, *De Rebus Ecclesiae non Alienandis ex Sententia Sacrae Romanae Rotae Tractatus* (Ferrariae, 1674), cap. I, nn. 1 and 2 (hereafter cited: *De Rebus Ecclesiae*); "Est enim regula, quod prohibitus alienare censetur etiam prohibitus actus facere, per quos alienatio sequi possit. (Rota dec. 480, n. 2, par. 1, divers.)"—Turricellius, *op. cit.,* cap. I, n. 14.

[50] "Limitatur autem primo in hypotheca generali in qua quidem contrahenda solemnitates non sunt necessariae . . . ratio est quia generalis hypotheca dicitur levioris praejudicii specialis autem gravioris, nam per specialem jus in re acquiritur per generalem autem jus ad rem, fortius autem est jus in re quam jus ad rem."—Merlinus, *op cit.,* lib. II, tit. II, q.

Merlin, however, qualifies this opinion, saying that General mortgage is not alienation only in two situations: when either the principal contract shall have been drawn up with the required solemnities,[51] or when it shall have been entered without them when they are unnecessary, as in the case in which the Church is financially bettered by the transaction.[52]

Pirhing considered a broadest interpretation of alienation to include every act through which a *jus in re* is transferred, and anyone not allowed to alienate as being equally unable to encumber the property with a Special mortgage. He felt that the reason behind this extension was the danger of alienation.[53] This

---

85, nn. 7 and 8. ". . . hypotheca generalis, per seipsam nihil sapiat alienationis, cum per eam non transfertur jus aliquod in re, utique eadem ratio videtur militare in terminis, Extravag. ambitiosae Pauli II . . . quod non potest compraehendere hypothecam generalem tamquam diversae naturae ab alienatione, quae fuit sola ratio praedictae Constitutionis Paulinae, quia ad eam non est directe et principaliter ordinata hypotheca generalis, sed ut magis creditori cautum sit, adeo ut cum non nisi in consequentiam possit per eam sequi alienatio, inde sequatur quod quousque non producatur in esse dictur effectus nunquam poterat dici (attenta primaeva sua natura) quod possit de ea censeri, quod de alienatione qua prohibita non potest dici prohibitum omne id per quod *ad illam potest deveniri,* non quidem directe et principaliter, sed secundario et in consequentiam, cum ea quae in consequentiam et secundario veniant non qualificent actum . . . et in terminis decreti [14 iul. 1638—Turricellius, c. VIII, n. 56]. Sacrae Congregationis Concilii data fuit eiusdem Sacrae Congregationis declaratio illus non compraehendere hypothecam generalem."—S. R. R. in *Amerina Bonorum coram Roias*—in Merlinus, *op. cit.*, p. 119, decis. 97. Cf. also Turricellius, *op. cit.*, cap. VIII, nn. 55-56.

[51] This could be the case, for example, when a diocese obtains permission from Rome for a loan without any mention being made as to the method of contracting or securing the debt. From private information the writer has learned that this is sometimes done.

[52] Ex. gr., obtaining a lower rate of interest. "Quae tamen, sunt intelligenda dummodo principalis contractus fuerit celebratus servatis servandis, et sic solemnitates necessariae intervenerint . . . vel ubi non sunt necessariae, ut quando Ecclesia acquirit . . ."—Merlinus, *De Pignoribus,* lib. II, tit. II, q. 85, n. 13. ". . . motus eadem ratione . . . nempe quod cum Ecclesia acquirat, potest sub hypotheca generali obligare sua bona, et talis hypotheca generalis non est comprehensa sub prohibitione alienandi bona Ecclesiastica."—cited in above-mentioned Rota decision, n. 1.

[53] ". . . sumitur alienatio latissime, pro omni eo actu, per quem . . . jus in re transfertur, ac proinde qui sic alienare prohibetur rem aliquam

most comprehensive meaning of alienation must be accepted in the prohibition to alienate Church property because it is legislation that is favorable to the churches, since the law, *Nulli,* was issued when the Church was being bled of its possessions.[54]

In discussing the limits of this extension of the concept of alienation, he concludes that a General mortgage is not prohibited. He does not say that it is not alienation in any sense. This should be a logical deduction because of the place in which he discusses it.[55]

In discussing the Constitution *Ambitiosae,* which he holds refers to solemnities of alienation,[56] he again discusses General mortgage, not as a method of alienation but as something prohibited without papal permission. He merely states that many (authors) hold it is forbidden because the constitution simply mentions mortgage, but that others hold only a Special mortgage is forbidden by reason of the canon *Nulli.* Not too explicitly does he seem to retain here his previously advanced opinion that General mortgages are not prohibited.[57] He reserves this unqualified

---

. . . neque etiam tradere in pignus [potest], aut hypothecam, saltem specialem; quia res ita obligata obnoxia manet alienationis periculo . . ." —Pirhing, lib. III, tit. 13, n. 1. It is not clear whether he intends to infer that property passes by transfer of possession in a Special mortgage, but even though he did not, his inclusion of a transfer of any *jus in re* would comprehend the Special mortgage.

[54] Pirhing, *ibid.,* n. 2.

[55] "Ex dictis infertur primo, etsi prohibitum sit, res Ecclesiasticas subjicere hypothecae speciali, non tamen prohibita est constitutio hypothecae generalis, ac proinde Praelatus ad firmandum contractum legitime institutum, bona Ecclesiae obligare potest sub hypotheca generali, etiam absque consensu Superioris, vel alia solemnitate Canonica . . . Ratio disparitatis est, quia per hypothecam generalem non ita facile devenire potest ad alienationem, seu venditionem rei generaliter solum obligatae, seu oppignoratae, quam per hypothecam specialem, per quam plus juris in rem transfertur in creditorem, cum periculo eam alienandi."—Pirhing, lib. III, tit. 13, n. 5. "Non potest Praelatus vel Rector Ecclesiae alienari prohibitas per specialem hypothecam obligare, etsi possint generalem ut constet ex . . . et dictum supra tit. 13, n. 5. . . . Quare licet Praelatus contrahens delicta, nomine Ecclesiae, bona eiusdem per generalem hypothecam obliget, nihil agit contra prohibitionem SS. Canonum de rebus Ecclesiae immobilibus non alienandis; . . ."—Pirhing, lib. III, tit. 21, n. 16.

[56] Pirhing, lib. III, tit. 13, n. 53.

[57] Pirhing, *ibid.,* n. 55, note 3. Schmalzgrueber avoids the question very

statement for that portion of his work devoted specifically to mortgages.[58]

Petra, the classical commentator on the Constitution *Ambitiosae*,[59] held that alienation by this constitution was to be understood in a broad sense to include the transfer of possession. Even a sale without execution was not alienation.[60]

He then refers to the sixth constitution of Pope Benedict XII for the discussion regarding alienation and mortgage.[61] There he reviews the vacillations of opinion on this point. Briefly, in March, 1626, the Congregation of the Council issued a decree wherein it was forbidden to monasteries to give a mortgage in return for a loan. The decree was re-issued in July, 1633. Still it was doubted whether General mortgages were comprehended, and if they were not comprehended, whether a resulting foreclosure sale on monastery or Church goods could be held without the *Beneplacitum Apostolicum*. Because of the general language of the Constitution *Ambitiosae*, some authors held General mortgage was included. But it was frequently and fully discussed in the Rota. At the first submission of the question on April 19, 1641 (*in Amerina Bonorum coram Verospio*), it was decided the contract was valid (hence was not considered alienation), but

---

nicely. After leading the reader to think he is in agreement with Pirhing, whom he cites, he concludes by saying he does agree because in a General mortgage those things are not included which are prohibited to be alienated by reason of some special favor to someone, and immovable goods of the Church are to be considered in this exemption.—Schmalzgrueber, lib. III, tit. 21, nn. 5, 15, 16, 17. What would be left? A General mortgage on movables—altogether beside the point and not in agreement with Pirhing.

[58] Pirhing, lib. III, tit. 21, n. 16.

[59] Raus, *Institutiones Canonicae Juxta Novum Codicem Juris* (2. ed. Lugduni: apud Vitte, 1931), p. 576, n. 1. Hereafter cited *Institutiones*.

[60] ". . . late sumitur sub hac prohibitione alienandi res Ecclesiae, itaut [ita ut] etiam simplicis dominii utilis alienatio sub hac prohibitione veniant; imo toties alienatio interdicitur a lege, . . . sumitur largo modo pro cujuscumque dominii translatione."—Petra, *Commentaria ad Constitutiones Apostolicas* (5 vols. in 2. Venetiis, 1729), Vol. V, comm. in const. V. Pauli II, sec. 1, n. 1. " Sed Venditio pura sine traditione, videtur hic non comprehendi, nam . . . alienatum non dici, quod venditum est; nam licet venditio sine traditione sequuta, sit proxima alienationi, non tamen est alienatio . . ."—Petra, *ibid.*, n. 4.

[61] Petra, *ibid.*, n. 3.

only the goods acquired at the time of the contract could be sold to pay the debt. Then before another judge (*coram Royas*), the validity of the contract was upheld but the ability to sell at foreclosure extended to all goods. This was vetoed by Pope Innocent X and again sent to the Rota. Again (*coram Royas*) the validity of the General mortgage was upheld but it was finally decided that the sale at foreclosure (of any or all property) had to have the prior approval of the Holy See.[62] Therefore, Petra concludes that a General mortgage is not comprehended under alienation for three reasons: first, it was not included in the canon *Nulli;* second, it was the common opinion of authors and of the Rota (in the foregoing account); third, it was declared by the Congregation of the Council on two occasions, January 13, 1691, and another decision not dated [14 iul. 1638?]. But in order that the foreclosure may take place, the Holy See's permission must be obtained for this resulting actual alienation.[63]

---

[62] Petra, *op. cit.*, Vol. IV, comm. in const. VI Benedicti XII, nn. 25–27.
[63] Petra, *ibid.*, nn. 28, 29, 30.

CHAPTER IV

Mortgaging and Solemnities of Law

ARTICLE I. PERIOD OF FORMATION LEADING TO THE BENEPLACITUM APOSTOLICUM

From the beginning of the Church, bishops were the administrators of its property,[1] and, therefore, when and if mortgages were to be placed on these possessions, it logically follows that they were the ones whose consent was legally necessary if they themselves were not the mortgagors. It has been shown that Roman law demanded the approval and consent of the bishop for mortgaging.[2]

It is almost impossible to find any early particular or general conciliar legislation in which mortgaging, as such, required this Episcopal concurrence. The term *obligare* was used.[3] This might be from the fact that mortgaging was not mentioned until Justinian's time; and that because Justinian required special solemnities (a method of procedure) for alienation and Special mortgage (regardless of their theoretical difference), succeeding Councils legislating on the solemnities necessary for alienation intended to include Special mortgage in their legislation. How long the Roman law concept of alienation, which was restricted to the transfer of dominion, persisted, and when Special mortgages were included, it is impossible to say, but the distinction seems still to have been used in Gratian's time.[4]

Therefore, the solemnities for Special mortgaging as pre-

[1] Cf. Hannan, *On Wills*, p. 419.

[2] *Supra*, Chapter II, p. 29.

[3] Cf. III (II), Council of Orleans (538), c. 26—*MGH, Legum Sectio III, Concilia*, Tom. I, p. 81; Council of Narbonne (589), c. 8—Hardouin, III, 493; I Council of the Lateran (1123), c. 4—Mansi, XXI, 282; Hefele—Leclercq, *Histoire des Conciles* (10 vols. in 19, Paris: Letouzey et Ané, 1907–1938), V, 630.

[4] ". . . alienare vel obligare absque permissu et subscriptione episcopi nihil liceat."—Ex Concilio Aurelianensi (506), in c. 41, C. X, q. 21.

scribed by Justinian[5] must have perdured as general Church law for many centuries.[6]

The incorporation of the fundamental law *(Nulli)* by Gregory IX into his Decretals did not change the ancient discipline of the Church. Though the consent of the bishop was needed for alienation through sale, donation, or exchange of Church property,[7] no legislation can be found in the decretals regarding the solemnities for mortgaging. One therefore concludes that the same solemnities were required for Special mortgaging as for alienation, namely, that the bishop had the right to mortgage because he had the right to administer Church goods;[8] that his consent was necessary for the validity of the mortgage when Church property was thus encumbered by abbots, priests, and other ministers;[9] but also that the consultation and consent of his chapter was necessary (since the twelfth century) before he gave his approval.[10]

The first general law requiring the *Beneplacitum Apostolicum* for mortgaging might seem to be contained in the *Liber Sextus* of Boniface VIII, promulgated March 3, 1298.

Among the many chapters from the II Council of Lyons (1274) which he incorporated in the *Liber Sextus,* Boniface VIII included one which prohibited administrators of monastic property from subjecting any rights regarding immovable Church property to the laity without first having the consent of their chapter and the special permission of the Apostolic See.[11] But this law was relative to the transfer of *dominium,* or real own-

---

[5] Cf. *Supra,* Chapter II, p. 29.

[6] Cf. also Cleary, *Alienation,* pp. 39–43. See also *supra,* Chapter III, pp. 32–35.

[7] C. 1, X, *de his quae fiunt a praelato sine consensu capituli,* III, 10.

[8] C. 7, C. X, q. 2.

[9] C. 41, C. X, q. 2.

[10] "Praelatus sine concilio capituli instituere vel destituere, vel alia negotia ecclesiae tractare non debet."—c. 4, X, *de his quae fiunt a praelato sine consensu capituli,* III, 10.

[11] "Hoc consultissimo prohibemus edicto, universos et singulos praelatos ecclesias sibi commissas, bona immobilia seu jura ipsarum laicis submittere, subiicere seu supponere absque capituli sui consensu et apostolicae sedis licentia speciali, . . ."—C. 2, *de rebus ecclesiae non alienandis,* III, 9, in VI°.

ership, i.e., a contract in which a new owner of the property *(dominus)* was created.[12] However, one feels that this was a definite step toward the later explicit provisions of the Constitution *Ambitiosae,* concerning mortgaging.[13]

The law was gradually being shaped, however, and the victory through the intrinsic rightness of the Church's cause in the Investiture struggle was becoming more evident by the increasingly assertive legislation. Pope Benedict XII, in 1339, ruled that monastic property could not be mortgaged without the approval of the Holy See.[14]

ARTICLE II. FROM THE CONSTITUTION AMBITIOSAE TO THE CODE

In the Constitution *Ambitiosae,* issued by Pope Paul II, on March 1, 1467, it was for the first time explicitly stated that the permission of the Holy See was henceforth necessary before a mortgage was placed on Church property.[15]

Because for nine hundred years Church laws had prohibited only Special mortgages, Pope Paul II would have saved five hundred years of discussion and debate had he either repeated the word "special" or expressly stated that both General and Special mortgages were meant. As it is, it is certain that the *Beneplacitum Apostolicum* was required for Special mortgages, which followed almost all the rules regarding alienation.[16] But

---

[12] Joannes Andreae, *Glossa,* ad. c. 2, *de rebus ecclesiae non alienandis,* IX, in VI°; Pirhing, lib. III, tit. 13, sec. 3, nn. 59, 60. It is therefore the introduction of the *Beneplacitum Apostolicum* for alienation and was merely confirmed and broadened in scope by Pope Paul II—Santi, III, 154, n. 11.

[13] Particular law in the Synod of Nîmes (1284) in France made the distinction between the pastor's and bishop's rights in the matter of obligating the Church for debts. The pastor was not to obligate his church for more than 100 solidi (of Tours) without the bishop's permission.—Mansi, XXIV, 541, n. 4. This possibly referred to mortgaging.

[14] Constitution VI of Benedict XII, *Ad Decorem,* 15 mai, 1339—*Bull. Rom. Taur.,* IV, 42. No distinction was made regarding General or Special mortgage, but he merely forbade their properties to be obligated. Cf. Chapter III, *supra,* p. 40, note 28, showing that *obligari* and *hypothecari* are the same.

[15] C. un., *de rebus ecclesiae non alienandis,* III, 4, in Extravag. com. Cf. Chapter III, *supra,* p. 41, for text.

[16] Redoanus, *De Alienationibus,* q. LI, n. 29, and q. II, cap. VI, nn. 12–16. Wernz, *Ius Decretalium,* III, n. 269 (cf. Chapter III, p. 45, *supra,* for text).

some held it was not required for General mortgage.[17] This did not mean that General mortgages were simply permitted without restrictions of any kind. As in every act of administration, there were definite limitations and requisites: a just cause;[18] a well-founded hope of meeting the obligation, which if not present reduced the contract to alienation;[19] a definite avoidance of frauds, as, for example, foreclosing immediately and selling a specific piece of property;[20] and in every case, permission from the Holy See before an auction sale on default.[21]

As could be expected from their ideas on alienation, some authorities specifically stated the *Beneplacitum Apostolicum* was required for both,[22] while many made no distinction of the types

---

[17] Petra, *Commentaria ad Constitutiones Apostolicas,* Vol. IV, comm. in const. VI Benedicti XII, n. 28; Merlinus, *De Pignoribus,* lib. II, tit. II, q. 85, n. 7; Turricellius, *De Rebus Ecclesiae,* cap. VIII, n. 55; Fagnanus, *Jus Canonicum,* III, *de rebus ecclesiae non alienandis,* cap. *Nulli,* n. 30. Rota decision in *Amerina Bonorum coram Verospio,* 19 apr. 1641; S. C. C. *in Romana Beneplaciti,* 13 jan. 1691—Petra, *ibid.,* nn. 27, 29. Rota decision in *Amerina Bonorum coram Roias,* 2 jun. 1645, Decisio XCVII, n. 6—in Merlinus, *loc. cit.,* Ferraris, *Prompta Bibliotheca, Canonica, Juridica, Moralis Theologica necnon Ascetica, Polemica, Rubricistica, Historica* (ed. Migne, 8 vols., Parisiis, 1860–1863), s. v. "Hypotheca," n. 23–25 (hereafter cited Ferraris, s. v.); Pichler, *Candidatus Jurisprudentiae Sacrae, seu Juris Canonici, secundum Gregorii Papae IX. Decretalium Titulos explicati* (5 vols., Augustani, 1723), lib. III, tit. 21, n. 6 (hereafter cited Pichler); Bouix, *Tractatus de Jure Regularium* (2 vols., Parisiis, 1857), II, 295, n. 10.

[18] The traditional causes were necessity (to church or for decent sustenance of clerics), piety (charity), utility, avoidance of harm and inutility—Rota dec. *Romana Census coram Penia,* 7 jan. 1579—Censius, *Tractatus de Censibus, cum Sacrae Rotae Romanae Decisionibus Recentissimus* (ed. novissima, Lugduni, 1730), dec. 314, n. 1; Redoanus, *op. cit.,* q. II, cap. VI, n. 13.

[19] Gutierrez, *Opera Omnia Civilia, Canonica et Criminalia, Decisionibus S. Rot. Roman. Recentissimis necnon Repertorio Generali* (16 vols., Coloniae, 1730–1731), Q. civ., lib. 2, q. 115, n. 2. Hereafter cited: *Opera Omnia.*

[20] Turricellius, *De Rebus Ecclesiae,* cap. VIII, n. 57, or mortgaging things of small value through separate mortgages, which, totaled, would exceed the sum for which permission is necessary—Santi, lib. III, tit. 13, n. 13.

[21] Cf. Pichler, lib. III, tit. 21, n. 5; cf. also Chapter III, *supra,* p. 49.

[22] Reiffenstuel, lib. III, tit. 21, n. 35; Schmier, *Jurisprudentia,* lib. III, tract. II, cap. V, n. 114; without saying it was alienation but requiring the *Beneplacitum Apostolicum* for general as well as special—Bonacina, *Opera Omnia* (3 vols. et *Tractationes Variae* in 1, Lugduni, 1639), Disp. II, Punct. II, n. 23.

but simply stated the requirements of the *Beneplacitum Apostolicum* for mortgage.[23]

The *Beneplacitum Apostolicum* was a most reasonable curb on the powers of prelates. Though all Church property cannot be said to be under the sole and complete ownership of the Holy See, yet individual Ordinaries are neither to be considered as having perfect proprietary rights. Not even imperfect ownership is attached to the office in either case. But as guardians of minors need authorization from judicial powers of society to alienate or encumber their ward's possessions, so also prelates of the Church, over the property of which they can be adjudged as holding a similar position, should obtain permission from the Supreme Judiciary of Catholic society as a whole, namely, the Holy See.[24]

The law affected all administrators of property, both secular and religious.[25] Many authors reported that the Constitution *Ambitiosae* was not received everywhere and, as a result, some

---

[23] Santi, lib. III, tit. 21, n. 4; for mortgages of more than 1000 florins' value in Austria—von Schulte, *Lehrbuch des katholischen Kirchenrechts,* p. 590, n. 4; for mortgages on immovables for more than 500 marks and on precious movables (res pretiosae), for more than 200 marks—Hergenroether, *Lehrhuch des katholischen Kirchenrechts,* n. 1100.

[24] Gonzalez, lib. III, tit. XIII, cap. 5, n. 10. The motivating cause is stated in the constitution itself; it was the conservation of Church goods to insure the continuance of divine services, the necessity and decent maintenance of the ministers, and the means to alleviate the distress of the poor. See also Santi, lib. III, tit. 21, n. 7. It was likewise held that the goods of Bishops, Prelates, and Clerics were tacitly (arising by operation of law) mortgaged against maladministration because, "Praelatus dicitur sponsus ecclesiae, et sicut sponsus carnalis habet obligata bona sponsae, ita sponsus spiritualis"—Merlinus, *De Pignoribus,* lib. III, tit. 1, q. 33, summarium, n. 5. Also interesting is the opinion that, if he wished, the Pope could alienate (*a fortiori* mortgage) any property of the Church through his plenitude of power—Redoanus, *De Alienationibus,* q. XLV, n. 1. Wernz held that the right of *dominium* of all ecclesiastical property rested in no single individual.—*Ius Decretalium,* III, 146.

[25] Cf. text of the Constitution *Ambitiosae, supra,* Chapter III, p. 36. Some religious societies were later given special privileges to mortgage and alienate without the permission of the Holy See, which privileges were revoked, because of abuses, from all European orders by decree of Pope Urban VIII, issued by the S. C. C., 17 sept. 1624—Santi, lib. III, tit. 13, n. 11.

territories were exempt from complying with its demands.[26] So also they were excused who, through any most urgent necessity in proportion to the gravity of its binding force, were unable to abide by its ordinances.[27] Nor did the constitution abrogate the centuries-old immunity granted by law for mortgaging property of little value.[28]

Besides the *Beneplacitum Apostolicum*, other requisites existed for mortgaging. These consisted in a just cause, such as necessity to Church (though some held to clerics also, as for decent sustenance), utility, charity (piety), inutility, and avoidance of harm.[29] Other solemnities required were, in their order of procedure: a meeting of the collegiate body governing the church to discuss and decide upon the contract; [30] the consulting of the parties interested in the transaction; [31] and the obtaining of the proper consent.[32] The recording of this consent through the

---

[26] At least in regard to its penalties.—Pirhing, lib. III, tit. 13, n. 51. This, in spite of the fact that any papal constitution inserted in the *Extravagantes* was presumed to be known and proof to the contrary was necessary by those pleading ignorance—Petra, *op. cit.*, vol. V, comm. in const. V, Pauli II, sec. 3, n. 39.

[27] Redoanus, *op. cit.*, q. XIII, n. 14, and q. XXXV, n. 7.

[28] C. 53, C. XII, q. 2; dec. S.C.C., 11 jan. 1596, referred to by Fagnanus, *Ius Canonicum*, III, *de rebus ecclesiae non alienandis*, c. *Nulli*, n. 25.

[29] For instance, Hergenroether, *Lehrbuch des katholischen Kirchenrechts*, n. 1100; Schmier, *Jurisprudentia*, lib. III, tract. I, par. II, cap. IV, nn. 75–85.

[30] C. 1, X, *de his quae fiunt a praelato sine consensu capituli*, III, 10, Schmier, *ibid.*, par. II, cap. IV, n. 84, et par. I, cap. IV, nn. 29, 119. Churches governed by a "rector ecclesiae" were not held to observe this "tractatus" —Hergenroether, *ibid.*, n. 1101.

[31] Hergenroether, *loc. cit.*; S. C. de Prop. Fid. ad Patriarch. *Armenien.*, 30 iul. 1867 ad 4—*Coll. S. P. C. F.*, n. 1310, and Zitelli-Natali, *Apparatus Iuris Ecclesiastici* (Romae, 1886), p. 54.

[32] The consent of the cathedral chapter was necessary for the Bishop to mortgage the chapter goods, his own *mensa*, or the goods of an inferior church—Glossa Ord., c. 52, XII, q. 2, ad. v. *vendere.* If an inferior prelate wished to mortgage the goods of his church, he needed the consent of his chapter, which if non-existent did not mean the consent of the cathedral chapter—C. 1, *de rebus ecclesiae non alienandis*, III, 4, in Clem. The Chapter's consent could be presumed when the duration of a contract was to be for less than ten years—Pirhing, lib. III, tit. 10, n. 2. In any event, the Bishop's consent was necessary—C. 41, C. XII, q. 2; Santi, lib. III, tit. 13, n. 10. Cf. also Provincial Council of Gnesen, in Poland (1577)—Mansi,

individual signatures of those voting, though needed for sales, exchanges, and donations, was not needed for mortgaging.[33] The proper authorization for submitting the petition was, however, necessary,[34] and finally, the forwarding of it to the Holy See.[35]

The question logically arises whether these latter solemnities were required for a General mortgage even though the *Beneplacitum Apostolicum* was not. It must be concluded that they were not, since even these preparatory steps were ordinances regarding alienation and prohibited acts of administration not classified as alienation in themselves but only in conjunction with alienation. And, therefore, since a General mortgage was not a prohibited act, it could be contracted by a rector of a church without even his own ordinary's consent.[36]

Should either the required solemnities not be observed, or no just cause exist when the solemnities were observed, many effects followed. Principal among these were the nullity of the mortgage[37] and its contestability.[38] However, if one of the req-

---

XXXVI bis, 717. Neither the Vicar General nor the Officialis had the power to give this consent in place of the bishop—Redoanus, *op. cit.*, q. 41, 60.

[33] C. 1, X, *de his quae fiunt a praelato sine consensu capituli*, III, 10; Redoanus, *De Alienationibus*, q. XL, n. 2. Lay approval could not legally supply for the consent of the proper ecclesiastical authorities—c. 12, X, *de rebus ecclesiae alienandis vel non*, III, 13. The consent of the majority was not judged solely numerically when voting as a collegiate body but also by their dignity, authority, and personal zeal—Redoanus, *op. cit.*, q. XXXVIII, n. 9.

[34] This was in the case of an inferior cleric wishing to mortgage the property of his church, in which instance he needed the authority of his bishop before applying for the *Beneplacitum Apostolicum*. Religious superiors of exempt religious applied directly to the Holy Father—Hergenroether, *Lehrbuch des katholischen Kirchenrechts*, n. 1101.

[35] After 7 sept. 1624, even religious had to apply to the Sacred Congregation of the Council—Pirhing, lib. III, tit. 23, n. 47.

[36] Ferraris, s. v. "Hypotheca," n. 25; Pichler, lib. III, tit. 21, n. 6; Pirhing, lib. III, tit. 13, n. 5. A mortgage which the Church held on property of others could not be remitted without the *Beneplacitum Apostolicum*—Petra, *Commentaria ad Constitutiones Apostolicas*, Vol. V, comm. in const. V, Pauli II, sec. 2, n. 27.

[37] C. 52, C. X, q. 2; c. 1, X, *de his quae fiunt a praelato sine consensu capituli*, III, 10; *Ambitiosae*—cf. *supra*, Chapter III, p. 38 for text. Cf.

uisite causes was the foundation of the transaction, a sanation was possible through petition to the Holy Father.[39] Even without a just cause as a motive for the mortgage, this sanation could be granted by him, but in this case there was ground for an action at law against the original mortgage.[40]

The resultant ecclesiastical penalties will be treated in the succeeding chapter.

The Second (1866) and Third (1884) Plenary Councils of Baltimore, without specifically mentioning mortgages, legislated that priests (of the United States) should not borrow money and thereby burden their churches, without having first obtained the permission of their bishop. This permission was to be given in writing.[41]

The Third Plenary Council of Baltimore, by virtue of an indult from Pope Leo XIII (1879–1903), granted through the Sacred Congregation of the Propagation of the Faith, suspended the

---

also Zitelli-Natali, *Apparatus Iuris Ecclesiastici,* p. 54, et al. Some classed this nullity among the penalties—cf. *infra,* Chapter V, p. 61.

[38] It could be contested by any alienator, successor, priest, patron, or even by any Catholic (!)—von Schulte, *Lehrbuch des katholischen Kirchenrechts,* p. 590, n. VI; a Papal Bull of Pius IV, *Apostolicae Sedis,* May 17, 1565, rescinded all alienations and mortgages made to the injury of the church—in Redoanus, *De Alienationibus,* p. 583; a Bull of Paul IV, *Iniunctum nobis,* July 14, 1555, rescinded all mortgages made without observing the solemnities required by the constitution, *Ambitiosae*—in Redoanus, *op. cit.,* p. 579, and *Fontes,* n. 88.

[39] Fagnanus, *Jus Canonicum,* lib. III, de rebus ecclesiae non alienandis, cap. *Nulli,* n. 46. The contract entered into with all requisites but the approval of the Holy See was considered *ipso jure null,* but the *Beneplacitum Apostolicum* could have a retroactive effect—Turricellius, *De Rebus Ecclesiae,* cap. XXII, n. 3.

[40] von Schulte, *loc. cit.,* if the just cause was lacking, the nullity of the original Papal permission and consequent contract followed on the necessity of the "preces" being true—Redoanus, *op. cit.,* q. XX, n. 161; it is interesting to compare this with our present Canon 40.

[41] *Concilii Plenarii Baltimorensis II., in Ecclesia Metropolitana Baltimorensi, a die VII. ad diem XXI. Octobris, A. D. MDCCCLXVI, habiti, et a Sede Apostolica recogniti, Acta et Decreta* (Baltimorae: John Murphy, 1868), n. 192; *Acta et Decreta Concilii Plenarii Baltimorensis Tertii A. D. MDCCCLXXXIV,* n. 279. The second Provincial Council of Quebec had required administrators of Church property to obtain the permission of the bishop for mortgaging.—*Coll. Lac.,* III, 657.

binding force of laws requiring the canonical solemnities for mortgaging. Henceforth, bishops were to seek the advice of their consultors regarding the justness of the cause.[42] The Council legislated that this advice must conclude in the consent of the Diocesan Consultors for any contracts exceeding five thousand dollars in value. Should this consent not be given, recourse to Rome would be necessary.[43] The special privileges of the indult were granted for a period of ten years, and were renewed for the last time in 1916 when mortgaging was again specifically stated among the exemptions.[44]

After the Code had been promulgated (May 27, 1917), the S. Consistorial Congregation, in revoking the above indult, directed the Ordinaries to Canon 1532 which was to grant them more extensive powers than they had previously enjoyed through indults.[45]

---

[42] *Acta et Decreta Concilii Plenarii Balitmorensis Tertii A. D. MDCCCLXXXIV*, p. ciii.

[43] *Op. cit.*, n. 20, 6.

[44] S. C. C., 31 iul. 1916—*AER*, LV (1916), 664 (private response).

[45] Decree S. C. Consist., 25 apr. 1918—*AAS*, X (1918), 190; *AER*, LIX (1918), 87. *De facto*, their powers were limited, because the Code was to require the *Beneplacitum Apostolicum* for mortgages exceeding six thousand dollars, whereas through the indults there was no limit above which this was necessary. It was only the Third Plenary Council of Baltimore's designation of the extent of Episcopal power to act without the consent of Diocesan Consultors which placed the sum at five thousand dollars. Barrett seems to have been unaware that this indult was revoked.—Cf. Barrett, *A Comparative Study of the Third Plenary Council of Baltimore and the Code*, The Catholic University of America Canon Law Studies, No. 83 (Washington, D. C.: The Catholic University of America, 1932), pp. 81, 82.

CHAPTER V

Mortgages and Ecclesiastical Penalties

ARTICLE I. ROMAN LAW INFLUENCE

By its nature, the Church has coercive power to enforce her laws and to punish any infraction which tends to subvert the ecclesiastical order. Because the maintaining of her temporalities is necessary so that she may accomplish her end, it is definitely a matter of the ecclesiastic order that her regulating the administration of these temporalities be observed. She has, therefore, always attached sanctions to her laws whose immediate ends were the conservation of valuable property. As will be seen, however, like the benevolent mother that she is, these punishments usually were inflicted only when the end of her laws was actually frustrated, namely, when Church property passed into the hands of some physical or moral person other than the particular subordinate unit which owned the property.

Justinian, in making the first laws regarding mortgaging of Church property, aimed his sanctions mainly at those contracting fraudulently (through which loss of property would naturally follow in almost every case) and at those who had obtained possession through contracting contrary to his legislation.[1]

Because even before the barbarian invasions and continuing through the Merovingian epoch (ended c. 750), churches were privately owned,[2] no subsequent legislation on penalties for mortgaging can be found until the revised chapter *Nulli* appears in the collections from the ninth to the thirteenth centuries, which extended the penalties inaugurated by the Roman Emperors for strict alienation to Special mortgaging.[3]

---

[1] Cf. Chapter II, *supra,* pp. 28–30; see also N. (120.11). Cf. also Council of Narbonne (589), c. 8, punishing those who have come into possession of property of the House of God through fraudulent transactions.—Mansi, IX, 1016.

[2] Clercq, *La Législation Religieuse Franque,* pp. 97, 303–305.

[3] Cf. Chapter III, p. 33, *supra.* "Sed omnes omnino sacerdotes ab hujusmodi alienatione abstineat, poenas timentes, quas Leonina constitutio

Sometime between the promulgation of Justinian's seventh novel in 535[4] and the Capitularia of Louis the Pious in 826[5] the word "mortgage" (*hypotheca*) was inserted in the canon *Nulli* in place of Justinian's original "pawn" *(pignus)*, and was carried over by Gregory IX to remain the common law of the Church until abrogated by the Constitution *Ambitiosae*, in 1467.[6]

This change meant that the Leonine penalties, which were never attached to mortgaging by Justinian, were applied, either through error or the deliberate falsification of the collectors, to mortgaging.

These penalties as they could affect mortgages meant that what was done contrary to the law was considered as not having been done at all; that the administrator involved in the legal transaction was to be deprived of his office, and any damages resulting to the Church were to be taken from his property; that, if necessary, his heirs, descendants, and even his successors, were liable to an action at law; that notaries to these contracts were to be punished by perpetual exile; and that a judge with jurisdiction in such matters and confirming such transactions was to lose his office and property.[7]

A few other scattered penalties appeared in the Decretals. The penalty for abbots', priests', and other ministers' mortgaging

---

minatur."—Burchard of Worms, *Decretum*, lib. III, c. 164—*MPL*, CXL, 706. None of the authors comment on the fact that this sentence follows immediately upon a definition of alienation in the preceding sentence of the same canon: "Alienationis autem verbum contineat venditionem, donationem, permutationem, et emphyteuseos perpetuum contractum."

[4] Cf. Chapter II, *supra*, p. 29.

[5] *Hludowici Pii Capitularia, Capitula e lege Romana Excerpta* (*826?*)—*MGH, Legum Sectio II, Capitularia Regum Francorum*, I, 310.

[6] ". . . nec per specialis pignoris occasionem tradere creditoribus."—Alciati, *De Iustiniani Novellis, Authentica* (Lugduni, 1549), Coll. II, tit. 1; ". . . nec magis specialis pignoris nomine creditoribus tradendi."—N. (7.1); ". . . neque creditoribus specialis hypothecae titulo obligare." *Hludowici Pii Capitularia*, in *MGH, Legum Sectio II, Capitularia Regum Francorum*, I, 310. This last reading is also in the *Collectio Capitularium Ansegisi* (834), Regino of Prüm (900), Burchard of Worms (c. 1025), Ivo of Chartres (1092–1115), *Iuliani Epitome* (ed. Haenel, 1873)—cf. *supra*, Chapter III, p. 34; c. 5, *de rebus ecclesiae alienandis vel non*, III, 13.

[7] C. (1, 2), 14, 3–7; Cleary, *Alienation*, p. 21.

Church property without the permission of the bishop was degradation.[8]

The penalty inflicted on prelates for mortgaging the goods of the Church to pay the debts of their clerical or lay friends was *ipso facto* suspension from spiritual and temporal administration, and *a beneficio* but not *ab officio ordinis.*[9] The penalty imposed by Pope Clement V on administrators who mortgaged Church goods without a just cause or without the proper solemnities was *ipso facto* suspension *ab officio et jurisdictione,* but not *a beneficio.*[10]

Sparse conciliar legislation was in harmony with the trend to inflict spiritual penalties only.[11]

ARTICLE II. FROM THE CONSTITUTION AMBITIOSAE TO THE CONSTITUTION APOSTOLICAE SEDIS

The Constitution *Ambitiosae* completely changed the common law of the Church regarding penalties for unlawful mortgaging. Though some interpreters of the constitution listed the nullity of the contract among its penalties,[12] others held that this was not a true penalty but rather an impediment to acquisition.[13] In either case, however, the nullity was *ipso jure* and consequently no

---

[8] C. 41, C. X, q. 2.

[9] C. 2, X, *de solutionibus,* III, 23; Thesaurus, *De Poenis Ecclesiasticis seu Canonicis Latae Sententiae a Iure Communi, et Constitutionibus Apostolicis Decretisque Sacrarum Congregationum* (Romae, 1640), pars II, s. v. "Obligantes," c. 1. Hereafter cited *De Poenis Ecclesiasticis.*

[10] C. 1, *de rebus ecclesiae non alienandis,* III, 4, in Clem. Notice the relaxation from degradation to suspension. Thesaurus, *De Poenis Ecclesiasticis,* pars II, s. v. "Alienatio," c. 5.

[11] Council of Avignon (1282), canon 3—Mansi, XXIV, 441; Synod of Nîmes (1284)—Mansi, XXIV, 541, n. 4; Council of Avignon (1326), canon 51—Mansi, XXV, 771.

[12] Redoanus, *De Alienationibus,* q. 76, cap. II, n. 29 and q. 77, cap. I, nn. 9, 16; Hergenroether, *Lehrbuch des katholischen Kirchenrechts,* n. 1101. Redoanus held that even if the Holy Father wished to derogate the law and alienated contrary to the existing law without cause, his successor could revoke the alienation.—*Op. cit.,* q. 76, cap. II, n. 29.

[13] Petra, *Commentaria ad Constitutiones Apostolicas,* Vol. V, comm. in const. V, Pauli II, sec. 4, n. 3. If the just cause was present and the Beneplacitum Apostolicum was not obtained, only the Church could rescind the contract—Fagnanus, *Jus Canonicum,* lib. III, *de rebus ecclesiae non alienandis,* c. *Nulli,* n. 46.

declaratory sentence was required, as in some of the true penalties.[14]

After the nullity of the contracts, the next penalty against any *male alienantes, accipientes, et subscribentes* was excommunication *latae sententiae nemini reservata.* This was applicable to all, regardless of their position or dignity even though it be episcopal. Abbots and bishops incurred, in addition, an interdict *ab ingressu ecclesiae;* and if within six months immediately following they did not repent and have the interdict lifted, they were *ipso facto* suspended from the spiritual and temporal administration of their monasteries or dioceses. These latter penalties were merely aggravating penalties.[15]

Inferior prelates and rectors, likewise, in addition to the excommunication, were *ipso facto* deprived of all dignities, offices, and benefices (with or without the care of souls) whose goods they had alienated. These benefices were thereupon considered as being vacant and able to be conferred on another.[16] Finally, all alienated goods must be returned.

To understand more correctly the Constitution *Ambitiosae,* a decree of Pope Urban VIII, issued through the Congregation of the Council on September 7, 1624, and the consequent resolutions of doubts concerning it are most helpful. This decree was descriptively called the *Decretum de rebus Regularibus non alienandis.* It abrogated any privileges which had been granted to, and any contrary customs which had arisen in, any religious

---

[14] Petra, *ibid.,* n. 4. But though *ipso jure* null it was urged that a declaration of nullity be given in order to save others from possible injury —Redoanus, *op. cit.,* q. 77, cap. II, n. 1.

[15] Petra, *ibid.,* n. 40. Thesaurus, *De Poenis Ecclesiasticis,* pars II, s. v. "alienatio," cap. 1, n. 2. That bishops and abbots incurred only the interdict and not the excommunication was held by Lega—*Praelectiones in Textum Iuris Canonici de Iudiciis Ecclesiasticis* (4 vols., Romae, 1896-1902), vol. III, 524; Bonacina, *Opera Omnia, Tractatus Variae,* disp. II, punct. V, n. 1. The excommunication was incurred if either the cause or the solemnities were lacking.—Maceraten, *Variae Practicabilium Rerum Resolutiones in Tres Libros Digestae* (Papiae, 1606), lib. I, resol. V, n. 7.

[16] Even after restitution or revocation of the contract, the benefice was not to be restored for the reason that his bad will had been manifested—Redoanus, *De Alienationibus, op. cit.,* q. 76, cap. II, n. 25. Though the privations were *ipso facto,* a declaration was necessary for the *foro externo*—Petra, *ibid.,* n. 39.

society whatsoever after the promulgation of the Constitution *Ambitiosae.*[17] Besides reaffirming the penalties of the Constitution *Ambitiosae,* it added another, applicable to religious, which consisted in the privation of either an active or passive voice and the perpetual inability to regain this right. No further declaration was necessary in this matter.[18]

Contrary to the almost unanimous opinion of authors that all these penalties applied only in a case of perfect alienation [19] the Sacred Congregation of the Council, with the approval of the Holy Father, replied in answer to a submitted question that for Regulars the very contracting of a mortgage on the occasion of a loan entailed the penalties of the aforesaid decree.[20] Since the decree in question had for its primary purpose to re-enact the Constitution *Ambitiosae,* this reply of the Sacred Congregation might be considered as authoritatively interpreting the Constitution *Ambitiosae* to mean that its penalties were applicable to unlawful mortgaging. However, it must be kept in mind that this was a particular response.

Inasmuch as a General mortgage was not comprehended under the terms of the Constitution *Ambitiosae,* it was consequently not included as a possible occasion of incurring penalties. The ex-

---

[17] Petra, *ibid.,* n. 3, and Vol. IV, comm. in const. VI, Benedicti XII, n. 5; Bouix, *Tractatus de Jure Regularium,* II, 286–289.

[18] Ferraris, s. v. "Alienatio," art. VI, n. 9. Some held this decree contained an added penalty of privation of offices for religious—R. de M., *Institutiones Juris Canonici Publici et Privati,* Vol. II (Parisiis, 1853), 432; but the Constitution *Ambitiosae* itself contains this penalty. Cf. text, *supra,* chap. III, p. 37.

[19] No penalties were incurred without *traditio*—Schmier, *Jurisprudentia,* lib. III, tract. I, par. II, cap. IV, n. 128; Engel, lib. III, tit. XIII, n. 18; Gutierrez, *Opera Omnia,* Q. civ., lib. II, q. 115, n. 2; Santi, p. 158, n. 16. Mortgage was not considered alienation in a strict sense—Pallottini, s. v. "Alienatio," II, n. 13. Alienators were anathematized so long as they did not restore the goods. [But there are no goods to restore in a mortgage.]—Conc. Trident., Sess. XXII, *de ref.,* c. 11; Ferraris, s. v. "Alienatio," art. IV, n. 3; cf. also Sabini, *Tractatus de Emptione et Venditione eorumque omnium quae ad eandem Materiam Pertinent* (Venetiis, 1575), p. 122, n. 11; Pirhing, lib. III, tit. 13, n. 77.

[20] Decree of 21 mart. 1626, repeated 4 iul. 1633—Petra, *op. cit.,* Vol. IV, comm. in const. VI Benedicti XII, n. 25. That no *traditio* or pacific possession by others was necessary to incur penalties was held by Bonacina, *op. cit.,* disp. II, punct. V, n. 2.

ception to this was the foreclosure sale resulting from a General mortgage.[21]

There were, moreover, other elements that required consideration in judging whether or not anyone had incurred the penalties. Because the law read "those presuming to mortgage," ignorance of law or of fact, so long as it was not crass or supine, as in other delicts, excused the delinquent from their incurrences.[22]

ARTICLE III. FROM THE CONSTITUTION APOSTOLICAE SEDIS TO THE CODE

On October 12, 1869, Pope Pius IX issued his memorable Constitution *Apostolicae Sedis,* which reaffirmed the Constitution *Ambitiosae,* by reference, but reduced all the various censures of the past to a single excommunication *latae sententiae nemini reservata.*[23]

It was doubted whether bishops guilty of unlawful alienation incurred this excommunication, or whether they were immune from all censures.[24]

The vindictive penalties of the former law against inferior prelates were not abrogated by the Constitution *Apostolicae Sedis.* These consisted in the privation of benefice and inability to receive the same benefice through a new *collatio;* the privation of an active and passive voice and the inability to regain it.[25] The nullity of the contract remained.[26]

---

[21] Cf. *supra,* chapter III, p. 49.

[22] Santi, II, 157; Ferraris, s. v. "Alienatio," art. IV, n. 3.

[23] "§ IV, Excommunicationes latae sententiae nemini reservatae, n. 3. Alienantes et recipere praesumentes bona ecclesiastica absque Beneplacito Apostolico, ad formam Extravagantis *Ambitiosae,* de rebus ecclesiae non alienandis."—*Fontes,* n. 552. Cf. Wernz, *Ius Decretalium,* III, n. 170. Cf. Aichner, *Compendium Juris Ecclesiastici ad Usum Cleri* (ed. 6, Brixinae, 1887), p. 781, n. 21. Hereafter cited *Compendium.*

[24] Cf. Aichner, *op. cit.,* p. 781, note 3.

[25] Wernz, *loc. cit.*; Santi, II, 157. That these privations no longer existed was held by many—cf. Lega, *De Iudiciis,* lib. II, vol. III, n. 452; Makee, *Institutiones Juris Ecclesiastici tum Publici tum Privati* (Parisiis, 1897), n. 910.

[26] Santi, *loc. cit.*

CHAPTER VI

The Mortgage Idea in Civil Law

ARTICLE I. EARLY FRENCH LAW

"Mortgage" is an interesting word. It has relatives in many fields of law, all with a common ancestor—gage. Some of the branches that have sprung from this single trunk can be seen in the English engagement, wage, wager, wed, wedding; the Scottish *wadset;* the Latin *gagium* (1174), *vadium, vadimonium, gageria, pignus, apotheca, hypotheca;* the Spanish *botica;* and the Frankish *wade, wadium, wetti, wedde, weddeshat.*[1]

The word gage is applied indiscriminately to movables and immovables, and a gage can be taken or given. The notion is expressed by our "security," and the possessor of it has something which secures the payment of money or the performance of some act by the person by whom it was given. But it is the giving of a gage of land that concerns us now.[2]

In French law, debtors gave lands to their creditors to secure the payment of their debts. The Frankish periods witnessed a transaction in which these lands were given for the enjoyment of the creditor who possessed the lands. This was called the land-gage. The creditor did not deduct the fruits of the land from the debt, and at default he acquired absolute ownership. Later, however, this was modified so that at times the profits were deducted, depending on the type of transaction. If so, it was called a "vif-gage" (live pledge). But because these lands could, at times, be an embarrassment for him (the creditor), and because the debtor had an interest in not giving up possession, a

[1] Cf. Pollock and Maitland, *History of English Law before the time of Edward I* (2 vols., Cambridge, 1895), II, 117 (hereafter cited: Pollock and Maitland); Du Cange, *Glossarium ad Scriptores Mediae et Infimae Latinitatis* (6 vols., Parisiis, 1733), s. v. "Apotheca"; Schulte-Fournier, *Histoire du Droit et des Institutions de L'Allemagne* (Paris, 1882), p. 482.

[2] Pollock and Maitland, II, 117.

method of removing these disadvantages was looked for. Moreover, the "mort-gage" was forbidden by the Church in the twelfth century because the profits were the same as interest and thus considered a form of usury. The feudal period brought a change in the form of a security which gave the creditor the same advantage as he previously had in the land-gage, but the debtor retained possession. At first it was known as a "bond" and could be general or special. The distinction depended on whether all goods, both present and future, movables and immovables, or only a particular immovable was offered in security. In the fourteenth and fifteenth centuries the bond became confused with the Roman mortgage, the *hypotheca,* except that the French law, at least from the sixteenth century on, demanded formalities and the old Roman law did not.[3]

ARTICLE II. ENGLISH LAW

In England, gages of land were known since the Saxon and early Norman periods. At the beginning of the thirteenth century, many lands were held as security for the large sums of money lent thereon. The form which these gages of land took is not so clear in many respects as might be desired. Ranulf de Glanville (a bishop c. 1180), in his manual for the use of judges, made one of the first attempts to explain the law. One of his distinctions is famous, namely, that between mort-gage and vif-gage, but there seems to be no direct proof that vif-gage was used in England.[4] So that the transaction could be considered valid, transfer of possession was necessary in both the vif-gage and mort-gage. If there was an express agreement to the effect that the mortgage of this period was given for a term of years, failure to pay before the expiration of the due date resulted in

---

[3] Brissaud-Howell, *A History of French Private Law,* The Continental Legal History Series, No. III (Boston, 1912), pp. 602–610. It is interesting to note that this giving of land as security for obtaining money instead of the highly logical *hypotheca* of the Roman civilization was a throwback to twenty centuries before Christ.—Cf. Harper, *The Code of Hammurabi, the King of Babylon about 2250 B. C.* (Chicago, 1904), p. 29.

[4] Cf. Pollock and Maitland, II, p. 117; Thompson-Johnson, *An Introduction to Medieval Europe 300–1500* (New York: W. W. Norton & Co., Inc., 1937), p. 450; Walsh, *On Mortgages,* p. 1.

the gagee acquiring absolute ownership without judgment. In the absence of an agreement on the term of the loan, an action had to be brought to fix the due date, failure to pay before which resulting in a similar absolute loss to the mortgagor.[5]

The mortgage for a term gave way to the ultimate common law mortgage in the form of a conveyance[6] in fee[7] to the mortgagee subject to payment of the debt as a condition subsequent. The performance of this condition gave to the mortgagor a right to re-enter and to the restoring of his estate. Default in the payment gave to the creditor an absolute title. Littleton explained this common law mortgage as being a gage which is dead to the debtor because if he fails to pay on the date due, he loses his land forever. Since the early part of the fifteenth century this has been the regular form of a mortgage.[8]

Though strict compliance with this condition of common law mortgages was insisted on by the courts of law, the court of Chancery quite early showed a disposition to relieve against this hardship. About 1625 it became a settled doctrine of the Chancery court that the debtor could redeem his land by paying the debt even after it had become due. This right of the debtor was called the "equity of redemption," and was recognized because the mortgaged property was understood to be primarily a security only.[9]

Still this required further development. This equity of redemption if allowed to continue indefinitely prevented the creditor from realizing his loan. The Chancery, therefore, began granting a decree of foreclosure by which the gagor's equity of redemption was "foreclosed" or cut off unless the debt was paid by a time named in the decree.[10]

It required some further time for the Chancery to adopt the view that the mortgagor was still the owner despite the transfer of possession. Logically, it had to regard the mortgagee

---

5 Walsh, *op. cit.*, p. 2.

6 A written instrument transferring the title to land or some interests therein from one person to another.

7 The quantum of the estate which was held of another.

8 Cf. Walsh, *op. cit.*, p. 4.

9 Tiffany, *Real Property*, p. 1166; Walsh, *op. cit.*, p. 9.

10 Walsh, *op. cit.*, p. 10; Tiffany, *op. cit.*, p. 1166.

as having merely a charge or lien on the land to secure his debt.[11]

Already in the fifteenth century the transfer of possession was not required by the Jews in England. Maitland says: "We may guess that if the Jews had not been expelled from England, the clumsy mortgage by way of conditional conveyance would have given way before a simpler method of securing debts, and would not still be incumbering our modern law." [12]

It might be added that had the Church not been reduced to a negative factor in England at about this time, the canonists might have revived the Roman law *hypotheca* to accomplish the same end.

However, at law the transfer of possession did not cease until the first half of the seventeenth century. This development was coincidental with that of the equity of redemption.[13]

Failure of the English law courts to recognize the actualities of the mortgage relation has resulted in some quite amusing, impossible, and conflicting theories as to the legal interest of the mortgagor in possession. Some held that he is a tenant at sufferance since the mortgagee has the right to eject him without notice similarly to a landlord. "But the spectacle of men of understanding seriously regarding the owner of land in possession of it as a tenant at sufferance merely because he has mortgaged it to secure a loan is about as unreal and fantastic as anything to be found in respectable human thought." [14] Neither can he be considered a tenant at will as some held. In 1820, it was decided that the mortgagor is tenant at will neither at law nor in equity.[15] English courts have ignored the solution of the problem as solved in New York and a great many of the states in this country. The Law of Property Act of 1925 did not solve their problems and, as a result, England lags far behind

---

[11] Tiffany, *op. cit.*, p. 1167. The term "equity of redemption" was now rather inappropriately applied to this entirely distinct right of ownership, in which sense it is most frequently used today, though still applicable to both. —Tiffany, *loc. cit.*

[12] Pollock and Maitland, II, 123.

[13] Walsh, *On Mortgages*, p. 15.

[14] Walsh, *op. cit.*, p. 17.

[15] Walsh, *op. cit.*, p. 18.

the United States in the law of mortgages, perhaps more so than in any other field of law.[16]

ARTICLE III. AMERICAN LAW

The early jurists of New York carried on with the English doctrine of mortgages, viz., that through a conditional conveyance the legal estate rests in the mortgagee, and thus the Eastern States in looking to New York as their leader early adopted this common law theory of mortgages.[17] In the early part of the nineteenth century, New York law courts began definitely to adopt the equitable theory that the mortgagee has merely a lien, a right of security incident to the mortgage debt, and that the legal estate continues in the mortgagor.[18] Following the later judicial authorities of the State of New York and its code which embodied the jurisprudence of these authorities, the newer states adopted this later theory rather than the old English idea of mortgages. However the fact that the Civil Law was established in Louisiana was an added factor in the adoption of the lien idea in most states west of the Mississippi.[19] Some of the States both west and east of the Mississippi arrived at their equitable consideration of the mortgage by law court decisions and others by statutory enactments or a combination of both, but it is immaterial. The important thing is that the development has taken place.[20]

This difference of evaluation of the rights vested in the mortgagor through the mortgage contract caused the States holding variant opinions to be called "common law" States and "lien theory" States depending respectively on whether they retained the English idea of transfer of legal estate or adopted the sensibly developed notion that the mortgage is only a lien upon the property for security of the debt. Because the "common law" theory States held for the transfer of the legal title they are also

---

[16] Walsh, *op. cit.*, p. 19.

[17] Cf. Jones, *A Treatise on the Law of Mortgages of Real Property* (8 ed., 4 vols., Indianapolis: The Bobbs-Merrill Co., 1928), I, 61. Hereafter cited *Mortgages.*

[18] Walsh, *On Mortgages,* pp. 21-23.

[19] Cf. Jones, *loc. cit.*

[20] Tiffany, *Real Property,* pp. 1167, 1168.

called "title theory" States, and because they follow the old English legal system are called also "legal theory" States. They include: Alabama, Arkansas, Illinois, Maine, Maryland, Massachusetts, New Hampshire, North Carolina, Ohio, Pennsylvania, Rhode Island, Tennessee, Vermont, Virginia, and West Virginia.[21]

The "lien theory" States, because allowing the mortgagee only the more equitable position of having a claim against the property, are also called "equitable theory" States, and, because of arriving at this doctrine by statute in many cases, are called also "statutory" States. They comprise Arizona, California, Colorado, Florida, Georgia, Idaho, Indiana, Iowa, Kansas, Kentucky, New York, North Dakota, Oklahoma, Oregon, South Carolina, South Dakota, Texas, Utah, Washington, Wisconsin, and Wyoming.[22] It might be noted that even in "lien theory" States the lien is a *legal* lien and that many "title theory" States have passed *statutes* to effect the transfer of title in a mortgage, but the former should not be called "legal theory" nor the latter "statutory" States on that account.

There are a very few States which have adopted a position midway between the lien theory and title theory. In them the common law doctrine has been modified to the extent that in the making of the mortgage only a lien is transferred to the mortgagee, but upon forfeiture and entry of the mortgagee he is regarded as having a legal title for the purpose of obtaining satisfaction out of the property. These are called "intermediate theory" States. They are Connecticut, Delaware, Mississippi, Missouri and New Jersey.[23]

Though for two hundred years and more a mortgage has been one thing at law and quite another thing in equity, the equitable view of the subject has largely encroached upon and sometimes superseded the legal, even in courts of law.[24] Thus the mortgagor is actually owner at law even in the "title theory" States for most all purposes other than the right of possession after

---

[21] Walsh, *On Mortgages*, p. 27. Jones has a slightly different listing, including Connecticut and New Jersey.—*Op. cit.*, 59.

[22] Cf. Jones, *op. cit.*, 60.

[23] Cf. Tiffany, *Real Property*, pp. 1168, 1169; Walsh, *On Mortgages*, p. 27.

[24] Cf. Jones, *op. cit.*, 11.

default; and in any case arising between the mortgagor or mortgagee and a third person.[25] The mortgagee holding title, whether at law or in equity, can use his legal title only for the purpose of securing his equitable rights under it.[26] Hence in both types of States the mortgagor's interest in the land may be sold upon execution; and his interest permits him to maintain a real action against a stranger, without the possibility of the mortgage's being set up as a defense. In both, the mortgagee has no such estate as can be sold on execution.[27]

This adoption at law, for most cases, of the modern (and ancient Roman) conception of a mortgage in these States should be applied consistently in all cases and thereby bring about the elimination of the distinction between the so-called "title" and "lien" States. "The legal title of the mortgagee is simply an unnecessary appendage left over from an earlier time as a remnant of a crude legal instrumentality long since outgrown, demanding excision as the vermiform appendix of the modern English law."[28] It seems the Christian Romans of 1400 years ago were not so "far behind the times"![29]

---

[25] Walsh, *op. cit.*, pp. 14, 15.

[26] Cf. Jones, *op. cit.*, 14, 15.

[27] Jones, *op. cit.*, 16.

[28] Walsh, *op. cit.*, pp. 28 and 32.

[29] In the modern theory, the lien is an hypothecation. The California Civil Code, defining a mortgage as "a contract by which specific property is hypothecated for the performance of an act, without the necessity of a change of possession," is held up as a model.—Cf. Walsh, *op. cit.*, p. 33, note 112.

PART TWO

CANONICAL COMMENTARY

CHAPTER VII

The Relation Between Alienation and Mortgaging

ARTICLE I. THE CONCEPT OF ALIENATION

The concept of alienation was anything but clear in pre-Code legislation. As was seen in Chapter III, every possible hypothesis was held at one time or another. These various and variant opinions were a result of no development of the mortgage idea. They resulted rather from the wording of the Constitution *Ambitiosae,* quoted in that chapter. Because this Constitution was the fundamental law up to the Code, the use of the term *hypotheca* without qualification caused confusion.

With the promulgation of the Code came a more clear determination but no explicit definition of the term alienation. An implicit definition can be found, however, in uniting one idea common to all commentators and canon 1533. All agree that alienation is a general term and as such has a restricted and an extended meaning, and while agreeing on the restricted signification, there are almost as many opinions on the extended sense as there are commentators.[1] The restricted meaning on which they agree is that alienation is a contract transferring the full dominion of ecclesiastical property.[2] In other words the owner-

---

[1] "Ut ex auctorum examine patet statim, plura incerta et obscura remanent in doctrina alienationis et obligationum post Codicem."—Larraona, *Commentarium Codicis,* in *Commentarium pro Religiosis* (Romae, 1920–1934; *Commentarium pro Religiosis et Missionariis,* Romae, 1935–), XIII (1932), 189, note (624). Hereafter cited *CpR.*

[2] ". . . alienatio . . . denotat omnem actum, quo bonum quoddam temporale ex dominio directo alicuius ecclesiae vel instituti ecclesiastici in dominium alterius subjecti . . . transfertur . . ."—Wernz-Vidal, *Ius Canonicum,* Tom. IV, Vol. 2, p. 222.

" (Alienatio comprehendit) . . . negotium seu actum quemlibet iuridicum per quae (quem) dominium, quod directum vocant . . . transfertur: . . ." —Larraona, *Commentarium Codicis, CpR,* XIII (1932), 188. Cf. also Beste, p. 744; Heston, *The Alienation of Church Property in the United*

ship is lost and the property, along with the proprietary title, passes into the complete and pacific ownership and possession of another.

By ordering the same solemnities both for the restricted meaning and for any contract wherein the condition of the Church can be made worse, canon 1533 extends the meaning of alienation

---

States, The Catholic University of America Canon Law Studies, No. 132 (Washington, D. C.: The Catholic University of America Press, 1941), p. 69, (hereafter cited *Alienation*); and others.

An evident error in the choice of the Roman law phrase to express transfer of ownership is found in the following: "Alienation is the transfer of the right of ownership (*ius in re*) of an object from person to person. This is the strict sense of the term. . . . Thus a sale or donation of an object would be alienation strictly speaking . . ."—*AER,* CII (1940), 167. "*Ius in re*" was unhappily used here instead of *dominium.* However, in all justice to the author of this article it must be admitted that these terms are used synonymously by American law writers because of a lack of understanding of Roman law.

The influence of Roman jurisprudence in the formation of the common law of England cannot be denied. The influence of the common law of England on American jurisprudence is readily admitted by all. One would think that American law would use Roman law terms which have been taken over bodily to express the definite legal meaning of those terms in Roman law. But such is not the case. Roman law terms have been kept intact as to their form but have been mutilated as to their meaning. This is explainable if not excusable when it is seen that authorities available to American law students give to these Roman law terms meanings which are erroneous in Roman law. As an example the reader with a knowledge of Roman law can detect the faultiness in the explanation of the terms *jus ad rem* and *jus in re* in the modern American law dictionaries and encyclopediae. (Ex. gr., *Bouvier's Law Dictionary* [New York: The Banks Law Publishing Co., 1928] s. v. "Jus ad rem.")

Since these sources show that the American law writers cannot agree amongst themselves as to the true meaning of these terms it is useless to follow any of their opinions. For the purposes of this dissertation, therefore, the writer will use these terms in their Roman law meaning. This procedure is justifiable because until 1918 the Church laws used Roman law in all matters of contract; because it is still used in Europe (except England), Canada, Mexico, all the countries of South America, Russia, and Louisiana (cf. *op. cit.,* s. v. "Civil Law"); and because the greater number of noted canonists have been subjects of, students of, and have written in countries wherein the Roman law is still basic.

The terms to be used according to their classical law concepts are: (1) *dominium,* or ownership (cf. Chapter IX, *infra,* for explanation); (2) *jura in re aliena,* or right *in rem* with respect to property owned by another,

to its broad sense.[3] This injury to the Church's condition is brought about by any legal act which exposes the property to loss through the grant of any property rights to another. These property rights are called, by the classical jurists, *jura in re aliena,* or individually a *jus in re.*[4] These contracts granting a *jus in re* limit the ownership of, or restrict the free disposal of, the property because the Church while retaining *dominium* has transferred some right or rights *in the property.*

The interpretation of canon 1533 can be projected still further. This would be extending it to prohibit as alienation the transfer of a *jus ad rem* according to the terminology of the classical jurists. There are arguments against this extension but their adequate refutation serves as the causes for projecting the definition of alienation to a transfer of a *jus ad rem.* The alleged reasons against, and the writer's reasons for, this extension are:

1. The amount of danger involved in transferring a *jus ad rem*

---

one kind of which is the *hypotheca* or mortgage; and (3) *jus ad rem,* or a right (resting on mere contract) in another's person. A difference between *dominium* and *jus in re* is that the owner can have the use, enjoyment, and possession of his property while another person has a *jus in re* enabling him, for example, merely to walk across the land. (American lawyers confuse *dominium* and *jus in re.*) A difference between a *jus in re* and a *jus ad rem* can be clearly seen in a mortgage: the holder of the *jus in re* received through a mortgage has the right to look to the land to secure his repayment, and regardless of into whose, or how many, hands the property has passed the *jus in re* (right in the thing itself) enables the mortgage holder to receive payment from the sale of that property and none other; whereas a *jus ad rem* merely gives to another person the right to demand something from the grantor personally. (American lawyers confuse this *jus in re* and *jus ad rem,* and consequently the related terms "*in rem* rights" and "*in personam* rights.")

[3] Cf. Beste, *loc. cit.* "Nomine alienationis bonorum temporalium ecclesiasticorum ius canonicum intelligit (a) omne negotium iuridicum, quo dominium rei temporalis ecclesiasticae ad alium proprietarium transfertur . . . (b) quemlibet contractu, quo conditio Ecclesiae peior fieri possit (Cf. can. 1533), . . ."—Schaefer, *Compendium de Religiosis ad normam Codicis Iuris Canonici* (3. ed., Roma: S. A. L. E. R., 1940), pp. 427, 428 (hereafter cited *De Religiosis*). Cf. also Woywod, "The Law of Contracts Concerning Ecclesiastical Goods,"—*The Homiletic and Pastoral Review* (New York, 1900–), XXX (1929), 269-277, esp. p. 273 (hereafter cited *HPR*).

[4] Cf. Raus, *Institutiones,* p. 576; Coronata, *Institutiones,* II, 481.

is not so great as in transferring a *jus in re*. But the amount of danger is irrelevant.

2. Canon 19 urges that administrators' rights be not restricted.[5] But canon 19 is inapplicable.

3. The interpretation of the meaning of canon 1533 should have as its extreme limit the transfer of a *jus in re*. But it will be shown that the extreme limit is to include the grant of a *jus ad rem*.

1. The canonists who limited the extension of alienation to the transfer of a *jus in re* sometimes gave as their reason the uncontested fact that there is not so much danger in the grant of a *jus ad rem* as there is in the concession of a *jus in re*, the danger to be feared being alienation.[6] The Code, it can be answered, does not seem to make any distinction in the degrees of danger, and where the law does not distinguish neither should the interpreter. These men were likewise writing before the promulgation of the Code and were basing their ideas on the Constitution *Ambitiosae* which specifically stated the types of contracts which were to be avoided, and did not legislate against dangerous contracts in general.

To support this restriction of the concept of alienation based on the diminished danger, it was explained by Pirhing that in the seizure of goods for non-payment of debts in the assuming of which only a *jus ad rem* was ceded, the movable property of the Church would be taken first and only in the event these movables were insufficient to satisfy the creditor, would the immovables be sold to pay the obligation. This was presented as being altogether proper because the natural law obliging the payment of obligations should precede the positive law of the Church forbidding alienation.[7] It must be kept in mind that before the Code the movables of the Church were alienable and that the laws affected only the immovables. Therefore, this reason seems ineffective today in that movables can no longer be freely alienated, but come under the same prescriptions as do immovables.[8] More-

---

[5] "Leges quae . . . liberum iurium exercitium coarctant, . . . strictae subsunt interpretationi."—C. 19.

[6] Merlinus, *De Pignoribus*, lib. II, tit. II, Q. 85, n. 8; Pirhing, lib. III, tit. 13, n. 5., cited in Chapter III, *supra*, p. 47, note 55.

[7] Pirhing, lib. III, tit. 21, n. 16.

[8] C. 1530, §1; "Quoad immobilia nota hac in re ius antiquum const.

over, there never was a law that absolutely prohibited the alienation of Church goods, and so there was no comparable positive law over which the natural law should take precedence. The Church has always permitted alienation if the proper solemnities were observed.[9] It is for the very observance of these solemnities that the extent of the concept of alienation must be determined. The Church would never have attempted to legislate to the non-observance of the natural law. It has always striven merely to prevent administrators from contracting to the detriment of the Church with the higher ecclesiastical authorities being in ignorance of the fact. Even in the less extended language of the Constitution *Ambitiosae,* the interpretation of the Congregation of the Council required the *Beneplacitum Apostolicum* for the sale of any property to pay the debts incurred by a contract not included in the law requiring the *Beneplacitum Apostolicum* for certain other contracts.[10]

2. Canon 19 requires the strict interpretation of laws which restrict the free exercise of rights.[11] The canonists who rely upon this canon to limit the extension of alienation to contracts granting a *jus in re* do so by saying that canon 1533, which extends alienation to any contract which can harm the condition of the Church, should be strictly interpreted because it restricts the free exercise of property rights,[12] and thus not only canon 19

Ambitiosae inde abrogatum esse."—Larraona, *Commentarium Codicis, CpR,* XIV (1933), 41; Cleary, *Alienation,* p. 58. Pope Clement V, in the beginning of the fourteenth century, had extended the law beyond immovables, but only for religious.—Cf. Ch. III, *supra,* p. 35.

[9] Though the laws in earlier times were posited in a negative command, they were always accompanied by laws regulating when alienations were permissible.—Cf. Roman Law, Ch. II, *supra,* pp. 27–30; Canon law, Chapter IV, *supra;* "Prohibitio illa (bona Ecclesiae) alienandi non est absoluta, sed hoc sibi vult, ut non fiat alienatio, nisi juxta praescripta juris;"—De Meester, *Juris Canonici et Juris Canonico—Civilis Compendium* (nova ed., Tom. III, pars prima, Brugis: Declee de Brouwer et Sii, 1926), Tom. III, pars prima, 400. Hereafter cited *Compendium,* III.

[10] Cf. Ch. III, *supra,* p. 49.

[11] "Leges quae . . . liberum iurium exercitium coarctant, . . . strictae subsunt interpretationi."—C. 19.

[12] Cf. Heston, *Alienation,* pp. 118, 121, 127–130.

would be applicable but also the juridical principle that *odia restringi, favores convenit ampliari.*[13]

First of all, it does not seem to be a question of limiting the exercise of anyone's property rights. The property rights in this whole discussion are the property rights of the Church,[14] and of the individual churches and moral persons juridically established.[15] The canons on contracts intend to preserve intact these rights of the Church, and therefore it would seem illogical to say that the laws intended to preserve these rights must be strictly interpreted so that the laws which state the administrators' rights resulting in harm to these rights of the Church might be kindly interpreted. The administrator of Church goods does not exercise his own rights but merely acts in the name of the Church, and his powers are dependent upon the concessions of the authority which placed him in the position to be able to administrate.

Secondly, it can hardly be denied that an administrator does not exercise his rights when he fulfills his office so much as he carries out his obligations. Title XXVIII of Book Three of the Code, which treats of the administration of ecclesiastical goods and seems to have been placed purposely just preceding title XXIX which treats of contracts (and the rules for alienation), has some very emphatic descriptions of the administrator's position. It is a duty of the Ordinary to keep a watchful eye on the acts of administration in his territory.[16] Persons related within specified degrees cannot assume the obligations of the Board of Administration which assists the Ordinary.[17] The members of the Board of Administration must take the oath *de munere bene ac fideliter adimplendo.*[18] Before any particular administrator enters upon his duty, certain regulations are to be carried out, among them being the same oath as the members of the Board of Administration.[19] After the assumption of his duties, specific directions are

---

13 R. J. 15, in VI°; Heston, *op. cit.*, p. 133.

14 C. 1495, §1.

15 C. 1495, §2.

16 C. 1520, §1.

17 C. 1520, §2.

18 C. 1520, §4.

19 C. 1522. The rubric of the article in which the commentary on this canon appears in Vromant is: "Obligationes adimplendae initio muneris

given to guide him in the performance of his task.[20] And they are bound so rigidly to their task that, even though they are not at the same time sharing in a benefice or ecclesiastical office, should they abandon their duties of their own accord and thereby cause damage to the Church, they are held to restitution.[21]

The reason for this seeming harsh attitude found in the canons is the nature of the canonical evaluation of the moral persons whose goods administrators manage. Ecclesiastical moral persons are considered minors in the eyes of the law.[22] As minors are in need of special protection, and as minors can easily be injured through lack of a desire to be a protector on the part of a guardian, or through the guardian's negligence, so also moral persons depend entirely on those who have been placed over them, i.e., their administrators, except through whom they cannot act, contract, or defend themselves.[23] Hence it is that canon 1527, §2, protects the juridical ecclesiastical persons from any possible injury caused by the negligence or maladministration of its "guardians" by freeing the moral person from any liability whatsoever in any contract which was executed without the consent of the proper superior, except only when and to the extent that the Church has profited by the transaction.

A further protection thrown about the moral person is the invalidating effect of the canons on any contract made by the administrator without the proper superior's permission. If it were the rights of the administrator that were to be protected by these

---

ineundi."—*De Bonis Ecclesiae Temporalibus* (Lovanii, 1934), p. 211. Though this and the rubric cited in the following note have no value as proofs, the writer feels that these rubrics do reflect Vromant's attitude toward the function of an administrator.

[20] C. 1523. Vromant's rubric here is: "De nonnullis obligationibus adimplendis perdurante munere administratore."—*Op. cit.*, p. 213; "The Sacred Congregation of Religious has considered for some time the necessity of formulating certain definite rules to assist religious superiors in their *grave and difficult obligations* in the administration of temporalities. The proper performance of such serious *obligations* requires special ability and prudence. Moreover, the duty demands . . ., etc." (italics added)—*Apostolic Delegation, Letter,* 13 nov., 1936—Bouscaren, *Supplement 1941*, p. 79.

[21] C. 1528.

[22] C. 100, §3.

[23] Cf. Beste, pp. 152, 153.

laws, the presumption of invalidity of these contracts in case of doubt would not be a corollary of the canons, but the laws would be differently worded to necessitate the proof of invalidity against the presumption of validity. But since the laws declare them invalid, it must be proven that they are not alienation before their validity can be upheld.

But even if it were the rights of an administrator that were considered, it still seems impossible to apply the strict interpretation because of Canon 19. Some commentators think this canon should apply to any law whatsoever which is an invalidating law. At first glance, this would apply to the laws on contracts which require the proper permission under pain of invalidity.[24] However, this is meant to be in reference to laws which grant inviolable rights to all persons.[25] Even then, those invalidating laws of the Church which are directly and primarily in favor of religion and the advantage of the Church itself cannot be said to be laws which restrict the free exercise of rights. The prescribing, prohibiting, or invalidating laws which regulate the administration of Church property are laws of this kind. The reason is that in regard to those things which are necessary to the very existence and operation of the Church, the natural rights of individuals are conditioned by the very fact of membership in the Church brought about by valid baptism. The restricted natural rights radically diminish the natural liberty of the faithful to those things which are not contrary to the rights proper to the Church. In this matter, therefore, the ecclesiastical law supervenes and cannot be said to be restrictive of the liberty of the subjects, but establishes and limits the liberty already fundamentally restricted by the conditioned natural right.[26] Neither by the divine natural law nor by the divine positive law is any liberty of the faithful acknowledged in these matters, and hence neither is

---

[24] C. 1530, §1, 3°. The application to all invalidating laws is held by Berutti, *Institutiones Iuris Canonici* (Vol. I, *Normae Generales,* Taurin-Romae: Marietti, 1936), I, 91.

[25] Berutti, *loc. cit.* Examples of these rights are those restricted by the irregularities and impediments to Holy Orders, the impediments to Matrimony, the prohibition of books, etc.

[26] Michiels, *Normae Generales Juris Canonici* (2 vols., Lublin-Polonia: Universitas Catholica, 1929), I, 447. Hereafter cited *Normae Generales.*

there any inalienable right, the exercise of which is restricted by a human law, acknowledged.[27] The rights of the local Ordinaries and other administrators come from no natural law or no divine positive law, but from the merely ecclesiastical laws of the Code and even as such they are not universal but particular rights restricted in the very act of concession.[28] In view of all of this it can be said that the laws of the Code which deal with alienation and its applicability to contracts should not be given a strict interpretation by reason of a fear to restrict the rights of administrators, because canon 19, which rules that laws restricting the exercise of rights should be strictly interpreted, does not apply to the administration of ecclesiastical goods.

3. Canon 1533, which finds no counterpart in previous legislation, presents the difficulty. Many of the authors writing since the promulgation of the Code try to make a distinction between the theoretical or proper meaning of alienation and those contracts which require the solemnities of alienation.[29] The distinction seems to be of little practical value, since the meaning of the word alienation depends on the legislator. Therefore, since he has demanded the same solemnities for strict alienation as for those contracts which can make the condition of the Church worse it is much simpler to use the word alienation in a wide

---

[27] Van Hove, *Commentarium Lovaniense in Codicem Iuris Canonici,* Vol. I, Tom. II, *De Legibus Ecclesiasticis* (Mechlinae-Romae: H. Dessain, 1930), 312 (hereafter cited: *De Legibus*). This is Van Hove's remark after agreeing with Michiels on the exclusion of the laws regarding administration of ecclesiastical goods from strict interpretation as cited immediately above.

[28] Cc. 1519, 1520, 1521, 485, 1182, 1476, 1489–1493.

[29] Vermeersch-Creusen, *Epitome,* II, 594, 598; Augustine, *A Commentary on the New Code of Canon Law* (8 vols., St. Louis: Herder & Co., 1925–1938. Vol. I, 6. ed., 1931; Vol. II, 6. ed., 1936; Vol. III, 5. ed., 1938; Vol. IV, 3. ed., 1925; Vol. V, 5. ed., 1935; Vol. VI, 3. ed., 1931; Vol. VII, 3. ed., 1930; Vol. VIII, 3. ed., 1931), VI, 593, 599 (hereafter cited *Commentary*); Ayrinhac, *Administrative Legislation in the New Code of Canon Law* (London-New York-Toronto: Longmans, Green and Co., 1930), p. 439 (hereafter cited *Administrative Legislation*); Larraona, *Commentarium Codicis, CpR,* XIII (1932), 187, 188 (line 10, p. 189, being evidently a typographical error in listing canon 1532); Cocchi, *Commentarium,* VI, 412.

sense and be done with it. This is done by some authors.[30] All that remains is to determine the mind of the legislator in using the phrase "*in quolibet contractu quo conditio Ecclesiae peior fieri possit*" and the extent of the meaning of alienation will be the same.

Those who wish to limit the meaning of alienation to those contracts which grant a *jus in re* do so on the strength of Wernz's definition of alienation in which he used a term similar to canon 1533. Wernz used the words "*pejoris conditionis fiunt.*"[31] The Code, while similar, is not the same, and there seems to be an oversight in basing the interpretation of the wording of the Code upon the meaning of Wernz. The word "*fiunt*" means "is made." The exact counterpart of Wernz's phrase would therefore have appeared in the Code thus: "*in quolibet contractu quo conditio Ecclesiae peior fiat.*"

This would have expressed the idea of an immediate effect on the condition of the Church. But since the Code uses the different words when its intent could have been phrased to express exactly what Wernz had in mind, the lawmaker must have intended to express a different idea. To interpret the meaning of the phrase of the Code there are definite rules of interpretation to be followed. This is an altogether new phrase in the legislation on alienation,[32] and therefore the laws of interpretation of canon 6 are not apropos. This canon failing, the next source of interpretation is the authentic interpretation of canon 17, whereby the legislator, his successor, or those to whom he has given the power to interpret are the only authentic interpreters. There has been no authentic interpretation of this phrase to the writer's knowledge. This also being lacking, the next step is to use canon 18 which legislates that ecclesiastical laws are to be understood according to the proper meaning of the words in their text and context. This is the primary means of interpeting law because the legislator presumes that words, which signify his mind, will be stu-

---

[30] Doheny, *Church Finance*, p. 22; Schaefer, *De Religiosis*, p. 428; Heston, *Alienation*, p. 70; De Meester, *Compendium*, III, 400.

[31] *Ius Decretalium*, III, n. 154.

[32] Cf. *supra*, p. 38, showing that the constitution *Ambitiosae* was the clearest statement of the common church law to the time of the Code.

diously and diligently adhered to.[33] The means of interpreting the sense of the words from their text and context is the grammatical interpretation.[34]

From this grammatical meaning of the words, the phrase in question has a future meaning and not an immediately present one. If we restrict this clause only to the contracts which grant a *jus in re,* we are following Wernz's explanation of alienation and limiting the meaning to those contracts which make the condition of the Church worse by the very fact of, and at the moment of, the contract. The contract grants the *jus in re,* and the Church *is made* worse *ipso facto.* Property encumbered by such a lien has less value from the very moment the lien is applied by means of the contract. Whereas the grant of a *jus ad rem* by contract has no instantaneous effect on the value of the property. It can have a future effect resulting from a suit at law in which an adverse decision is rendered against the church corporation. This then seems to be the contract by which the condition of the Church *can be made* worse. The Code terminology has the textual significance of a possible result harmful to the condition of the Church.[35] This possibility lasts as long as a *jus ad rem* is retained by a creditor, and can happen any time in the future. We cannot divorce the creditor's rights against the debtor from the possibility of damage, because even at law a creditor has always a potential right *in rem* when he has a right *in personam.*

This process of the examination of the text seemingly takes precedence over any other method prescribed in canon 18 to interpret law, and this process immediately reveals the mind of the legislator. The law is clear and *in se certa.* "And," as Schmidt says, "there is immediately applicable the traditional principle enunciated by Reiffenstuel (1703): '*Verba clara non admittunt interpretationem neque voluntas coniecturam.*' In fact,

---

[33] Van Hove, *De Legibus,* p. 258.

[34] Van Hove, *loc. cit.*

[35] "The Canon Law regards all transactions which *may* (italics added) render the financial condition of the Institute, Province, or religious house less secure, as alienations."—*Apostolic Delegation, Letter,* 13 Nov., 1936—Bouscaren, *Supplement 1941,* p. 79.

according to the express terms of canon 18, further investigation is not permissible."[36]

However, to show that the writer is not attempting to project an altogether new theory of the extension of the meaning of the word alienation, attention is called to the fact that in the old law some able canonists explicitly held that the most wide interpretation of the word included the transfer of *jus ad rem.*[37]

Since the promulgation of the code no commentator can be found who explicitly extends the meaning to a transfer of a *jus ad rem,* but several do so implicitly. Thus, Teodori, Vermeersch-Creusen, Cocchi, Larraona, and Vromant can be said to ascribe to this notion of alienation. Teodori uses the phrase of Reiffenstuel[38] to define the wide sense of alienation: *"vel ius in alium transfertur."*[39] Roman law knew no term such as *ius in alium* and therefore its exact meaning can only be estimated from a comparison to the Roman law terms, *jus ad rem* and *jus in re.* It is immediately evident that much depends on the prepositions, *ad* and *in. Ad,* meaning "to" or "unto," signifies motion *to* a place, and often *to* a person. *In,* when with the accusative, signifies direction or motion to a place and also to persons. When *in* is used with the ablative, it signifies being, rest, state, or condi-

---

[36] Schmidt, *The Principles of Authentic Interpretation in Canon 17 of the Code of Canon Law,* The Catholic University of America Canon Law Studies, No. 141 (Washington, D. C.: The Catholic University of America Press, 1941), p. 133.

[37] "Alienatio lata continet actus et negotia quibus aliquod jus in re vel ad rem ab uno in alium transfertur. . . ."—Schmier, *Jurisprudentia,* lib. III, tract. I, par. II, cap. IV, n. 57. That a transfer of *any* right was comprehended under forbidden alienations—cf. Santi, lib. III, tit. XXI, nn. 5, 6. Contrary to Heston's ascribing the originating of the term "conditio Ecclesiae peior fieri possit" to Wernz (Heston, *Alienation,* p. 115, note 17), Santi had used this term two centuries previously and meant by it the transfer of any right. Cf. Santi, *loc. cit.* Cf. also *S. C. C.,* in *Camerin. Fabricae,* 30 jul. 1774—Pallottini, cited in Chapter III, note 32, *supra.*

"Alienationis nomen in proposito sumitur large, ac prout complectitur omnem actum quo . . . jus in alterum transfertur."—Reiffenstuel, lib. III, tit. XII, n. 3.

[38] See previous footnote.

[39] "Alienantes bona ecclesiastica sine beneplacito Apostolico."—*Consultationes Iuris Canonici* (Romae, 1934—), I (1934), 318–322, esp. p. 321.

tion.[40] The *jus* which is *in re* is directed toward the state or the condition of the property. The *jus* which is *ad rem* does not affect the state of existence of the property but rather is directed toward a person, in this case the administrators of the property. The *jus* which is transferred *in alium* has the same meaning as the *jus ad rem* since the word "*in*" is used here with the accusative to denote the idea of movement by contractual transfer of a right to a person.

It is admitted that the unqualified *jus in alium* of Reiffenstuel and Teodori can be understood in two ways to signify the type of *jus* which is transferred or to mean that some kind of *jus* is transferred to someone. Both the *jus in re* and *jus ad rem* are transferred *ad alium,* or *in alium.* But in either case these authors can be said to mean the transfer of a *jus ad rem* because if it is the type of *jus,* it is synonymous to a *jus ad rem* as shown, and if it is not the type of *jus* they wish to describe but rather to mean that *some jus* is transferred to another their very lack of specifying and limiting signifies the generic quality of the type transferred.

Vermeersch-Creusen, while not using canon 1533 to show the extent of the concept of alienation, does hold that this canon signifies the transfer or ceding of a *jus litis,*[41] which Cocchi interprets as meaning a right to a lawsuit.[42] Now the right to a lawsuit can be the result of any contractual pecuniary obligation and is not limited to the enforcement of a *jus in re.* If a person has only an *in personam* right, which is equivalent to the *jus ad rem,* he can sue to enforce it. As Larraona holds, every contract, money transaction, or legal act by which a right is granted to others to demand the performance of some action entailing an economic burden, is included under the provisions of canon 1533, because the condition of the Church can be made worse by having accepted this duty to fulfill the contract.[43]

---

[40] Freund-Leverett, *Lexicon of the Latin Language,* s. v. "ad" and "in."

[41] "Talis contractus (quo conditio Ecclesiae peior fieri possit) est cessio iuris, vel litis vel actionis . . ."—*Epitome,* II, 598, n. 855.

[42] "Hinc, non tantum cessio domini alicuius rei, sed cessio cuiuscunque iuris *ut* ius crediti, ius litis, ius actionis iam quaesitae comprehenditur."—*Commentarium,* VI, p. 412, where in his reference on this point he notes (note 9) that his authority is Vermeersch, II, 855.

[43] He distinguished between alienation properly so called and improperly

Vromant gives the General mortgage as an example of a contract by which the Church can be made worse. Though he makes the distinction between this type of contract and alienation we have seen that this is an arbitrary distinction.[44] By placing the General mortgage under the prescriptions of canon 1533, he extends alienation to the transfer of a *jus ad rem* because that is the type of right transferred by a General mortgage.[45]

The writer herewith submits an added reason, perhaps the most evident, why the meaning of canon 1533, and automatically of alienation, must be extended to the transfer of a *jus ad rem*.

---

so called. (This is not the same as alienation in the strict and wide sense, because he already has said that the wide sense includes the transfer of ownership, real rights or legal possession.) He designates the contracts of 1533 as *obligationes* rather than as *alienationes*. He then adds: "Nomine obligationis, hac in re, venit omnis contractus seu negotium vel actus iuridicus quibus alii ius conceditur ad aliquam praestationem, actionem, omissionem exigendam quae aliquod onus oeconomicum secumfert. Ex hoc suscepto onere merito dicitur conditionem Ecclesiae peiorem fieri (c. 1533). *Obligatio* potest sumi sensu latissimo, quatenus contractus et negotia etiam complectatur quae, iuxta superius dicta, alienationem secumferunt. Sensu *magis proprio,* de quo in can. 534 et in can. 1533, *obligatio* ab alienatione distinguenda est et ad illos actus, contractus, negotia restringenda videtur, quae cum imponant Ecclesiae in favorem alterius personae, onus oeconomicum ex quo ipsius Ecclesiae conditio peior redditur, tamen alienationem proprie dictam non continent. Obligationes huiusmodi *simplices* i. e. absque alienatione, quoad plura alienationibus aequiparantur et sensu lato *alienationes* dici possunt et non raro dicuntur, tamen nec sunt proprie dictae alienationes, nec nomine *alienationis* veniunt, non solum *in poenalibus,* sed nec in aliis ad quae aequiparatio ex lege non extendatur . . . can. 1533 . . . est unice fundamentum aequiparationis.—Larraona, *Commentarium Codicis, CpR,* XIII (1932), 189, 190. Hence his distinction between alienation and obligation is made with a purpose not to fuse canon 1533 with the penalties for illicit alienations, but as far as the contractual laws and the solemnities of alienation, these contracts which do not grant *real rights* (which are *jura in re aliena*) but do grant the right to the performance of an action (which is a *jus ad rem*) are contained in canon 1533 as forbidden without the proper solemnities.

[44] Speaking of canon 1538, he says: "Cum canone praesenti agatur de contractu alienationis (hypotheca speciali vel oppignoratione) vel de contractu quo condicio Ecclesiae peior fieri possit (hypotheca generali vel aere alieno contrahendo), administratores ecclesiarum . . . qui . . . contractum legitime perficiunt, etc."—*De Bonis Ecclesiae Temporalibus*, p. 344. (Parentheses in original.)

[45] Cf. *infra,* Article V, p. 101.

The grant of a *jus ad rem* rests on contract alone, so that the recipient gains nothing, nor can he exercise or enforce his right, without proof of the contract on which it is based. Once the contract is proven, the right to the economic value contained in the contract is ascertained and if it can affect the stable capital alienation would result when the right is enforced. Since canon 1533 mentions nothing about the contractual transfer of a *jus in re* but speaks merely of contracts in general, it definitely seems to include all contracts and all rights which as a result rest on the contracts. Canon 1533 is primarily concerned with contracts, not the transfer of a *jus in re*. Since the *jus ad rem* rests on contract, the canon must include the transfer of a *jus ad rem*. If the Code merely wished to extend the solemnities to the transfer of a *jus in re*, it could have worded the law much more clearly by saying, "*Solemnitates . . . requiruntur . . . in quolibet contractu quo jus in re transfertur.*" This would have distinguished between the admittedly forbidden contractual transfer of the *jus in re* and the defended permissible transfer of a *jus ad rem*. Yet the law does not make this distinction. Neither then, it seems, should the interpretation.

Since, then, there is some danger in the grant of a *jus ad rem* by contract; and since canon 19 demanding the strict interpretation of laws restricting the rights of administrators is inapplicable but on the contrary these laws demand a wide interpretation; and since the meaning of the law itself embraces a possible future harm and would not be understandable if meant to embrace an immediate harm since alienation itself does this; and since the prohibition of the law is directed toward contracts generally, and the *jus ad rem* rests on contract, canon 1533, to the extent of its prohibition, extends the definition of alienation to the transfer of a *jus ad rem* when this right can be juridically enforced.

ARTICLE II. RESTRAINTS AFFECT ONLY STABLE CAPITAL

Not all goods that are ecclesiastical are subject to the laws of alienation. Alienation is had only when the stable capital or patrimony of the Church is diminished. The stable capital is all those assets which are not in ordinary circulation and which, therefore, form the permanent basis of the financial condition of the church corporation.[46] All real estate, both land and buildings, would be considered a part of the stable capital, except in the case where through some extrinsic cause these cannot be annexed to the patrimony of the corporation. Examples of real estate which is not stable capital are: (a) property which is given to be *used* for some special purpose of the donor, such a purpose being perhaps that it be sold to provide manual mass stipends; (b) property given to *serve* some special purpose, such as to provide the funds for anniversary masses from the revenue; (c) property which ecclesiastical law will not permit the church body to retain, such as a religious community which may not own immovables or is obligated by law to use all its resources to prosecute the purpose of its existence.[47]

However, since even from the times of the Roman law the alienation of immovable property was forbidden in contradistinction to movables, and only in the Code has the movable property been subjected to the laws of alienation, a distinction can be drawn between real estate and stable capital. Real estate is by its nature the basis of economic security. Money was brought into use as a medium of exchange, and in itself has no stability. It is only when the money is invested as an endowment fund in some comparatively permanent form, as ex. gr., at interest in a bank or in interest-bearing or dividend-paying securities, that it takes on this quality of permanency and can be considered stable capital.

Conversely, as has been shown, real estate can be considered non-stable capital at times. If money held for current use or expansion (not belonging to the stable capital) were invested for a time in houses or buildings as a medium of security (e.g. against inflation), or for any fruitful purpose, this real estate represents free money not yet incorporated into the stable capital and the buildings can be sold without any solemnities of alienation.[48]

---

[46] A very fine exposition of this point is presented by Heston. Cf. Heston, *Alienation*, pp. 72–79; Heston, " The Element of Stable Capital in Temporal Administration."—*The Jurist* (Washington, D. C., 1941—), II (1942), 120–133.

[47] Larraona, *Commentarium Codicis, CpR*, XIII (1932), 191.

[48] Cf. Vromant, *De Bonis Ecclesiae Temporalibus*, p. 299; passage found also in Larraona, *Commentarium Codicis, CpR*, XIII (1932), 190, note 630.

Hence it can be seen that the distinction between immovable property (real estate) and stable capital is made because real estate by its nature is not freely alienable though accidentally (and rarely) it might be, whereas money by its nature is freely alienable though accidentally it might not be.

Because of the respective ease or difficulty of alienating movable or immovable property as has just been shown, one is justified in arriving at a *presumptio facti* in a doubtful case. In case of doubt as to whether any certain amount of money is stable capital, the presumption would favor not regarding it as such.[49] But in case of doubt as to the status of any piece of real estate, the presumption would be in favor of its being regarded as stable capital. Therefore unless some extrinsic cause can be proved to show the contrary, the presumption still stands and causes real estate to be considered as subject to the laws of alienation.

ARTICLE III. MORTGAGE AS A CONTRACT OF ALIENATION

It is necessary to consider the mortgage contract specifically in order to determine if and when it is to be classed under the contracts demanding the formalities of alienation. Having determined the meaning of canon 1533, the interpretation of canon 1538 is no longer difficult, for if a mortgage does make the condition of the Church worse it requires all the solemnities of alienation; whereas if the mortgage does not and cannot make the condition of the Church worse, it does not require these added solemnities. The intermediary type which does not at the moment of contract, but can, as a result, make the Church's condition worse will require the solemnities.

The pre-Code and even some post-Code authors make a distinction between General and Special mortgages. The Special mortgage in canonical literature is the contract offering as security for a debt some certain and determined piece or pieces of immovable property without the transfer of possession to the creditor, the creditor receiving only the right to institute proceedings to sell the property if the debt is not paid. The General mortgage obligates all the goods of the debtor, both present hold-

[49] Heston, *op. cit.*, p. 75.

ings and those to be acquired in the future, even though no mention of these future goods were made.[50]

As is immediately evident, there are marked differences between the Special and General mortgages. The Special obligates a particular and certain piece of property, or several parcels so long as they are a part of a group, even though not individually expressed.[51] Even if every piece of present and future property were obligated it created a Special mortgage on each piece because of the use of the words "omnia et singula." [52] The General mortgage occurred when one's goods (simply) or all one's goods were obligated as security, even though the future holdings were not expressly mentioned.[53] Property specially mortgaged made it impossible to transfer *dominium*, whereas a General mortgage did not prevent this transfer.[54] And perhaps the greatest distinction so far as any effect on administration of Church property is concerned was that a Special mortgage transferred a *jus in re* (*in rem* rights), while a General gave only a *jus ad rem* (*in personam* rights), to the creditor.[55]

From this it can be seen that the Special mortgage of the canonists is what is known in American law simply as a mortgage, namely that certain specified property is obligated to secure the payment of a debt, through which act of obligating a lien is created on, and colors the title to, the property. In American law there is such a thing as a mortgage on property in possession and after acquired property,[56] but the mortgage on property in possession is so imposed that *in rem* rights are granted, whereas in the property to be acquired only *in personam* rights are granted

---

[50] Cf. Schmalzgrueber, lib. III, pars II, tit. XXI, nn. 2, 3, 4, 5; Pirhing, lib. III, tit. XXI, nn. 1, 2, 3; Vromant, *De Bonis Ecclesiae Temporalibus*, p. 342.

[51] Merlinus, *De Pignoribus*, lib. I, tit. II, q. XI, n. 2.

[52] Though this was disputed.—Merlinus, *op. cit.*, lib. I, tit. II, q. XI, n. 5.

[53] Merlinus, *op. cit.*, lib. I, tit. II, q. XI, n. 8.

[54] Merlinus, *op. cit.*, lib. I, tit. II, q. XI, n. 12.

[55] Redoanus, *De Alienationibus*, q. II, cap. VI, n. 16; Merlinus, *op. cit.*, lib. II, tit. II, q. 85, n. 8.

Because no transfer of possession takes place in a mortgage, some maintained that even a Special mortgage transferred only a *jus ad rem*.—Cf. Redoanus, *De Alienationibus*, q. II, cap. VI, n. 14.

[56] Cf. Walsh, *On Mortgages*, p. 54.

until such a time as they come into possession and the mortgage is recorded or not, as the law demands, when *in rem* rights arise. This, too, is rather the Special mortgage of the canonists because of the grant of the real rights.

The General mortgage of the canonists would be an imaginary American law mortgage whereby all present and future property, both personal and real, is offered as security for a debt without coloring the title to the property, so that during the running of the debt, the property can be sold or otherwise alienated with a clear title; yet should the debt not be paid, a personal action at law is available to the creditor with the debtor having a right to present personal property in satisfaction thereof before real estate. If the debtor's present holdings should fail to satisfy the debt, all future acquired property would be available to attachment. In case of bankruptcy or failure of the corporation, the creditor would have a prior right over unsecured creditors. Such a contract does not exist in American law.

What then does canon 1538 mean to include in its transactions forbidden without the proper solemnities of alienation? Since it is one of the canons describing specifically the contracts mentioned generally in canon 1533, these of canon 1538 must be legally enforceable contracts which can harm the stable capital of the corporation entering them. There must be a transfer of *jus in re* or a *jus ad rem* in reference to the stable capital.

It matters not whether the contract was entered into for the sake of realizing a financial profit for the Church, since the Church is inclined to choose the safer method of procedure in all acts of administration and to forego a profit that is certain rather than suffer a loss that is possible.[57] Nor does the fact that both parties to the contract are ecclesiastical corporations lessen the restrictions of the law or change the nature of the transaction.[58] If a church has non-stable capital which it wants to loan to another church rather than deposit it in a bank temporarily, this transaction on the part of the investing church would not be alienation,[59] but on the part of the borrowing church it would be

[57] Cf. Cleary, *Alienation,* p. 3; Larraona, *Commentarium Codicis, CpR,* XIII (1932), 189, note (625).

[58] Cf. Doheny, *Church Finance,* p. 39.

[59] Cf. Heston, *Alienation,* p. 75.

the granting of rights either personal or real which would necessitate the borrowing corporation's compliance with the laws of alienation. In a word, the quality of the corporation or person from whom money is borrowed does not change the nature of the contract if the same transaction in any case whatsoever can be termed alienation.[60]

Since each ecclesiastical corporation has its own distinctive rights to retain its temporal goods,[61] it seems hardly within the law for anyone to demand one corporation to mortgage its property or in any way to endanger its stable capital by the grant of rights to a third person or corporation in order to come to the assistance of another ecclesiastical corporation, without at the same time observing the formalities of alienation. Schmalzgrueber entertains the question of whether a bishop, or similar prelate having quasi-episcopal jurisdiction, can transfer the goods of one church to another. He is of the opinion that it is permissible if there is a just cause and if no privation to the rector or other ministers of the church occurs. And the reason given is that individual churches, as members of one body of the Church universal, ought to come to the assistance of each other.[62] This is a most praiseworthy motive, but it is merely supplying a cause. The law demands a just cause in any case.[63] If the mortgage cannot be placed on a church without a just cause, the presence of a just cause (in this case the assistance of another church) certainly does not remove the necessity of the other requirements. Nor does the presence of a just cause change the nature of the transaction. Administration is either ordinary or it is not. When it exceeds the limits of ordinary administration only some acts are alienation.[64] But the quality of a motive or the presence of any particular motive in any one act of administering Church property does not cause the act to be classified any differently and changed either from alienation to an act of extraordinary administration that is not alienation, or to an act

---

[60] Cf. Schmalzgrueber, lib. III, pars I, tit. XIII, n. 22; Coronata, *Institutiones,* II, 482. Many others likewise.

[61] C. 1495, §2.

[62] Lib. III, pars I, tit. XIII, n. 23.

[63] Cc. 1530, §§1, 2; 1538, §1.

[64] Cf. Vromant, *De Bonis Ecclesiae Temporalibus,* pp. 185, 186.

of ordinary administration. Moreover, Canon 1519 calls bishops only supervisors and indicates their authority over ecclesiastical property in their jurisdiction is limited in many ways, thus nullifying the lax view of Schmalzgrueber who seems not to require any formalities whatsoever.[65]

ARTICLE IV. SPECIAL MORTGAGE IS ALIENATION

The word *hypotheca* as contained in canon 1538 must necessarily include at least the Special mortgage in its meaning[66] since of the two types of mortgage, *viz.*, General and Special, the Special mortgage grants the greater rights and exposes the Church to the greater harm. To deny that the word means at least this in the canon would be to deprive the term of any meaning whatsoever. The rights transferred in the Special mortgage are real rights and immediately restrict the ownership of the Church. However, the transfer of a *jus in re* should not be confused with the transfer of *dominium* or ownership.[67] The fusion of these leads to absurdity. While it is true that the creditor receiving a *jus in re* has some rights, specifically to demand the sale of the property given in security for the debt, he by no means is the owner. Before default the creditor cannot sell the property or in any way alienate it; nor can he eject trespassers, but rather can in fact be ejected as any other trespasser; nor is he bound to the payment of taxes and repairs; nor is he entitled to the fruits of the land or to the minerals discovered beneath the surface. These are the rights of ownership and remain with the debtor, subject only to the creditor's equitable right of repayment of the loan.[68] Even in the case of default the creditor receives only his loan (with interest, of course) and the debtor receives

---

[65] Cf. Woywod, *Laws of the Code on the Temporal Goods of the Church, Homiletic and Pastoral Review,* XXX (1929), 44.

[66] Cf. Doheny, *Church Finance,* p. 56.

[67] It is regrettable that this distinction is not observed by some authors, ex. gr., Pirhing, lib. III, tit. XIII, n. 41; Arregui, *Summarium Theologiae Moralis* (3. ed., Bilbao, 1919), p. 158; Heston, *Alienation,* p. 127.

[68] "Courts of law have so far adopted the principles of equity that they allow the legal title of the holder of the mortgage to be used only for the purpose of securing his equitable rights under it."—Jones, *Mortgages,* I, 14.

any surplus brought by the sale.[69] The only purpose of the mortgage is to give specific security for the repayment of a loan, and since in a Special mortgage (or any American law mortgage) this grants *in rem* rights, it has always been considered alienation because the thing mortgaged is put in danger of being lost to the Church in case of default. The hope to pay the debt is always present, so much so that if no means of repayment were forthcoming, good business would suggest selling the property immediately rather than mortgage it, because in an outright sale the expenses of a foreclosure action and the lower bid at auction would be prevented.

ARTICLE V. SOME CONSIDERATIONS ON GENERAL MORTGAGE

Though the General mortgage of the canonists does not exist in American law, it is necessary to show the similarity between a General mortgage and other transactions, in order to see whether and in what circumstances this type of contract or one approximating it would fall under the law of canon 1538.

A. Similarity to Borrowing on a General Credit Rating

The word "credit" in this connection has the meaning of ability to borrow on the opinion conceived by the lender, that he will be repaid. The Church as a whole may be considered as having a reputation of meeting its obligations, but, since each ecclesiastical corporation owns its own property and is the sole debtor in any credit negotiation, it seems the quality of the general credit rating of the borrowing corporation, whether it be an individual parish or a diocese, should be the norm for determining the quality of the loan. The method of forming his opinion is, on the part of the lender, variable. There are two extremes.

[69] "The money realized on the sale on foreclosure is first applied to reimburse the mortgagee for taxes paid by him, and to pay any taxes on the property still unpaid, together with the cost of the foreclosure and the sale; then to pay the mortgagee the amount of the mortgage debt with interest. The balance is the surplus money, and the general principle under which it is distributed is that it takes the place of the land and is distributed to those having interests in the land which have been foreclosed in the action. If there are no junior mortgagees or other lienors, the mortgagor or his successor or successors in interest are entitled to the money."—Walsh, *On Mortgages*, p. 233.

One is to look upon the past record of the Church in this country in faithfully meeting obligations based on the generosity of the faithful. The other is to have an auditing of the books by a certified public accountant to determine the excess of the assets, both current and fixed,[70] over the liabilities to determine the nature of the risk undertaken in granting the loan.

The writer feels neither of these methods to be satisfactory. If only the reputation of the Church is considered some individuals will, at times, suffer greatly in loaning large sums to individual churches. The right of the creditor to repayment may never be overlooked. In what position is a particular corporation to offer assurance of repayment when it is borrowing to meet interest payments, at times interest payments on a loan which will likely not be substantially repaid in case the bonded indebtedness were foreclosed? If a secular business goes into voluntary bankruptcy, there is no injustice to the creditors. Injustice would occur only when a business remained in operation while constantly becoming worse and constantly becoming less able to repay its creditors. True, not all churches borrowing on a general credit rating of this kind are in such a poor condition, but the fact that there may be some would detrimentally affect the negotiation of loans in the future.

The latter method is equally unbusinesslike because it does not take into consideration the recognition by the Church of its moral responsibility, and makes no allowance for the records of the centuries of the Church giving " good paper."

A combined procedure would seem desirable. The Church authorities themselves should establish and recognize the ability of any particular corporation to meet its obligations, so that they give the creditor, whether secular or ecclesiastical, moral security; while, on the other hand, the creditor should know he is not loaning *merely* on the record of the Church, but that he has a sound financial investment. A true credit rating then will always consider the assets and liabilities of the ecclesiastical corporation even though no security is given.

It is not quite exact to say that a General mortgage is equiva-

---

[70] This is not necessarily the same as stable and non-stable capital.

lent to a general credit rating.[71] The General mortgage is an actual contracting of a loan; it is one of the *instruments* of credit. The general credit rating is a mere qualification of the ecclesiastical corporation as a good or a bad risk, and security will be waived or not, respectively. No contract need be entered at all, and yet the general credit rating exists. Credit is extended by means of a General mortgage, but the general credit rating merely serves as a basis for credit which may or may not be actually extended.

B. *Similarity to Borrowing on Unsecured Notes*

After the general credit rating is established, a loan may be negotiated on an unsecured note. Notes are either secured or unsecured. If secured, that portion of the assets given in security is available to satisfaction.[72] It is easily seen that if the security given is a portion of the stable capital, the contract follows the rules of alienation. And, if the security given is non-stable capital, it does not follow the rules of alienation,[73] provided the non-stable capital security is amply sufficient to satisfy the debt at default.[74]

Where no security is given, the entire assets of the corporation are subject to the repayment of the debt, *in personam* rights are given to the creditor along with potential *in rem* rights, so that in the event of default, a judgment can be obtained against the corporation. If the judgment is not paid, the property can be attached and automatically *in rem* rights are seized by the creditor.

The General mortgage seems for these reasons to be very similar to the unsecured note, because in both a contract is made,[75]

---

[71] This is done by Heston, *Alienation*, p. 132.

[72] The security of a co-signer is not under consideration, for if the co-signer is an ecclesiastical corporation, it follows the rules of alienation and secured notes, since in the case of default, all the assets of the co-signer are available to satisfy the debt.

[73] Cf. Heston, *op. cit.*, p. 166.

[74] When not sufficient, it would follow rules of a General mortgage, depending on whether or not it could make the condition of the Church worse, as explained *infra*, this Chapter at "E" and "F."

[75] If the requisite legal formalities are complied with, both are enforceable at law; if they are not, both are enforceable in equity. "And so we may say it (a contract) is an agreement enforceable at law, made between

the same property or properties of the debtor are available to satisfy the debt, the same type of rights—*in personam,* or *jus ad rem* —are given, and the debt must be collected in the same way in case of default, i.e., by suit, judgment, and attachment.

C. *Similarity to Debts*

Canon 1538 places the contracting of debts (*aere alieno contrahendo*) in the same category as Special mortgages.[76] It is disputed whether this is new legislation.[77]

Debts other than those secured by a Special mortgage can be: (a) current debts, for ordinary expenses, provided for in the regular budget; (b) debts consequent upon annuity agreements; and (c) debts arising from loans.

(a) Current debts are not comprehended under "*aere alieno contrahendo*" because of the moral and even physical impossibility of compliance with the solemnities of the law on the part of ecclesiastical administrators,[78] and a law impossible to comply with does not bind.[79] Therefore current debts are outside the discussion of the similarity between General mortgages and contracting of debts.

---

two or more persons, by which rights are acquired by one or more to acts or forbearances on the part of the other or others."—Bays, *Cases and Materials on Business Law* (4. ed., National Casebook Series, Chicago: Callaghan and Company, 1939), p. 64 (hereafter cited *Cases*). "In every case of contract, without exception, the breach thereof entitles the opposite party to sue at law for monetary compensation."—*Op. cit.,* p. 65.

[76] "*To contract an obligation* means to give another the right to demand payment in kind, or the performance or omission of an act. *To contract a debt* almost always means to obligate oneself to pay a sum of money within a specified time, or to supply something of equivalent value."—Creusen-Garesche-Ellis, *Religious Men and Women in the Code* (3. English ed., Milwaukee: Bruce, 1940), p. 116. Hereafter cited *Religious.*

[77] "Per se nihil alienat qui aes alienum contrahit sine speciali pignore vel hypotheca. Quare, ante Codicem, obligationes huiusmodi sine beneplacito apostolico contrahi poterant."—Vermeersch-Creusen, *Epitome,* II, 602. "Contractio debiti per se non est stricte alienatio, dummodo nec pignus nec hypotheca in ea interveniat; aliquam tamen speciem alienationis induit, quia qui aere alieno erga alterum ligatur eo ipso suis iuribus detrahit; ideo ante Codicem in contrahendis debitis, ecclesiae solemnitates iuris pro alienatione praescriptas servare debebant; . . ." Coronata, *Institutiones,* II, 491.

[78] Heston, *Alienation,* p. 165; Creusen-Garesche-Ellis, *op. cit.,* p. 123.

[79] Van Hove, *De Legibus,* p. 89.

(b) Debts consequent upon annuity agreements have no exact counterpart in pre-Code law.[80] They can be defined as a "bilateral contract whereby one party agrees to pay another a fixed sum at specific periods in return for a gross amount of money or equivalent property received." [81] In American law, an annuity is a personal charge on the corporation, and no *jus in re* in any assets of the corporation is given as specific security for the guarantee of payments because "in case of the insolvency or bankruptcy of the debtor, the *capital* of the constituted annuity becomes exigible." [82] Therefore, the acceptance of an annuity obligation grants a *jus ad rem* and in this agrees with a General mortgage. A General mortgage cannot be perfectly assimilated to an annuity except insofar that all goods are liable primarily in a General mortgage and only secondarily in an annuity agreement.[83]

(c) Debts arising from loans. The remaining type of debts is borrowing on promissory notes. A promissory note is a written promise to pay a certain sum of money at a definite future time, unconditionally. It has been considered under the similarity of a General mortgage to borrowing on notes. It was shown that a General mortgage is similar to borrowing on *unsecured* notes because of the similarity in the nature and amount of property liable to the satisfaction of the debt, in the transfer of *in personam* rights, and in the method of seeking payment. A difference could possibly exist in the manner of contracting a General mortgage and a debt on an unsecured note. The General mortgage would expressly bind all the goods of the debtor

---

[80] For the comparison of annuities to *census, precaria,* and trusts, see Heston, *op. cit.*, pp. 167, 168.

[81] Heston, *op. cit.*, p. 168.

[82] S. v. "Annuity"—*Bouvier's Law Dictionary.*

[83] The annuity fund itself is subject to the primary liability. It is immediately noticeable that since annuities are comprehended under canon 1533 (cf. *Apostolic Delegation, Letter,* 13 Nov., 1936—Bouscaren, *Supplement 1941*, p. 79), and since there is a grant only of a *jus ad rem,* this discussion of the General mortgage and its possibility of being likened to the contracting of debts forbidden by canon 1538 is not altogether amiss. It moreover is a substantiating argument of the writer's conclusion in Article I above that canon 1533 and the concept of alienation may be extended to contracts granting a *jus ad rem.*

while the unsecured note would only implicitly take these goods into account.[84] In the latter written instrument, these goods would not be mentioned. However, one may be sure that the creditor will never loan large sums of money on an unsecured note without having first satisfied himself as to the nature of the assets of the borrowing corporation, so that, in the event of necessary action for repayment, the amount and nature of the goods liable to attachment might be known. No sane business man will loan money to another person with whose financial position he is not well acquainted.

Because of the similarity, one may reasonably conclude that the General mortgage of the old law can therefore be said to be included in the forbidden contracting of debts of canon 1538, and the consequent assumption of financial obligations. Without an explicit statement to this effect, Vermeersch-Creusen reasons that in itself contracting a debt without specific security is not alienation, and before the Code was not forbidden; but because these contracts are dangerous and detrimental, they now fall under the same regulation as a Special mortgage.[85] Vromant, even more definitely, seems to affirm this opinion by saying: "*Cum canone praesenti* (1538) *agatur . . . de contractu quo condicio Ecclesiae peior fieri possit* (*hypotheca generali vel aere alieno contrahendo*), etc. . . ."[86] However, it is difficult to determine whether his use of the conjunction *vel* means to have a disjunc-

[84] "Generalis hypotheca, quae vix differt a debito seu aere alieno contrahendo, verificatur, quando omnia bona personae moralis, in genere, absque ulla specificatione, expresso gravantur. Haec hypotheca generalis alienationi non aequiperatur [aequiparatur], sed potius debito annumeratur. In debito enim seu aere alieno contrahendo, bona ecclesiae in genere revera gravantur, quamvis id expressis verbis non definiatur. Hypotheca vero generali expresse firmatur creditoris securitas quam, in aere alieno contrahendo, obligatio a debitore diserte assumpta iam implicite tutabatur."—Vromant, *De Bonis Ecclesiae Temporalibus,* p. 343.

[85] *Epitome,* II, 602. "Eaedem praescriptiones observandae sunt cum agitur de aere alieno contrahendo (can. 1539), ex quo bona ecclesiastica frequenter periculo et damno exponuntur. Olim generatim auctores tenebant aes alienum contrahere absque oppignoratione aut hypotheca speciali non requirere beneplacitum apostolicum, cum per se non sit alienatio."—De Meester, *Compendium,* p. 411, n. 1493, and note 2.

[86] *De Bonis Ecclesiae Temporalibus,* p. 344. Cf. *supra,* Article I, p. 88, for complete text.

tive or a copulative force. But in either case, a General mortgage would be forbidden by canon 1538, according to his view. The reason an explicit statement that *aere alieno contrahendo* means General mortgage cannot be found is that the Code phrase is more far reaching than General mortgage. As was seen, annuities and borrowing on secured notes likewise are included.

D. *Similarity to a Bond* [87]

A bond is a written instrument under seal or unsealed evidencing an obligation.[88] It can be single or conditional. The single bond obligates the obligor (maker), his heirs, executors, and administrators to pay a certain sum of money to another at a day named. The conditional bond, which is the kind more generally used, becomes void if the obligor does some particular act, or else remains in force, as evidencing the obligation of payment of rent, performance of the covenants of a deed, or repayment of a principal sum of money borrowed of the obligee, with interest.[89] Bonds are similar to notes in that they can be secured or unsecured. A bond issued by a corporation is (generally) a unit of an issue evidencing an aggregate indebtedness secured by a mortgage on corporate assets. As each bond is for a principal sum to be paid at the expressed maturity, it is in form and effect a promissory note secured by mortgage (or trust deed).[90] The mortgage security would be a Special mortgage and come under the rules of alienation. If no mortgage or other collateral secures the bond only *in personam* rights are granted.[91] From this

---

[87] A bond is used here as a credit contract between creditor and debtor and is not to be confused in thought with a bond as a contract of indemnity or as a contract of surety.

[88] Cf. *Words and Phrases,* II, s. v. "Bond."

[89] S. v. "Bond"—*Bouvier's Law Dictionary.*

[90] Bays, *Cases,* p. 721. Cf. also Cleveland-Hall, *Funds and Their Uses* (New York: D. Appleton and Co., 1922), pp. 175–182.

[91] "If in a bond the obligor binds himself, without adding his heirs, executors, and administrators, the executors and administrators are bound, but not the heir; . . . for the law will not imply the obligation upon the heir."—S. v. "Bond," *Bouvier's Law Dictionary.* The unsecured bond is also called a debenture bond, but unsecured does not spell insecurity.—Hoagland, *Corporation Finance* (New York: McGraw-Hill Book Co., Inc., 1933), p. 81. "A bond is an obligatory instrument in writing whereby one

viewpoint a General mortgage is similar to a bond since any or all the goods of the debtor would be subject to attachment in the case of a suit and judgment award. Here too the same exception exists as in the comparison of a General mortgage with unsecured notes and the contracting of debts, i.e., that no express mention is made that all the goods of the debtor will act as security. But here too the same solution is available—the creditor may sue, get judgment, and attach specific property to satisfy the same, becoming to all intents and purposes a mortgage bondholder.[92]

Summary.

Because of the grant of a *jus ad rem* (*in personam* rights), and because of the nature and amount of goods liable to seizure by attachment, unsecured bonds and unsecured notes are similar to a General mortgage. Because a General mortgage would be included in the *aere alieno contrahendo* of canon 1538, a General mortgage, unsecured notes, and unsecured bonds are all subject to the rules of alienation and can be considered alienation in the widest sense when by them the condition of the Church may be made worse.[93]

E. *When a General Mortgage or Similar Contract Makes the Condition of the Church Worse*

Herein lies the application of Article I, which extends the concept of alienation to a *jus ad rem.* Having already mentioned in Article II that alienation concerns only stable capital, it logically follows that *it is only when the stable capital is endangered that the transfer of a jus ad rem is considered alienation.*

How and when is this possible? The method of determining stable capital already being given it follows that the amount of the debt less the non-stable capital will either leave a balance chargeable or not. For example, if the debt to be contracted

---

doth bind *himself* to another to pay a sum of money."—*Words and Phrases,* II, s. v. "Bond." There was no word such as "bond" in Civil Law, but its equivalent under that law was the word "obligation."—*Ibid.*

[92] Cf. Hoagland, *op. cit.,* p. 82.

[93] A general credit rating is not mentioned here because it has been shown it is not one of the contracts by which credit is obtained.

were $75,000, and the non-stable capital totaled $40,000, the stable capital would be acting as security for the debt to the extent of $35,000. Even though no specific piece of the stable capital were offered as security, nevertheless since the non-stable capital is not sufficiently large, some specific portions of the stable capital would be attached in the case of a default judgment, the condition of the Church not only could but thereby actually *would* become worse, and therefore in entering the contract, all the solemnities of alienation must be observed.[94] The amount of the stable capital endangered in any transaction will determine the requisite permissions necessary.

This General mortgage then is one which does not at the time render the juridical condition of the Church worse, but which can do so at some time in the future and for that reason follows the procedure of Special mortgaging. The objection that the number of court actions to collect on General mortgages (and unsecured notes and bonds) is small, or that the number of actual sales of stable ecclesiastical property to satisfy creditors is a rather rare thing, should not be a blinding veil hanging before the mind shutting out the dangers to the condition of the Church. The absence of harmful actions in the past is by no means a guarantee of the continued prosperity of the future. Many of these contracts are entered on the strength of past contributions of parishioners, in most cases the only means of revenue. But long-term loans are sometimes far from being completely paid when financial or social conditions of this relatively limited source of income change and cause untold and unnecessary hardships on those charged with the duty of seeing that unwisely contracted debts are paid.

This may seem more severe than what some commentators contend the law intends, but a study of the history of the legislation convinces the writer that the Holy See is constantly limiting administrators in their powers when large sums are concerned. It is usually a matter of large sums in the case of mortgages and notes and bonds, or, in a word, debts generally.

---

[94] Schmalzgrueber seems to have envisioned the trend of legislation when in less definite terms, he said: "Neque hypothecae generali subjici possunt ecclesiae bona, si pignus sit constitutum pro magna quantitate."—Lib. III, tit. XIII, n. 21. Cf. also Aichner, *Compendium*, p. 776.

In negotiating short- or long-term loans good management demands that the proposed borrowing be indicative of an adequate financial program. This is true on the basis of the inexorable axiom that the last dollar is the most expensive dollar. A series of piecemeal and unrelated borrowings, whether accompanied by a mortgage, note, or bond, is not only expensive, but bad business practice.

It may seem paradoxical, but it is true that any credit agency would far rather loan a larger sum in one amount than a smaller total in several or more smaller borrowings, yet this is based on good sense and sound finance. Repeated attempts to contract loans express not only imprudent management, but a lack of planning, budgeting, and foresight, all of which undermine faith in the intelligence of the leadership so important in all credit transactions.[95]

This being the case the permission of the Holy See will frequently be necessary. Far from giving the impression that it wishes these requests to be referred to that authority less frequently, legislation is constantly increasing the necessity of this reference. The original law (in 535) of the Church forbade pawning.[96] Between 535 and the first half of the ninth century this was broadened to forbid the burdening of Church property by Special mortgage.[97] At the beginning of the fourteenth century Pope Clement V extended the previous laws which referred only to immovable property, so that thereafter they referred to movables when the contract was entered by religious.[98] Only a century later (March 1, 1467), Pope Paul II enacted the law which required the *Beneplacitum Apostolicum,* heretofore unknown. Though applying only to immovables it used the general term mortgage without making any distinction between Special and General mortgages.[99] The Code again restricted adminis-

[95] Cf. Frommelt, *Church Property,* p. 31.

[96] Transferring possession of the Church's property to secure a financial obligation.—Cf. canon *Nulli, supra,* p. 60.

[97] Cf. *Hludowici Pii Capitularia (826?), MGH, Legum Sectio II, Capitularia Regum Francorum,* Tom. I, 310; c. 5, X, *de rebus ecclesiae alienandis vel non,* III, 13.

[98] C. 1, *de rebus ecclesiae non alienandis,* III, 4, in Clem.

[99] C. un., *de rebus ecclesiae non alienandis,* III, 4, in Extravag. com.; "Quod in hac Constitutione (Ambitiosae) prohibita sit etiam generalis

trators by extending the law to include movables,[100] and was not content to forbid mortgages, but extended the restriction to include the contracting of debts,[101] or any contract that might harm the Church.[102] And finally after these laws were interpreted to be applicable only when stable capital was affected [103] it was authoritatively announced that they affected some funds not stable capital.[104]

F. When a General Mortgage or Similar Contract Does Not Make the Condition of the Church Worse

Should a General mortgage not in any way be of such a type that the condition of the Church may be made worse, administrators of Church property are not for that reason free to contract them without any solemnities of law whatsoever. In any amount, except what perhaps may be authorized by diocesan statutes, the General mortgage, note, or bond exceeds ordinary administration,[105] beyond which the administrator acts invalidly without the bishop's permission.[106]

---

hypotheca, quia simpliciter loquitur de hypotheca, tenent plures, apud *Quarant. c.1.n.17,* alii vero dicunt, prohibitam tantum esse hypothecam specialem, *juxta c. Nulli, 5. h. t.* de qua ibi tantum fit mentio, non de generali, *Molin. Tract. 2. dis. 466. n. 1, Redoan. in cit. Tract. q. 51. c. 29."*—Pirhing, lib. III, tit. XIII, sec. 3, par. 2, n. 55.

100 C. 1530, §1.

101 C. 1538, §1.

102 C. 1533.

103 *Quaesita Varia,* n. 18—*Periodica,* XI (1923), p. (157); Vromant, *De Bonis Ecclesiae Temporalibus,* n. 281; Larraona, *Commentarium Codicis, CpR,* XIII (1932), 191.

104 They applied to annuities which are a personal obligation on the payor. Cf. *Apostolic Delegation, Letter,* 13 Nov., 1936—Bouscaren, *Supplement 1941,* p. 79.

The writer realizes that the distinction between stable and non-stable capital is tenable because of the many authors who have made this distinction without rebuke from the Holy See, and because none can be found who explicitly hold the opposite viewpoint. Yet he is fully convinced that primarily because of the nature of the endowment of parishes in the United States, this distinction will one day be obliterated by the Holy See in accord with the trend of legislation over the centuries.

105 Cf. Vromant, *De Bonis Ecclesiae Temporalibus,* p. 185; Augustine, *Commentary,* VI, 589.

106 C. 1527, §1.

Therefore, in the last analysis, it will be for the Ordinary of the place to decide whether the stable capital is endangered, and whether, therefore, permission from the Holy See must be obtained when the amount exceeding non-stable capital pledged is more than $6,000.

ARTICLE VI. CONSTRUCTION MORTGAGES AND PURCHASE MONEY MORTGAGES

These are two types of mortgages which are frequently encountered in ecclesiastical administration. Both are Special mortgages. They are frequently confused but for the sake of accuracy should not be used synonymously. Both follow the same canonical provisions.

A *construction mortgage* is a mortgage given to a creditor to secure a loan used in building an edifice. The instruments are in much the same form as other bonds and mortgages, but may contain a reference to the loan agreement which has been made between the parties. This agreement contains the names of the parties, the amount, rate of interest and due date of the loan, the description of the property, a statement of the kind of building to be erected, a schedule of payments, and various other agreements and conditions.[107]

The only property mortgaged is the building under construction and the land on which it is erected. Because nothing can be mortgaged which is not in existence at the time of the mortgage,[108] the land must be sufficient security to warrant the loan of sufficient funds to begin construction or some funds must be on hand. Thereafter the schedule of payments in the loan agreement sets forth at what times and in what amounts portions of the loan shall be paid by the lender to the Church corporation. The time of payment is described as the various stages of construction, as "enclosure," "brown mortar," "white mortar," "standing trim," and "completion." The amounts to be paid may be stated as definite sums, or in the form of percentages of the total loan. Often, to give more payments at intermediate stages, or to limit the total number of payments to two or three,

---

[107] Montgomery, *Financial Handbook,* p. 1061.

[108] 41 C.J. 371.

no definite schedule is agreed upon, the statement being that the loan shall be advanced at such times and in such amounts as the lender may approve. The proper proportion of value that may with safety be loaned on a construction mortgage is a matter of individual judgment.[109]

A *purchase money mortgage* is one contracted in a sale, wherein the vendor is the mortgagee and the purchasing Church corporation is the mortgagor. For example, a church or institute purchases a building and pays one fourth the price and the vendor takes a mortgage on the remaining three fourths. The effects are immediately noticeable. The creditor (vendor) not only has a mortgage to secure the payment of the balance due, but in title theory States the vendor transferring the title in the contract of sale receives it back immediately in the contract of mortgage. Ownership (*dominium*) is transferred to the ecclesiastical corporation however, because the title is vested in the mortgagee merely to secure his equitable rights.

In deciding the canonical validity and licitness of these two types of mortgages there are three considerations, any one of which might be a factor as would imply alienation:

(a) The nature or source of the initial expenditure;
(b) The property mortgaged;
(c) The amortization and interest.

(a) The nature or source of the initial expenditure. This element of these contracts is not discussed by the authors but certainly merits consideration. The sum used to begin construction of, or as partial payment in buying, a building can come from either the non-stable or stable capital. Funds previously gathered and destined for such an enterprise, though considered a part of the stable capital so far as any other use is concerned,[110] may be used without complying with the solemnities of alienation when used for the originally designated purpose.[111] *A fortiori* money

[109] Cf. Montgomery, *op. cit.*, pp. 1061, 1062. The legal limit for savings banks in New York State is 60%, but when costs are above normal the loan will probably be only 50% or less of sales price.—*Ibid.*

[110] Ferraris, s. v. "alienatio," n. 41. Hence any diversion from the specific purpose for which originally gathered is alienation.—Doheny, *Church Finance*, p. 45.

[111] "Et si pecunia destinata aedificationi ecclesiae interim fructuose col-

definitely non-stable capital can be used for this initial purpose without being a species of alienation.[112] The use of stable capital not destined for this purpose would be alienation, and the opinion that it is merely a conversion of assets seems untenable. Canon 1539 permits the conversion of only one particular kind of assets and decrees the nature of the assets into which they may be converted.[113] Therefore only if the genus of an investment of stable capital is retained is its conversion permissible.[114] Otherwise the consequences would be illogical: Supposing instead of stable-capital-money being used to erect buildings, a mortgage were placed on some piece of stable capital property for the same purpose. If the mortgage must be foreclosed and the property sold the corporation would still retain the newly erected edifice. This is certainly not a conversion of assets, but the very placing of the mortgage is an act of alienation.[115]

(b) The property mortgaged. To escape the rules of alienation the mortgage may cover only that property being added to the assets of the Church. A difference in the two transactions appears here. In a construction mortgage the lot on which the building is to be erected can be viewed under the same aspects as the funds in the previous consideration, viz., as stable, or non-stable capital, and also as being bought for the specific purpose of erecting the building thereon. Since in the event of foreclosure the structure cannot be separated from the lot, and therefore the lot will also serve as security for the loan, the mortgage on a building under construction would be alienation when the lot on which it is being erected is a portion of the stable capital not destined for that purpose; otherwise, not. Because in a pur-

---

locetur, non putabitur esse alienatio, simplex venditio istorum titulorum ut obtenta pecunia aedificationi inservire possit."—Vermeersch-Creusen, *Epitome*, II, 596.

[112] Cf. Vromant, *De Bonis Ecclesiae Temporalibus*, p. 295.

[113] "Administrators may exchange notes payable to bearer for other valuable papers which are at least equally safe and profitable, but must avoid any kind of barter or trading; . . ."—Woywod, *Practical Commentary*, II, 189.

[114] "Si autem genus idem maneat, aberit alienatio, ex ipso sensus communis iudicio, quando ipse collocationis modus variationem istam secum ferat."—Vermeersch-Creusen, *Epitome*, II, 596.

[115] Cf. Heston, *Alienation*, p. 77, note 23, for opposite opinion.

chase money mortgage the building and lot are bought, there is no alienation from the viewpoint of the property subjected to the mortgage.

(c) The amortization and interest. To the writer's knowledge only two authors consider this question in deciding the procedure to be followed. McManus thinks that individual cases should be examined cautiously before considering these as non-alienation contracts because of the possibility of loss of the money paid by the moral person on the mortgage either as interest or part payment on the principal.[116] In evaluating this cautionary suggestion the writer feels that its basis must be canon 1410 which allows the endowment of a benefice to consist in the reliable contributions of the faithful, and, if this is lacking, canon 1415, §3, which permits parishes to be erected if it is prudently foreseen that the necessities will not be lacking.[117] Thus, Connolly thinks the prospective offerings of the faithful are considered a part of the patrimony, provided it is certain that these offerings will be made, even though the exact amount is indefinite. Among these offerings are included subscriptions of free-will offerings, pew-rent, and offertory collections.[118] Heston, on the contrary, maintains the money from current resources paid out in interest and amortization is not a part of the stable capital;[119] while Cleary

[116] He is speaking of purchase money mortgages, but the opinion applies equally as well to construction mortgages.—*The Administration of Temporal Goods in Religious Institutes,* The Catholic University of America Canon Law Studies, No. 109 (Washington, D. C.: The Catholic University of America, 1937), p. 125, note 22. Hereafter cited *Administration.*

[117] Cf. also *Letter of Apostolic Delegate, U. S.,* 10 Nov., 1922—Bouscaren, I, 151: ". . . all the parishes of the United States having the three necessary qualifications, viz., (1) a resident pastor; (2) endowment (resources or revenue according to the provisions of canons 1410 or 1415, §3); and (3) boundaries, are not only parishes in the strict canonical sense, but are also ecclesiastical benefices."

[118] Connolly, *The Canonical Erection of Parishes,* The Catholic University of America Canon Law Studies, No. 114 (Washington, D. C.: The Catholic University of America, 1938), pp. 81, 82. It seems these offerings are more similar to the fruits of a benefice, the revenue; and the patrimony is rather the obligation of the laity to make these offerings. After sums necessary to support the priest and for current expenses are deducted, excess offerings can be used to add real estate to the assets of the corporation.

[119] *Alienation,* p. 163, note 9.

feels that in the event of foreclosure, it is no longer money but real estate into which the money was transformed that is in danger of being lost.[120]

It seems the solution lies in this: To the extent that these monies are converted into stable capital, they are inalienable. If invested in real estate the presumption is in favor of the property being stable capital. Now when property is bought the Church receives *dominium* over it. If bought in a contract wherein a note secured by a mortgage on the acquired property serves as a partial payment, the Church acquires *dominium* restricted by the amount of the mortgage. In this act of buying the Church loses nothing which it previously owned. But because these funds have been converted into stable-capital-property over which the Church has *dominium,* a foreclosure of the mortgage would result in the loss of *dominium.* This would be a new act, an act of alienation, a new contract.

It might be alleged that this loss of *dominium* happens as a result of the mortgage, and that therefore the original mortgage was an act of alienation requiring the solemnities. It is answered by saying that the loss of *dominium* is not a necessary result of every mortgage. It is the result of poor administration in entering the original mortgage contract, or a result of circumstances beyond control. The original mortgage at the time it was entered was not one which made the condition of the Church worse because it did not affect stable capital existing at the time of contract—it affected only the property in process of being acquired. The conversion of revenue to stable capital at the time of the mortgage in the down payment and after the mortgage by payment of amortization and interest increased the patrimony of the Church and bettered the corporation's condition which it enjoyed on the mortgage date. Therefore the sale at foreclosure would make the condition of the Church worse on the sale date, since it would lose a certain portion of the stable capital which it did not have at the time of the mortgage. Hence permission to alienate this property through the foreclosure sale seems necessary, but need not be obtained until the sale is imminent.

Nor does the fact that the foreclosure sale takes place by order

---

[120] Cf. Cleary, *Alienation,* p. 9.

of the State seem to relieve the necessity of securing the required ecclesiastical permissions,[121] since there seems little actual difference between the State in this case and an agent. The State in legislating for the foreclosure sale,[122] attempted to seek an equitable settlement of the debt, so that a mortgagor might not, by seizure at default, lose property valued at a considerably higher price than the mortgage debt. Moreover, recourse to the Superior may avert the necessity of sale and consequent loss of property. The local Ordinary and the Holy See, as the case may be, are not merely automatons issuing alienation licenses. They are the superior officers of a corporation having vast financial resources, and it is not improbable that sums sufficient to avert an impending loss through the foreclosure sale might be made available through these offices to brook the financial embarrassment of a particular "branch house." [123]

Summary.

In the light of the foregoing it can be said

(1) that the solemnities of alienation are *not* required in:

A. Construction mortgages verifying these conditions:

(a) The plot of ground on which the building is to be erected has been acquired for that purpose.

(b) The initial payment to begin construction comes from non-stable capital or from a fund destined for that specific purpose.

---

[121] It would seem apparent that the Ordinary capable of granting the permissions is to be computed according to the value of the property, not the value of the mortgage.

[122] Cf. *supra*, pp. 26, 67, 96.

[123] Cf. *infra*, p. 158, for exposition of the difference between transfer of *dominium* and conveyance of title in a mortgage. The facts presented there, combined with above, seem to certify that permission for the foreclosure sale is necessary also in the case of a mortgage which in itself was alienation and for which permission had been previously obtained. The permission to mortgage is not a permission to sell; the Holy See never inquires as to the value of the property to be mortgaged, thereby hardly granting permission to mortgage to the future sale of the property; the law of the Code demands the amortization for the very purpose of assuring the avoidance of foreclosure and thereby shows that the Church grants permission to mortgage only when the mortgage debt according to prudent judgment can be repaid without loss of the property encumbered.

(c) The amortization and interest is paid from current revenue.

B. Purchase-money mortgages, when,

(a) The initial partial payment for the property comes from non-stable capital or from a fund destined for that purpose.

(b) The amortization and interest comes from current revenue.[124]

(2) that the solemnities of alienation are required for the foreclosure sales on these properties.

---

[124] With these conditions present the authors' statements on the ability of administrators to contract these mortgages without complying with the laws of alienation can be understood. Re purchase money mortgages, cf. McManus, *Administration*, p. 125; "Nam si, in ipso actu emptionis, hypotheca constituatur ad securitatem dandam de solutione pretii, ecclesia minus acquirit, sed nihil alienat."—Vermeersch-Creusen, *Epitome*, II, 601; Coronata, *Institutiones*, II, 492; Bastien, *Directoire Canonique* (4. ed., Paris: Bloud et Gay, 1933), p. 245; De Meester, after quoting Vermeersch-Creusen, adds: "tamen illud dominium exponitur periculo alienationis, v. gr., ex non soluto foenore."—*Compendium*, III, 410, note 3.

Re construction mortgages, cf. Doheny, *Church Finance*, p. 48, and p. 57; Heston, *Alienation*, p. 162.

Re both, cf. Vromant, *De Bonis Ecclesiae Temporalibus*, p. 296.

CHAPTER VIII

PROCEDURE IN MORTGAGING

AFTER having defined, compared, and projected the concepts of alienation, mortgage, debts, etc., it remains to examine the method of placing a mortgage on Church property. Since a General mortgage does not exist in American law, and since this monograph is to consider mortgages, only Special mortgages will be treated.[1]

Before entering any contract the administrator must see that certain canonical provisions are fulfilled, some of which are necessary for its lawfulness while others are required for its validity. While the process of mortgaging cannot exactly follow each step in the canonical procedure for alienation, adherence to the laws of alienation must be as near as possible, while at the same time the special canonical provisions for mortgaging must be observed.[2] These measures, which will be individually discussed in the following Articles, are:

I. Verification of Prerequisites (C. 1530, §1, 2°).
II. Appraisal of Property Value (C. 1530, §1, 1°).
III. Choice of Mortgagee and Agent (C. 1531, §2).
IV. Submission of Statement of Financial Status.
V. Obtaining the Necessary Permission (C. 534; C. 1530, §1, 3°; and C. 1532).
VI. Amortization (C. 1538).
VII. Observance of State Laws (C. 1529).

---

[1] Any contract resembling a General mortgage which is considered alienation in the light of Chapter VII will follow the same rules as about to be given in this Chapter.

[2] Cf. canon 1533.

". . . his contractibus (pawn and mortgage) applicandi sunt, servatis servandis, canones de alienationibus. Quaedam specialia praescribuntur can. 1538 prae natura hujusmodi contractus, . . ."—De Meester, *Compendium,* III, 410.

ARTICLE I. VERIFICATION OF PREREQUISITES

Canon 1538, in stating that a legitimate cause must be present to mortgage, states no new law nor does it supplement nor derogate from canon 1530, §1, 2°, which states the need of a just cause to alienate. It is a mere reminder that the same causes are required for mortgaging as are necessary for alienating,[3] namely, either urgent necessity, evident utility, or piety.[4]

The presence of the just cause is necessary only for the liceity of the mortgage,[5] but it is required under a grave obligation,[6] so much so that if a cause is lacking through culpability, and the transaction turns out to harm the Church, the culprits are bound to make good the loss.[7] Only the Holy See can dispense from this condition.[8]

ARTICLE II. APPRAISAL OF PROPERTY VALUE[9]

That there must be an appraisal of property to be mortgaged is not specifically stated by the authors, yet the fact that all the

---

[3] Cf. De Meester, *Compendium,* III, 410.

[4] This is a closed enumeration, and no other is a legal cause.—Cleary, *Alienation,* p. 63. All authors writing on alienation explain these causes, and any space given them in this monograph would be sheer repetition.

[5] Fanfani, *De Iure Parochorum,* pp. 200, 201; Larraona, *Commentarium Codicis, CpR,* XIII (1932), 353; Schaefer, *De Religiosis,* p. 437; De Meester, *op. cit.,* 404; Vromant, *De Bonis Ecclesiae Temporalibus,* p. 302; Ayrinhac, *Administrative Legislation,* p. 441; Nevin, *ACR,* XIII (1936), 241.

Wernz-Vidal, *Ius Canonicum,* Tom. IV, Vol. II, 227, vigorously maintains the just cause to be necessary for validity, but without convincing argument, without notice of the explicit requirement of permission alone for validity, and without adverting to canon 11 requiring express or equivalent mention of invalidity in invalidating laws.

[6] Larraona, *op. cit.,* 355. There is a possibility of parvity of matter in other alienations, but hardly in a mortgage contract.

[7] Nevin, *ACR,* IV (1927), 38.

[8] Schaefer, *De Religiosis,* p. 437.

[9] Though the Code places the appraisal of property before the cause, there is really no need to have the property evaluated if no cause to mortgage exists. Given the need for money, the administrator should completely satisfy himself that the need is so great as to verify one of the causes listed as a legal reason for mortgaging. Only then should he proceed to the appraisal and submission of his request for permission. The Superior likewise must pass judgment on the sufficiency of the cause.

requisites of alienation proper apply ***servatis servandis*** to mortgaging [10] and because a proper appraisal is to the best interests of the Church, it seems very necessary that this provision be carried out. Regardless of what may be said concerning the ability of the corporation to discharge the mortgage debt, the very necessity to burden a portion of the stable capital shows the inability to obtain unsecured loans and thus the danger of borrowing more than prudent administration would suggest is present.

The appraisal is not necessary for the validity of the mortgage. But because it is required in order that the mortgage be a licit contract,[11] its omission would be truly an injustice [12] to the respective ecclesiastical body which owns the property. The offenders would be liable in case harm would result to the Church through its omission.[13]

The appraisal should be made with a view to alienation,[14] which means that the actual commercial sale value of the property must be estimated.[15] It should include the valuation of land, buildings, machinery, and mineral and oil deposits.[16] Factors in the appraisal are:

I. Type of land:
   A. Agricultural:
      (a) fertility;
      (b) closeness to transportation;
   B. Urban:
      (a) location in financial, high grade retail business, high class residential and apartments, private dwellings, and factories sections;
      (b) actual sales of similar land;
      (c) unit value, i.e., per lot, adding 50% to

---

[10] De Meester, *op. cit.*, 410.

[11] It follows the law of necessity for a just cause, *supra*, Article I.

[12] Larraona, *Commentarium Codicis*, *CpR*, XIII (1932), 358.

[13] Nevin, *loc. cit.* While speaking of the appraisal in mortgaging, Nevin does not show the obligation of having one made.

[14] Cleary, *Alienation*, p. 62.

[15] Cf. Doheny, *Church Finance*, p. 29.

[16] Frommelt, *Church Property and its Management* (hereafter cited: *Church Property*), (New York-Milwaukee-Chicago: The Bruce Publishing Company, 1936), p. 44.

value of corner lots, and 10% to value of lots next to the corner;

(d) nuisances in neighborhood, as noisy or offensive manufacturing plants;

(e) transit facilities, both existing and proposed;

(f) plottage, adding 10% to value of every lot.

II. Type of buildings:

A. Cost to reproduce, less depreciation;

B. Improvements not visible to the eye, such as water mains, sewers, plumbing and electrical conduits.

The desirable appraisal report will contain a list of all components of the property with their value besides a summed-up value of the entire property.[17]

One expert might be sufficient in some other matters of law,[18] but in this instance one alone is not accepted by the law itself [19] and thus at least two must be used.[20] These should be honest and efficient, having no personal interest in the transaction, but they need not necessarily be professionals.[21] Their qualities are judged by the superior,[22] but whether the superior himself must appoint them is disputed.[23] Since the law does not decide, it rests with the superior who consents to the mortgage to be satisfied with the appraisers (not their report) appointed by the petitioner. If not, the superior may appoint others. Therefore if

---

[17] Cf. Montgomery, *Financial Handbook*, pp. 1065–1069; Frommelt, *op. cit.*, p. 45. For further information on appraising consult: Arthur, *Appraisers' and Adjusters' Handbook* (New York: Scientific Book Corporation, 1929); Babcock, *Appraisal of Real Estate* (New York: Macmillan & Co., 1924); Reeves, *Appraisal of Urban Land and Buildings* (New York: Municipal Administration Service).

[18] Cf. C. 1793, §3, which uses the phrase: "unum pluresve peritos eligere."

[19] "Aestimatio rei a probis peritis scripto facta."—C. 1530, §1, 1°.

[20] "Pluralis locutio duorum numero est contenta."—R. J. 40 in VI°; cf. Cleary, *Alienation*, p. 62; Doheny, *Church Finance*, p. 29.

[21] Heston, *Alienation*, p. 83.

[22] Cf. Larraona, *Commentarium Codicis, CpR*, XIII (1932), 355.

[23] In the affirmative—Doheny, *Church Finance*, p. 29. Seemingly to the contrary—McManus, *Administration*, p. 135. The mortgagee will frequently appoint his own appraisers, in which case they can be accepted by the superior.

the appraisal is made prior to consultation with the superior granting the permission, their names, or, if not known to the superior, their qualities should be mentioned in the petition, together with the date of the appraisal and the purpose for which it was made.

In any case their report must be submitted in writing.[24] This may be a single report subscribed by both or all as the case may be, but differences of opinion should be carefully noted.[25]

Payment of the experts, just as the printing of any bonds and other expenses, can come from the money received by the mortgage.

Should the superior not have appointed them, and not be satisfied with their report, he can appoint his own to make a second appraisal.[26] Even when originally appointed by him the superior can demand another appraisal,[27] or appoint other appraisers.

There is a dispute whether the superior can demand that the appraisers take an oath. Doheny thinks an oath can be demanded to *confirm* the appraisal in special cases.[28] Heston thinks it can be an oath of fidelity to duty.[29] While Cleary feels that no oath as to truthfulness can be demanded.[30] Since the Code provides for the taking of oaths outside of trials [31] it seems that when a just cause demands it an oath can be administered either before or after the appraisal.[32] The ability of the Superior to appoint other appraisers to furnish a new appraisal would in most cases

---

24 C. 1530, §1, 1°.

25 Cf. C. 1802 together with canon 20.

26 Cf. C. 1803 together with canon 20.

27 Larraona, *op. cit.*, 356.

28 *Church Finance*, p. 29.

29 *Alienation*, p. 83.

30 *Alienation*, p. 63.

31 Canons 1316–1321 should have been in the Fourth Book of the Code were oaths to be considered in trials exclusively. Cf. also Coronata, *Institutiones*, II, 233.

32 It might be noted that since not all appraisers will be Catholic and because an oath is the invocation of the name of God to witness the truth, an oath is of no value if he who takes it is an atheist.—Cf. Coronata, *Institutiones*, II, 232.

militate against the presence of a just cause as demanded by canon 1316, §1.[33]

A most interesting consideration then presents itself. What is to determine the proper superior who has the authority to grant the permission? Should it be the amount of the mortgage or the valuation of the property to be mortgaged? Suppose a $6,000 mortgage is to be imposed upon a piece of real estate valued at $40,000. Should the $6,000 mortgage enable the Bishop to grant permission by canon 1532, §3, or would the $40,000 appraisal valuation of the property to act as security necessitate the permission of the Holy See by canon 1532, §1, 2°? Nevin, who stands alone and unwaveringly, writes:

> Though a mortgage is not alienation of property, it prepares the way for alienation. . . . Regularly to alienate property over the value of 30,000 lire or francs . . . a parish needs the permission of the Holy See. In the same way, then, the same authority would have to be approached when there is question of *mortgaging property whose valuation exceeds the above sum.* In case of *property of less value,* the local Ordinary, observing certain formalities, may give the permission.[34]

Vromant and Cleary explicitly hold the opposite opinion: that it is the amount of the mortgage contemplated and not the valuation of the property which is to be considered.[35] Without considering an alternative, Cocchi,[36] Wernz-Vidal,[37] Vermeersch-Creusen [38] and Doheny [39] determine the superior by the value of the mortgage. Nevin alone gives a reason for his position. Perhaps the best argument that could be supplied for those who hold the common opinion is that a mortgage is one of the contracts which can make the condition of the Church worse, and since

---

[33] " Iusiurandum . . . praestari nequit, nisi in . . . iudicio . . ."—C. 1316, §1; cf. Coronata, *op. cit.*, 234.

[34] *ACR*, X (1933), 349. (Italics added.)

[35] " Si valor non rei gravatae, sed ipsius hypothecae vel debiti contrahendi, superet triginta millia libellarum: . . ."—Vromant, *De Bonis Ecclesiae Temporalibus*, p. 343; Cleary, *Alienation*, p. 99, note 21.

[36] *Commentarium*, III, 425.

[37] *Ius Canonicum*, Tom. IV, Vol. 2, 345.

[38] *Epitome*, II, 601.

[39] *Church Finance*, p. 56.

canon 1533 requires the solemnities for the contract itself and not for the possible subsequent harm to the property, it is the value of the original contract of mortgage which governs. At worst, i.e., foreclosure, no more than the mortgage amount is being alienated since the surplus goes to the mortgagor who could reinvest this surplus in other real estate. Moreover, a mortgage is an act of alienation in itself even though it be in the wide sense of the term,[40] and, therefore, is judged as any other act of alienation by the actual amount of the contract.

It might be objected that the practice of the Sacred Congregations, i.e., to grant permission to mortgage without inquiring about the value of the property to be mortgaged,[41] is not a solution to the problem since they reply according to the petition submitted. Yet the fact that this is a practice and not an isolated occurrence shows the mind of the Congregation has been interpreted correctly by the canonists who hold the common opinion. Therefore in accord with the common opinion Ordinaries can grant permission for mortgages up to $6,000 even though the building mortgaged has an appraised valuation of many times that amount.

ARTICLE III. CHOICE OF MORTGAGEE AND AGENT

The Code requires alienations to be made by public auction or at least in a public manner and the property to be given to him who, everything considered, offers most.[42] Applying the principle that mortgages should follow the laws of alienation as far as possible, it would seem that this canon imposes an obligation on administrators to choose their Bond Houses or Mortgage Brokers, trustees, paying agents, and, in case of an individual lender, their creditor with all due regard for the financial interests of the Church and not *merely* on the basis of cheapest interest, less financial cost or good-fellowship. The safeguarding of the financial interests of the Church can be viewed as the primary factors which should control the choice, and other circumstances as secondary.

---

[40] Beste, p. 749.

[41] Cf. *CpR*, XIV (1933), p. 29; Doheny, *op. cit.*, p. 89. Cf. also *Apostolic Delegation, Letter,* 13 Nov., 1936—Bouscaren, *Supplement 1941,* p. 79.

[42] C. 1531, §2.

The bases just suggested which should be secondary factors can be motives that are present in three possible cases: (a) when, all other things being equal, they are only additional factors that control the choice; (b) when, even though some disparity exists among the advantages offered by the creditors, the condition of the Church would be as well provided for by selecting the very one who offered these secondary advantages as an added attraction; and (c) when the choice would be contrary to prudent judgment and these secondary reasons which controlled the choice (and thus became primary factors) could in no way counterbalance the danger to the institute or parish. In (a) and (b) the administrator would be following an irreproachable path. In (c) it seems the administrator would be liable for any harm resulting to the Church when his negligence was culpable.[43] In no case would the mortgage be invalid because of the imprudent choice of the creditor, etc. The canon demanding the safeguarding of the Church's interests through negotiating alienations in a public manner [44] does not do so under pain of invalidity.

Should a choice be made wherein a person or company has the reputation of less tolerance in the matter of interest payments or even of harsh promptness in foreclosure actions there can be no objection so long as the transaction is financially sound, since these are not legal considerations, but psychological ones. In law the rights and duties of one creditor or trustee are identically the same as those of another.[45] However, in those localities where by law the trustee has greater powers than a simple mortgagee, ex. gr., in the method of foreclosure, it seems that when at all possible the mortgage should not be given to a trustee. Where it will be necessary that this be done, it is, of course, permissible.

Hence it can be readily seen that it is not left to an arbitrary decision to make these choices, nor to a seeming "beggar's need" wherein any concern which accepts the proposition is snatched up. The law demands it to be a result of a prudent business investigation.

---

[43] It seems that in virtue of canon 1534, §1 the deliberate choice of the less advantageous creditor would be a case falling under the provisions for an action for damages against such an alienator.

[44] C. 1531, §2.

[45] Cf. Hannan, "Refinancing a Mortgage."—*The Jurist,* II (1942), 58.

ARTICLE IV. SUBMISSION OF STATEMENT OF FINANCIAL STATUS

Under the pain of invalidity, canon 534, §2 requires the petition for consent to contract debts to be accompanied by a financial statement listing all previous debts and obligations on the same moral person. This canon, and therefore its requirements, and especially its sanction apply only to religious.[46] The rules of the Sacred Congregation for Religious, in its now well known letter issued through the Apostolic Delegation at Washington,[47] supplemented canon 534, §2 with respect to the completeness of the financial statement. Religious must now submit a detailed (a) report of current assets and liabilities; (b) statement of receipts and expenditures over a sufficient number of years to give an accurate estimate of normal receipts and expenditures; and (c) a separate list of obligations which do not occur under the listing of current liabilities (such as guarantor, indorser, surety, trustee, bondsman, etc.).[48] Though the general law does not demand these statements for administrators of non-religious property, they could be ordered by particular law of a diocese.[49] Whether or not this is the case, it seems imperative that this detailed report be submitted in all cases of petition to mortgage. Without it the Superior granting permission cannot fulfill in the best manner, if at all, his obligation of determining the amortization plan as canon 1538 demands.[50]

---

[46] This is the unanimous opinion. Canon 676, §2 extends this to societies of men or women living in communities without vows.—Cf. Vromant, *De Bonis Ecclesiae Temporalibus*, p. 323, note 1.

[47] Nov. 13, 1936.—Authorized form in Bouscaren, *Supplement 1941*, pp. 78–82.

[48] Cf. Doheny, *Church Finance*, pp. 88, 89 for typical formula for financial statement.

[49] In virtue of canon 1530, §2 these particular laws would then have the same binding force as Code laws. Even without a particular law the Bishop could legally demand the financial statement in a particular case in virtue of the same canon.—Larraona, *Commentarium Codicis*, *CpR*, XIII (1932), 357.

[50] The submission of this statement was not a necessary provision of this title of the Code because in virtue of canon 1525 the Ordinary has the annual report from parishes and non-collegiate bodies in his jurisdiction. Since petitions going to the Holy See should be sent through the Ordinary, it seems possible to conclude that whether it is the Ordinary or Holy See who is the legitimate superior this information is thus available to them.

ARTICLE V. OBTAINING THE NECESSARY PERMISSIONS

The petition for permission to mortgage, together with the financial statement, should be forwarded to the proper superior. In some cases there will be more than one superior involved.

A. Permission Necessary for Validity

Regardless of what superior or superiors must be approached, their permission or permissions, as the case may be, must be obtained for the validity of the mortgage.[51] The legal superior of canon 1538 is the superior designated by canon 1532, because canon 1533 has already implicitly determined that the legal superior for mortgaging is the same as for alienation strictly so called. Canon 1538 merely in express terms designates the superior indicated in canon 1532 as the one to be approached, and it determines which superior has the obligations to be stated in the following part of canon 1538. In referring to canon 1532 as a whole, canon 1538 definitely determines the necessity of permission for validity, for in turn canon 1532 directs its subjects to canon 1531, §3, wherein it is expressly stated that the permission of the legal superior is necessary for the validity of alienations, and therefore also for the validity of mortgages.

The petition must mention that a mortgage is to be imposed on Church property, because if the permission is obtained merely to contract a debt it does not suffice for the added mortgage.[52] It would seem that this is necessary for validity. The contracting of a special mortgage and a debt are distinct types of alienation and therefore permission for the debt alone would furnish no permission for a mortgage. It is not a question of interpretation of law but of fulfillment of the law. Since no permission is given for the mortgage it cannot be valid.

The practice seems to be that the Holy See depends on the approval of the Ordinary to the petition before granting permission. This information could be obtained by checking back on the annual reports, but it seems this places an unfair burden on those who have access to the records. Since a favor is being asked, all information necessary and helpful to its concession should be supplied by the petitioner.

[51] Cf. McManus, *Administration*, p. 129.

[52] *Jus Pontificium*, II (1931), 112.

The superior petitioned can be either the religious superior, the local ordinary, or the Holy See.

B. *The Religious Superior*

It is left to the constitutions of the community to determine: (a) which one or more of the religious superiors is the legitimate superior; (b) whether it is the Council or the Chapter whose consent the religious superior must obtain by vote, but the secrecy of the balloting, though ordered, does not affect the validity.[53]

C. *The Local Ordinary*

Nuns and Sisters of Diocesan approval must have the permission of the local Ordinary for every mortgage.[54] Seculars must have the permission of their local Ordinary for every mortgage of $6,000 or less.[55] Canon 1532, §3 demands that the local Ordinary, in granting permission to alienate this amount, have the consent of three groups: (a) the Cathedral Chapter, which is supplied in this country by the Diocesan Board of Consultors,[56] (b) The Diocesan Council of Administration,[57] and (c) the interested parties.

---

[53] Cf. C. 534, §1; McManus, *Administration*, pp. 128, 129. The constitution can provide that in the whole Institute (*Religio*) there is only one subject of *dominium*, and hence only one administrator of temporal goods, who would be a member of the general Curia thus requiring the permission of only one religious superior.—Schaefer, *De Religiosis*, p. 416.

[54] C. 534, §1; McManus, *loc. cit.*

[55] C. 1532, §§2, 3. It is not necessary to consider a mortgage of less than $200.00 as is provided for by canon 1532, §2. For the method of computing the value of 30,000 lire or francs, cf. *infra*, this chapter at E.

[56] Cf. canons 423 and 427. It might be noted that canon 427 considers this Board as the Senate of the Bishop. So as a Senate this Board should be called and vote in session, and not through individual approach.—Cf. C. 105, 2°. The consents of the Board of Consultors and Council of Administration need only be elicited in the majority. The consent of either cannot be supplied by the local Ordinary. If consent is obstinately refused and seemingly without reason withheld, recourse to the Holy See can solve the difficulty. But should the proposed mortgage be calmly opposed by both the Council and the Board, it should suggest to the local Ordinary that their denial of consent is reasonable.—Cf. S. C. C., 14 ian. 1922, in *Jus Pontificium*, II (1922), 56, 57; *AAS*, XIV (1922), 160.

[57] Required in every Diocese by canon 1520. In many Dioceses this Council's membership is identical with that of the Board of Consultors.—

> Canon 1532, §3: Si denique de rebus quarum pretium continetur intra mille libellas et triginta millia libellarum seu francorum, est loci Ordinarius, dummodo accesserit consensus tum Capituli cathedralis, tum Consilii administrationis, tum eorum quorum interest.

Canon 1533 demands that this threefold consent be obtained before the local Ordinary grants permission for any contract which can make the condition of the Church worse.

> Canon 1533: Sollemnitates ad normam can. 1530–1532 requiruntur non solum in alienatione proprie dicta, sed etiam in quolibet contractu quo conditio Ecclesiae peior fieri possit.

It would seem therefore that this same threefold consent would be needed for the local Ordinary to grant permission for a mortgage, because a mortgage certainly can make the condition of the Church worse.[58]

However canon 1538 requires that the legitimate superior (in this case the local Ordinary) should demand that the interested parties previously be heard.

> Canon 1538: Si ecclesiae bona . . . hypotheca nomine obliganda sint, . . . legitimus Superior, qui ad normam can. 1532 licentiam dare debet, exigat ut antea omnes, quorum interest, audiantur, et curet ut, cum primum fieri poterit, aes alienum solvatur.

From this it seems that the local Ordinary need merely hear the interested parties and need not have their consent as required by canon 1532, §3. This would mean that canon 1538 is in accord with the pre-Code law since the consent of the interested parties was not required for alienations and mortgages before the Code,[59] and that canon 1532, §3, which requires the consent of the interested parties is a change from the old law.

Beste, p. 739; cf. ex. gr., *Synodus Dioecesana Bellevillensis Quinta* (Belleville: Buechler Printing Co., 1940), p. 20. In this event they would meet and vote as members of both the Board and of the Council simultaneously.

[58] Cf. *supra*, p. 96.

[59] Cf. *supra*, Chapter IV, p. 55. A patron is considered one of the interested parties (cf. *infra*, p. 129), yet the consent of the patron was not

If canon 1538 does not require the consent of the interested parties it is retaining the old law. It would seem that a lone exception from the general principle requiring their consent, as established by canon 1532, §3, and a lone exception to the change from the old law to the new, should have been more explicitly stated by the legislator if this lone exception were intended.

This difficulty is treated by only one of the available authors. Pistocchi holds that because of the use of the word *audiantur* the consent of the interested parties is not necessary, but that the mortgage is valid even if the Ordinary permits it over the objections of the interested parties; and that if he does not hear them at all he acts only illicitly.[60] The writer agrees with Pistocchi. The prime principle of interpretation is that laws must be understood according to the proper meaning of the words in the text and context.[61] The words *quorum interest audiantur* can be interpreted to mean something other than "the interested parties are to be heard" only by doing violence to the meaning of the text. The Code itself supports this interpretation of *audire.*[62] Hence the only warranted solution of this conflict between canons 1532, §3 and 1538 seems to be that of Pistocchi, who evidently interpreted canon 1538 according to the proper meaning of the text and exemplified the principle: *Generi per speciem dero-*

---

required for alienations by any law before the Code (cf. Schmalzgrueber, lib. III, tit. XIII, n. 111). If the consent of one so deeply concerned as the patron was not required, then it seems also that the consent of none of the interested parties could have been required.

60 "Ibi *consensus* eorum quorum interest requirebatur, heic tantummodo edicitur ut *audiantur,* deficiente consensu de quo §2 §3 can. 1532 negotium in irritum cedit, ac proinde praeceptum Superiori factum illud exquirendi est ad validitatem: id veritatem non habet in praesenti. Superior—exigat ut . . . audiantur—sed neque dissensus eorum quorum interest negotium invalidat, neque omissio eorum consultationis: in hoc ultimo casu Superior tantummodo *illicite* procedit."—*De Bonis Ecclesiae Temporalibus* (Taurini: Marietti, 1932), p. 435. (Hereafter cited *De Bonis.*)

Without pointing out this difference in the two canons, Ayrinhac, Cocchi and Pruemmer say that the interested parties need only be heard for liceity, and therefore seem to support the interpretation of Pistocchi.—Cf. Ayrinhac, *loc. cit.;* Cocchi, *loc. cit.;* Pruemmer, *loc. cit.*

61 C. 18.

62 Cf. C. 105.

gatur,[63] in the present case canon 1532 being the general law for all alienations and canon 1538 the specific law for mortgages.

In saying that the Ordinary acts only illicitly when he does not even hear the interested parties Pistocchi evidently is interpreting the canon according to the more lenient interpretation of canon 105, 1°. This canon lays down the principle that "if consultation only is demanded, it suffices for the validity of the action if the superior consults the persons specified." [64] The common opinion of canonists who comment on this canon 105 is that the omission of holding the consultation would cause the act to be invalid.[65] Yet "until such a time when an official reply will be given, it seems indicated to acknowledge the extrinsic probability of the less common opinion, and hence, not to be disturbed about the consequences of acts which superiors might execute in violation of the demand of canon 105, n. 1." [66] Therefore since the less common opinion, that hearing the persons who are ordered to be heard is a necessity only for licitness of the action of the superior, has this extrinsic authority, there is ground for doubting whether it is necessary for the validity of the Ordinary's consent to the mortgage that he call in the interested parties mentioned in canon 1538. Hence, if the Ordinary does not summon them the validity of the mortgage cannot be attacked. In practice, by virtue of canon 15,[67] and canon 209,[68] the consent of the

---

[63] R. J. 34 in VI°.

[64] "Si consensus exigatur, Superior contra earundem votum invalide agit; si consilium tantum, per verba, ex. gr.: *de consilio consultorum, vel audito Capitulo, paricho,* etc., satis est ad valide agendum ut Superior illas personas audiat;"—C. 105, 1°; translation from Woywod, *Practical Commentary,* I, 46.

[65] Cf. Coronata, *Institutiones,* I, 187, note 8.

[66] Bastnagel, *The Appointment of Parochial Adjutants and Assistants,* The Catholic University of America Canon Law Studies, No. 58 (Washington, D. C.: The Catholic University of America, 1930), p. 228; cf. also Coronata, *loc. cit.;* Vromant, *De Bonis Ecclesiae Temporalibus,* p. 53; Meier, *Penal Administrative Procedure Against Negligent Pastors,* The Catholic University of America Canon Law Studies, No. 140 (Washington, D. C.: The Catholic University of America Press, 1941), p. 178.

[67] "Leges, etiam irritantes et inhabilitantes, in dubio iuris non urgent."

[68] "In . . . dubio positivo et probabili sive iuris sive facti, iurisdictionem supplet Ecclesia pro foro tum externo tum interno." Cf. Miaskiewicz, *Supplied Jurisdiction According to Canon 209,* The Catholic University of

Ordinary and the subsequent mortgage will be regarded as valid despite the simultaneously acknowledged unlawfulness of the Ordinary's manner of acting.

The Diocesan Council of Administration and the Diocesan Board of Consultors are not mentioned in canon 1538. This should not leave the impression that they need not even be heard, much less give their consent. If this were the case, canon 1533 requiring the same solemnities for all contracts making the condition of the Church worse, would be useless; there would be no reason to state in canon 1533 that the solemnities of canons 1530–1532 should be observed and at the same time mean that only those solemnities mentioned in canons 1538, 1540, 1541, 1542 for the individual contracts of mortgage, sale, or lease to relatives, lease in general, and emphyteusis respectively should be observed.

The Code wisely points out that the superior should hear the interested parties before all else. Whereas the consent of the Council of Administration and the Board of Consultors need not be unanimous, but will be valid if only elicited in the majority, the viewpoint of the interested parties, which is not necessarily obtained in session, should not be considered unreasonable if it be not unanimous. The interested parties are not members of a committee of any kind; neither are their interests pooled necessarily. Whereas the Council and the Board have one common interest, namely, to assist the local Ordinary in the administration of his diocese, the interests of the " interested parties " may be as diverse as they are numerous. Since matters which concern all as individuals must be approved by all,[69] there seems no reason for submitting the interpretation that these interested parties can elicit a majority consent in other alienations,[70] or a majority approval in mortgaging.

Therefore, for the licitness of his action, the Ordinary should hear these interested parties, not necessarily *collegialiter*, and

---

America Canon Law Studies, No. 122 (Washington, D. C.: The Catholic University of America Press, 1940), pp. 194–210, 221, 281.

[69] C. 101, §1, 2°. Translation of canon from Woywod, *Practical Commentary*, I, 45.

[70] This is done by Coronata, *Institutiones*, II, 487.

only then for the validity of his action, obtain the consent of the Council and of the Board.

The interested parties are those involved in the contract: the possessor of the benefice, the administrator, the rector, the members of a collegiate juristic person, the canonical patrons, and the rector of a non-collegiate moral person as the case may be.[71]

That permission to mortgage, when obtained by Religious, must be in writing, is evident.[72] Larraona is of the opinion that the general law of the Code does not require the permission to be in writing.[73] The conclusion would therefore be that a written permission is necessary for Religious alone. But if Vromant's division of acts of administration is accepted (and there seems to be no sound argument against it), namely, that mortgaging is an act which exceeds the limits of ordinary administration,[74] then canon 1527, §1 is applicable. This canon decrees that administrators act invalidly in actions that exceed ordinary administration unless they first obtain the faculty in writing from the local Ordinary.[75] Though the validity of the transaction does not depend on the committing of the permission to writing, the prescription that it

---

[71] Cf. Coronata, *Institutiones,* II, 486; Ayrinhac, *Administrative Legislation,* p. 455. The charter of a non-collegiate person could determine others beside the rector whose opinion would be necessary to obtain.—Cf. C. 1489, §3.

It must be noted that the interested parties must be the same people that are referred to in canon 1532, §3.—Pistocchi, *De Bonis,* p. 435. The same phrase, *quorum interest,* is used in both canons and therefore there seems to be no reason for determining them in one canon to mean a certain group and in another canon to mean a different group. Thus Ayrinhac, Cocchi, and Pruemmer think that in canon 1538 the interested parties would include those who might have to pay the interest.—Ayrinhac, *Administrative Legislation,* p. 452; Cocchi, *Commentarium,* III, 425; Pruemmer, *Manuale Iuris Canonici,* p. 41. Whether they mean the administrator, who really pays nothing but only writes a check perhaps, or whether they mean the people who through their contributions are the ones who finally must bear the burden of the mortgage, they do not say.

[72] C. 534, §1. McManus concludes an unwritten permission would be sufficient to insure the validity of the transaction.—*Administration,* p. 30.

[73] *Commentarium Codicis, CpR,* XIII (1932), 357.

[74] *De Bonis Ecclesiae Temporalibus,* pp. 185, 186.

[75] "Nisi prius ab Ordinario loci facultatem impetraverint, scriptis dandam, administratores invalide actus ponunt qui ordinariae administrationis fines et modum excedant."—C. 1527, §1.

be a written permission nevertheless binds.[76] The enactments of the Second and Third Plenary Councils of Baltimore to this effect are still in force as being in complete accord with canon 1527, §1.[77] Good administration would suggest that both grantor and grantee attempt to have anything of such import in writing, especially since the validity of the mortgage depends on the consent.

D. *The Holy See*

When a mortgage of more than $6,000 is to be contracted on a single piece of property, or when several pieces of real estate are individually mortgaged at the same time by the same corporation exceeding $6,000 in the total, the Holy See must be petitioned for permission.[78] This applies to Religious as well as to seculars.[79] Administrators are not bound by the law of the Code to obtain the permission of any intermediary superior in these cases where the permission of the Holy See is necessary. This condition could be imposed as a *sine qua non* by the Holy See in its grant.[80] But to avoid the difficulty of perhaps having their petition returned administrators should always obtain the *votum* of the Ordinary or Religious superior and have the petition forwarded to the Holy See by them.

By the Holy See is meant:

1. The S. Congregation of the Council for seculars.[81]
2. The S. Congregation of Religious for Religious Institutes, Third Orders, and Societies of men or women living in community without vows.[82]
3. The S. Congregation of the Propagation of the Faith for those within the territories under its jurisdiction, and even for Institutes and Associations placed under its complete jurisdiction.[83]

---

[76] Vermeersch-Creusen, *Epitome,* II, 591, 592.

[77] Cf. *supra,* Chapter IV, p. 57.

[78] Canons 1538 and 1532, §1, 2°; cf. also Cleary, *Alienation,* p. 76.

[79] C. 534, § 1, governing Religious, C. 1532 seculars.

[80] Coronata, *Institutiones,* II, 486.

[81] C. 250, §2.

[82] C. 251, §1 and C. 676, §2.

[83] C. 252, §1; cf. also Vromant, *De Bonis Ecclesiae Temporalibus,* p. 305, note 2.

4. The S. Congregation for the Oriental Church for those who administer goods belonging to a moral person of an Oriental discipline.[84]

5. The S. Consistorial Congregation if the mortgage is to be placed on property strictly diocesan.[85]

6. The S. Congregation of Seminaries and Universities if the property of a diocesan seminary is to be mortgaged.[86]

After the *Beneplacitum Apostolicum* has been granted, the administrator is still free to use it or not. There is no obligation to contract the mortgage simply because permission to do so has been received.[87]

E. *The Value of 30,000 Lire or Francs*

Should a mortgage contract exceed in value the local Ordinary's authority to grant permission by only a very little amount, the consent and the consequent mortgage would be invalid.[88] Therefore it is necessary to be very exact in determining the equivalent of 30,000 lire or francs in dollars, above which the Code requires the permission to be obtained from the Holy See.[89]

Four opinions as to the value of 30,000 lire or francs have been advanced since the promulgation of the Code. They are as follows:

First Opinion. The limit, above which the *Beneplacitum Apostolicum* to mortgage would have to be secured, should be a sum whose *purchasing power* today would be the equivalent of $6,000 before the depreciation began. To compute this sum it is suggested that statisticians be approached to supply the reliable figures.[90] This could hardly be a practical solution. The purchasing power could change daily and the statisticians' figures be of no value by the time they reached the local Ordinary. The

---

[84] C. 257, §1; cf. also Vromant, *loc. cit.*

[85] Vromant, *loc. cit.*

[86] Cf. Ayrinhac-Lydon, *Penal Legislation in the New Code of Canon Law* (New York, Cincinnati, Chicago, San Francisco: Benziger Brothers, 1936), p. 236 (hereafter cited *Penal Legislation*); Heston, *Alienation*, p. 105.

[87] Cf. Larraona, *Commentarium Codicis, CpR,* XIV (1933), 44.

[88] Cf. Larraona, *Commentarium Codicis, CpR,* XIV (1933), 41.

[89] Canon 1532, §1, 2°. Canon 534, §1 is applicable to Religious and the Religious superior's authority.

[90] Cf. Nevin, in *ACR,* XIII (1936), 244, and IV (1927), 39.

proposer of this opinion himself feels that "the problem is intrinsically difficult and no private interpreter can solve it."[91] But some solution is necessary that administrators, Religious superiors, and Ordinaries have some means without which observance of the law is impossible.

Second Opinion. The legislator meant the market value of Italian or French currency as a standard of valuation. In normal times this would be about $6,000 but in 1938 about $10,000 or $12,000. This would correspond to the intention of the Code because land as well as building materials have risen so much in value.[92] The author here uses two determinants of the mind of the lawgiver, namely the market value of Italian or French currency and the purchasing power of American money. Surely both cannot be simultaneously used since the market value of money may remain constant while its purchasing power might fluctuate.[93]

Third Opinion. Any question of gold content, grams, price of gold, etc., appears to be unnecessary and may be disregarded in this particular relation, and $6,000 should be the equivalent as indicated in the letter of the Apostolic Delegate of Nov. 13, 1936.[94] Just why the gold value of the lire or franc should be disregarded the author does not state. He makes no mention of the statement in the same letter of the Apostolic Delegate which reads:

> The aforesaid sum of six thousand dollars should be understood, in connection with the terms of the Code,

---

[91] *ACR*, XIII (1936), 244.

[92] Augustine, *Commentary*, III, 186.

[93] In all fairness to Augustine, the criticism of his opinion by Coronata seems a bit harsh and on the illogical side. Coronata states that the lire should be the gold lire and hence in March 1924, 30,000 lire would have been the equivalent to 120,000 paper lire. He says Augustine's view is absurd because $12,000 that month was equivalent to 288,000,000 paper lire.—Cf. Coronata, *Institutiones*, I, 697, note 4. Moreover, if $12,000 equals 288,000,000 paper lire, then the 120,000 paper lire, which Coronata says was the equivalent at that time to the 30,000 lire of the Code, would equal $5.00! Perhaps by correcting an error, which could hardly have been typographical, one could explain increasing this valuation of 30,000 lire to $5,000, but $6,000 had been accepted long before, and $6,000 on the same basis at that time would have been 144,000 paper lire or 36,000 lire of the Code!

[94] Cf. *AER*, CI (1939), 560, author not identified in the periodical.

> as the equivalent of "thirty thousand lire or francs" and in reference to the value of currency based upon gold in distinction to other currencies, gold being the true unit of value. In this connection the value is based upon such stable gold content and rate of exchange.[95]

It is true that the Apostolic Delegate says stable gold content and not the intrinsic worth of the dollar. Yet the intrinsic worth of the dollar caused the pre-1934 standard to be five francs to one dollar. Before 1934 this ratio was not absolutely permanent; otherwise it could not have been altered in 1934. Perhaps the present ratio may not be permanent considering the possibility of change. Moreover many reputable canonists do not disregard the gold value, and though it might be objected that none disregards it as such and that it should merely be disregarded in the search for a standard rate of exchange, the writer feels that the standard rate of exchange in any event will be merely a rate based on a gold value which the dollar had at some specific time. Why any period of history should be selected, in preference to the present, to possess the standards for succeeding periods is difficult to see.

The writer admits the probability of this opinion, yet favors the opinion to be developed subsequently.

Fourth Opinion. This theory advances the use of the gold value of money as the standard for computing the equivalent of 30,000 lire or francs. This is the most common opinion because of the consistently uniform view of canonists, and it can be considered not only probable but indubitably a certain opinion.[96] The use of the gold value of money brings independence from exchange fluctuations,[97] which the Code was trying to prevent in its

---

[95] Cf. Bouscaren, *Supplement 1941*, p. 79.

[96] Cf. Doheny, *Church Finance*, p. 41. This opinion is held by Pruemmer, *Manuale Iuris Canonici*, p. 263, note 109; Vermeersch-Creusen, *Epitome*, I, 474 and II, 569; Ellis, *Triginta Millia Libellarum seu Francorum—Periodica*, XXVII (1938), 349; Creusen-Garesche-Ellis, *Religious*, p. 117; Coronata, *Institutiones*, I, 697, note 4; Schaefer, *De Religiosis*, p. 432; Ayrinhac, *Administrative Legislation*, p. 443; Blat, in Ayrinhac, *loc. cit.;* Cocchi, *Commentarium*, III, 417; Wernz-Vidal, *Ius Canonicum*, Tom. IV, Vol. 2, 230; and those to be cited subsequently.

[97] Cf. Cocchi, *Commentarium*, III, 417.

legislation.[98] Paper money is not suitable as a norm for perpetual and universal law and so cannot be the norm of valuation which the lawgiver had in mind.[99]

Three statements emanating from the Holy See favor the use of the gold evaluation of 30,000 lire. The S. Congregation of the Council advocated the use of real money instead of fictitious money.[100] The S. Congregation of the Propagation of the Faith permitted the Japanese to alienate $15,000 as the equivalent of 30,000 francs.[101] The Apostolic Delegate in transmitting the Instruction of the S. Congregation of Religious to the religious superiors in the United States expressly said that $6,000 (the accepted equivalent) was to be understood in reference to the value of currency based upon gold, which is the true unit of value.[102]

Accepting then the gold value as the standard, it is possible to find three variations in establishing the amount above which recourse must be had to Rome. Cleary thinks that even using the gold standards the ratio is 5 lire or francs to the dollar.[103] His method of arriving at this ratio is not quite clear and does not seem to take into consideration the change which occurred in the gold standard of this country in 1934. Heston considers $10,000 as the present equivalent, but no method of computation is shown.[104] Doheny alone gives an accurate equivalent based

---

[98] Woywod, *HPR*, XXX (1929), 272.

[99] Beste, *loc. cit.*

[100] *Resolutio circa redemptionem canonis,* 23 ian. 1923—*AAS,* XV (1923), 513.

[101] Cf. Schaefer, *De Religiosis,* p. 433. No reference is given to the source where the document can be found.

[102] *Apostolic Delegation, Letter,* 13 Nov., 1936—Bouscaren, *Supplement 1941,* p. 80. "Respectus monetae aureae *practice* sed nondum formaliter et explicite in S. Congregatione admittitur."—Vermeersch-Creusen, *Epitome,* I, 474, note 2. The gold criterion is used in the Apostolic Chancery.—Larraona, *loc. cit.*

[103] *Alienation,* p. 78.

[104] *Alienation,* pp. 110–112. Heston shows that Ellis, a professor of Canon Law at the Pontifical Gregorian University in Rome, and Consultor of the S. Congregation of Religious, estimated the 30,000 lire as being the equivalent of $10,000 in the United States and Canadian currencies and published this as a safe procedure at a time when he was thoroughly conversant with the attitude of the S. Congregation.

on gold valuation and relative values of money prior and subsequent to the President's official reduction in 1934 of the gold weight of the dollar. The gold value was reduced to .5906 of the par established in 1900, making the $6,000 of 1900 to 1934 equivalent now to 10,159 devaluated dollars. Therefore the 30,000 lire of the Code which were equivalent to $6,000 during that same period are now equivalent to $10,159.[105] Roelker feels that the legal worth of this, Doheny's opinion, depends on the permanency of devaluation of U. S. currency, being tenable or not as this present devaluation is permanent or not respectively.[106] For practical purposes: it seems that because of the tremendous governmental debts already assumed and more contemplated, and the consequent economic impossibility to reestablish the higher valuation of money, the new equivalent of 30,000 lire and other sums quoted in special faculties may be safely followed.

The method of arriving at the equivalent established by Doheny was not explicitly shown, but it was evidently based on the use of either of two equations. 1: .5906::X:1.00 can be used to establish the equivalent relative value of U. S. currency. The product of the extremes, 1.00, divided by the denominator, .5906, gives the quotient, 1.69319. Multiplying this by the number of dollars will give the equivalent in gold valuation. The equation .20: .5906::X:1.00 produces the quotient .338638, which multiplied by the number of lire will give the equivalent dollars in gold valuation. Thus 1.69319 × $6,000 = $10,159.14; .338638 × 30,000 = $10,159.14. Accordingly the faculties of the local Ordinaries to mortgage up to $10,000[107] refers to gold dollars[108] and may be considered as being $16,931.90 in present United States currency.[109]

---

[105] Doheny, *Church Finance,* p. 42; "Church Finance and Problems of Alienation."—*The Jurist,* I (1941), 102.

[106] *The Jurist,* II (1942), 87.

[107] Quinquennial Faculties of Ordinaries: Formula IV (1939-1944) for the United States—Bouscaren, *Supplement 1941,* p. 31. The indult of November 18, 1924 authorizing the bishops of the United States to permit alienations up to $50,000 was not renewed in 1934.—Heston, *Alienation,* p. 49.

[108] Cf. Doheny, *Church Finance,* p. 42.

[109] Doheny's estimate is $16,931—*loc. cit.* With Vermeersch-Creusen in projecting the view that gold valuation is to be used, the writer includes his

F. *The Use of Canon 81* [110]

Very few authors treat the possibility of the Ordinary's use of canon 81 in relation to alienation or mortgage. Those who do either give no reason why its use is possible [111] or do not establish the juristic principles with a completeness sufficient entirely to dispel the doubts regarding the possibility of its use. This is without fault since their purpose was not analysis but direction.[112] The intention of the writer is not to differ with their suggestion as to its use, but to show the canonical reasons on which the employing of it is based.

(1) *A Proposed Difficulty.*

Canon 81 requires the presence of three contingencies, namely, difficulty of recourse to the Holy See, danger of grave harm in delay, and a case in which the Holy See usually dispenses. These conditions must simultaneously occur in a particular case, so that if one is lacking the Ordinary has no power to dispense.[113] But the *Beneplacitum Apostolicum* [114] which is required by the canons for mortgages exceeding the sum of $6,000 [115] is, in the Code's own words, a permission, which is granted by the Holy See.[116] A permission and a dispensation are not identical. The Code itself defines the word dispensation to mean the relaxation of a law in a particular case.[117] This means it is an act by which the

views as stated above: "Verum haec sunt dicta ut animum nostrum simpliciter et modeste aperiamus, salvo proin meliore iudicio et salva authentica S. Sedis responsione."—*Epitome,* I, 474.

[110] "A generalibus Ecclesiae legibus Ordinarii infra Romanum Pontificem dispensare nequeunt, ne in casu quidem peculiari, . . . nisi difficilis sit recursus ad Sanctam Sedem et simul in mora sit periculum gravis damni, et de dispensatione agatur quae a Sede Apostolica concedi solet."

[111] E. g., Augustine, *Commentary,* VI, 599.

[112] E. g., Doheny, *Church Finance,* pp. 82-85.

[113] Cf. Coronata, *Institutiones,* I, 122.

[114] This is the term used in canons 534, §1 and 2347, 3°.

[115] For gold equivalent, cf. *supra,* section E.

[116] "Licentia legitimi Superioris, sine qua alienatio invalida est."—C. 1530, §1, 3°; "Legitimus Superior de quo in can. 1530, §1, 3° est Sedes Apostolica, si agatur: De rebus quae valorem excedunt triginta millium libellarum seu francorum."—C. 1532, §1, 2°.

[117] "Dispensatio, seu legis in casu speciali relaxatio, concedi potest a conditore legis," etc.—C. 80.

legitimate superior either himself or through another removes, as far as some one else is concerned, the specific obligation of some determined law by which the recipient of the dispensation would otherwise be bound.[118] Whereas a permission is simply a faculty according to the law, which has the effect not of taking away the obligation of the law which is absolutely imposed, but of permitting an act to be legitimately placed or omitted. The law makes the condition on which the act can be placed or omitted respectively.

The *Beneplacitum Apostolicum* is not then, as a dispensation is, contrary to the law or an injury to the law, but it is in accord with the law or a condition, which, once obtained, the act is permitted by the law itself.[119] Therefore since the *Beneplacitum Apostolicum* is not a dispensation, the third requirement of canon 81 is not fulfilled, namely, the *Beneplacitum Apostolicum* is not a dispensation which the Holy See is accustomed to grant because it is not a dispensation at all. The use of canon 81 would not therefore be possible to *supply* a permission to mortgage.

(2) *The Solution.*

From certain private information it seems safe to assert that the *praxis Curiae* recognizes the possibility of the use of canon 81 in reference to mortgages. Having what should otherwise be a conclusion thus anticipated in practice, it remains only to search for the premises and the reasons why authors may have affirmed the use of canon 81 in these cases.

It seems that the dispensation which Ordinaries can grant is that which relaxes the law of canon 1530, §1, 3°, requiring the Holy See's permission. Automatically canon 1532, §1 loses its binding force because it merely explains canon 1530, §1, 3°, which has been dispensed from. The contract is entered then without any *Beneplacitum Apostolicum* because the relaxation of the law has caused these particular canons to lose their binding force and, as it were, not to exist in reference to the particular case.

For the grant of this dispensation the contingencies of canon 81 can be verified.

---

[118] Cf. Michiels, *Normae Generales,* II, 452.

[119] Cf. Michiels, *op. cit.,* p. 455.

(a) Difficulty of recourse to the Holy See. It is not necessary that extraordinary difficulties of recourse to Rome be present, but only that there is not sufficient time to apply in the particular case.[120]

(b) Danger of grave harm in delay. The doubt of the presence of this condition is possible when it is a case in which a proposed mortgage will serve only to the advantage of the Church, and hence its lack will seemingly cause no harm. But this doubt is dispelled when it is realized the *damnum* can be interpreted to mean the probable loss of temporalities,[121] or a probable economic loss.[122] This loss must be grave, but certainly the loss of a substantial sum of money would entail the necessary gravity.[123] In a refinancing program in which a lower rate of interest can be obtained, the loss would be the excess interest paid if the refinancing did not succeed.[124] In a new mortgage for the purpose of building, etc., the probable higher costs in the future would be a loss to the extent of the difference over present costs.

(c) It must be a dispensation which the Holy See is wont to grant. Since it has been shown[125] that the Holy See recognizes the possibility of the use of this canon in reference to mortgages,

---

[120] Cf. Van Hove, *Commentarium Lovaniense in Codicem Iuris Canonici,* Vol. I, Tom. V, *De Privilegiis, De Dispensationibus* (Mechliniae-Romae: H. Dessain, 1939), p. 378 (hereafter cited *De Dispensationibus*). The time under ordinary circumstances is computed as between 40 and 50 days for the United States, by the use of the mails, to the Holy See, so that even though the amount were within the faculties of the Apostolic Delegate, this canon can be used.—*Ibid.*

The letter of January, 1942, to the Diocesan and Religious Ordinaries and Superiors of the United States from the Apostolic Delegate does not seem to contradict any of the principles of law or any of the accepted authors' interpretations, but merely to preclude the use of canon 81 for any and all dispensations when there is sufficient time for recourse.—Cf. *The Jurist,* II (1942), 182–183.

[121] Van Hove, *op. cit.,* p. 379.

[122] Coronata, *Institutiones,* I, 123.

[123] Doheny, *Church Finance,* p. 84.

[124] Hannan is of the opinion that in a refinancing, a new permission is not needed, because, though in strictly legal application it is a different mortgage, substantially and in equitable application it is the same mortgage.—"Refinancing a Mortgage," *The Jurist,* II (1942), 58; cf. also Doheny, *Church Finance,* p. 63.

[125] Cf. *supra,* p. 137.

it is implicitly saying it is one which it customarily grants.[126] No information is available as to whether the Holy See may have given dispensations in other countries, during emergencies, from applying for its *Beneplacitum,* but it is certainly not improbable that this may have been done. But even if it has not, the condition of the canon can be verified. There are certain dispensations which the Holy See never grants,[127] and others which it is not wont to grant.[128] The writer can find no opinion that a dispensation from the necessity of the *Beneplacitum Apostolicum* is considered as being in either of these two groups. Thus by elimination it must be considered among those referred to by canon 81.[129]

Therefore since the contingencies required by the canon can be simultaneously present, canon 81 is a possible instrument in the mortgaging of church property.

(3) *Advisability of Its Use.*

It might be objected that the use of canon 81 will often be a needless instrument since frequently cases will arise in which the causes for its use are sufficiently grave to be at the same time causes excusing from the law requiring the *Beneplacitum Apostolicum.*[130] In which case only a declaration on the part of the Ordinary, to the effect that in the particular case there exist

---

[126] Doheny summarily says: "It is well known that dispensations are granted in matters of alienation by the Holy See."—*Church Finance,* p. 85. However the very statement leaves doubt in the reader's mind whether or not the specific dispensation in question is granted by the Holy See, and whether he may not be confusing the terms dispensation and permission. No other writers can be found who refer to this point.

[127] As in cases involving the matrimonial impediment of affinity in the direct line arising from a consummated marriage, or when there is a doubt of law or of fact regarding the existence of certain other impediments of the natural law.—Van Hove, *De Dispensationibus,* p. 380.

[128] Such as in the case of the public impediment of crime arising from conjugicide.—*Ibid.*

[129] "(C. 81) extendit ad omnes leges ecclesiasticas omnesque casus in jure non expresse exceptos; quod enim in genere conceditur, ad omnes species extenditur, nisi expresse derogetur;"—Michiels, *Normae Generales,* p. 485.

[130] That under certain conditions the solemnities are unnecessary, cf. De Meester, *Compendium,* III, 403.

causes sufficient in themselves to excuse, need be issued. Since a greater cause is required to excuse than to dispense from the law, when such a cause is *de facto* present the Ordinary's dispensation will be as useless as dispensing a person gravely ill from the law of fasting when in reality the person is already excused.[131]

It can be answered that since the mortgage is always a matter of extraordinary administration it would have to be referred to the Ordinary[132] for either the declaration of the existence of an excusing cause or a dispensation. Since the declaration is merely an act of the intellect and requires no jurisdiction the obligation of the law is not removed should the declaration rest on error. Whereas the dispensation, which is an act of ordinary jurisdiction,[133] if granted with a doubtful cause will remove the binding force of the law.[134] In the former case the mortgage would be invalid, in the latter, it would be valid.

As there is a presumption for the validity of a challenged dispensation[135] so there is a presumption for the invalidity of a challenged mortgage entered without permission.[136] The presumption of validity of a dispensation from the necessity of permission is sufficient to destroy the presumption of invalidity of a mortgage entered without permission, because the dispensation removes the binding force of the canon requiring the permission. The excusing cause, whatever it may have been, enjoys no presumption of having been *de facto* sufficiently grave to excuse from the law, and thus a plaintiff's proving the contract was en-

---

[131] Cf. Van Hove, *De Dispensationibus,* pp. 314–315.

[132] Cf. Vromant, *De Bonis Ecclesiae Temporalibus,* p. 186; S. C. Con. Feb. 17, 1906—Schaefer, *De Religiosis,* p. 430, and *CpR,* XIII (1932), 192, note 635.

[133] Reilly, *The General Norms of Dispensation,* The Catholic University of America Canon Law Studies, No. 119 (Washington, D. C.: The Catholic University of America Press, 1939), p. 72.

[134] Cf. C. 84, §2; Van Hove, *op. cit.,* p. 315.

[135] C. 84, §2; Wanenmacher, *Canonical Evidence in Marriage Cases* (a revised and augmented form of *The Evidence in Ecclesiastical Procedure Affecting the Marriage Bond,* The Catholic University of America Canon Law Studies, No. 9, Washington, D. C., 1920), (Philadelphia, Pa.: Dolphin Press, 1935), p. 246.

[136] Cf. Canons, 1538, §1, 1530, §1, 3°.

tered without permission would throw the burden of proof on the one alleging the excusing cause.[137] Therefore, should the validity of a mortgage contracted by either a declaration of the existence of a cause excusing from, or a dispensation from, the *Beneplacitum Apostolicum* ever be called into question the presumption of invalidity would exist in the former case whereas the presumption of validity would be present in result of the dispensation.

After using canon 81 there is no obligation of informing the Holy See. The Quinquennial Faculties expressly mention this obligation if a mortgage is permitted in virtue of these faculties. If canon 81 were used after the petition for the *Beneplacitum Apostolicum* had been sent to Rome[138] notification of its use would have to be transmitted also.[139]

ARTICLE VI. AMORTIZATION

C. 1538, §1: . . . legitimus Superior . . . curet ut, cum primum fieri poterit, aes alienum solvatur.

§2: Hac de causa annuae ratae ab eodem Ordinario praefiniantur quae exstinguendo debito sint destinatae.

The Code orders "the legitimate Superior to see that all debts are paid off as soon as possible. The same Ordinary shall for this purpose determine the annual rate at which the debt is to be extinguished."[140] This is the incorporation into the Code of the sound business principle that money should not be borrowed except in cases where the revenue is such that the parish or institute can surely pay the interest charges out of current revenue and meet the principal at maturity.[141]

The Code leaves a great deal to the judgment of the superior in determining just how soon it is possible to pay off the mort-

---

137 Cf. C. 1827.

138 This necessity is possible.—Cf. Reilly, *op. cit.*, p. 78.

139 Cf. C. 204, §2; Coronata, *Institutiones*, I, 123.

140 Translation of canon from Woywod, *Practical Commentary*, II, 188.

141 Cf. Montgomery, *Financial Handbook*, p. 569. A basis frequently followed is that the average surplus revenue over a considerable period of time should be at least twice the interest requirements, whereas the minimum surplus during periods of economic depression should be equal at least to the interest requirements.—*Ibid.*

gage, but certainly the mind of the Church is plainly shown to be averse to the contracting of mortgages when a prudent judgment that they will be paid within a reasonable time is absent. The canon provides for the more efficacious and practical fulfillment of this duty of the Ordinary by directing him in its second section to determine the annual payment on the principal,[142] or to determine the amortization.[143] The source of the money for the amortization is not stated by the canon. An Instruction of the S. Congregation of the Propagation of the Faith permitted a portion of the fixed revenues to be set aside for this purpose.[144] But if no such endowment or fixed revenues are available (which is the usual condition in this country), a "sinking fund" or amortization fund should be established to wipe out the debt,[145] and thus enable the direction of the Ordinary as to the amount of annual payments to be fulfilled.

There are three principal methods of handling this amortization fund. The Ordinary can determine the amount and require it either to be invested or to be deposited in a bank each year;[146] to be paid to a trustee or other worthy person who deposits or invests the same at his discretion, according to agreement;[147] or to become due each year for the redemption of bonds of an issue which were arranged to mature in series.[148]

---

[142] Cf. Cocchi, *Commentarium,* III, 425; Vromant, *De Bonis Ecclesiae Temporalibus,* p. 344.

[143] C. 536, §5 is the parallel for Religious: "Caveant Superiores religiosi ne debita contrahenda permittant, nisi certo constet ex consuetis reditibus posse debiti foenus solvi et intra tempus non nimis longum per legitimam *amortizationem* reddi summam capitalem."

[144] Ad Patriarch. *Armenien.,* 30 iul., 1867—*Coll. S. P. C. F.,* n. 1310, par. 4; Fontes, n. 4867. Although revenues are usually considered income and not stable capital, it must be that in this response the revenues called "fixed" were considered a type of endowment according to 1410 and hence stable capital. Only with the permission of the proper superior, as obtained in this instance, could such fixed revenues be alienated in this manner.

[145] Augustine, *Commentary,* VI, 604.

[146] Coronata, *Institutiones,* II, 491.

[147] Ellis, "Some Canonical Terms Dealing With Temporalities—Bona Temporalia"—*Theological Studies,* I (1940), 174. This method differs from the former in that one is managed by the administrator and the other by a third person.

[148] Ellis, *loc. cit.*

Naturally canon 1538, §2 must be observed only when it is beneficial to the Church's interests that the debt be amortized. The amortization of debts is in itself the result of the highest type of administration, but some circumstances may arise in which it is beneficial to the Church to have its property remain encumbered. In these circumstances this section of the canon would not apply.[149]

In determining the amortization plan the best interests of the Church will be safeguarded by providing a plan most suitable to both the creditors and to the parish or institute. Hence in virtue of canon 1538, §2 the Ordinary might guard against any proposed plan being too rapid and thus throwing an unreasonable burden on those who in the last analysis will have to pay the money, or being too slow and thus causing the prospective creditors (in most cases, prospective bondholders) to doubt the financial resources of the debtor parish or institution.

ARTICLE VII. OBSERVANCE OF STATE LAWS

" Whatever the civil law of a country decrees on contracts and payments of all kinds is to be observed also by Canon Law in ecclesiastical matters, and has the same effects, except in so far as the civil law is contrary to the divine law, or Canon Law rules otherwise." [150] Hence in the matter of mortgaging Church property in this country there is an obligation arising from the ecclesiastical law to follow the American law on contracts in general and mortgages in particular. Since the laws of the individual States vary, it is not within the scope of this monograph to examine the individual laws with the purpose of judging whether any conflicts exist between American law and Code law, or between American law and divine law, but since the Code laws have been stated and explained the administrators of Church property are well able from this explanation and from their knowledge of divine law to detect any conflict with either canon law or divine law which may arise through a particular State's legislation.

---

[149] Vermeersch-Creusen, *Epitome*, I, 601; Vromant, *De Bonis Ecclesiae Temporalibus*, p. 344.

[150] C. 1529. Translation from Woywod, *Practical Commentary*, II, 183.

Needless to say the importance of having expert legal advice on American mortgage laws in drawing up contracts of mortgage cannot be overstressed.[151] To present herein all the laws of the States, or examples of mortgages and mortgage bonds with a view to enabling the administrator to draft these documents personally would certainly lead to disastrous results. To depend on the creditors (individual or corporate) for this may be equally calamitous, without malice necessarily on their part.

Yet administrators should be acquainted with the more general matters regarding which State laws have been enacted and judicial decisions rendered. Summarily then, these concern the form, the formal parts, the condition or defeasance clause, and the solemnities.

No particular form is necessary to constitute a mortgage, only a written instrument of some kind which clearly indicates a mortgage, the debt secured, and the property encumbered.[152] The form can be also a statutory form of mortgage, or a trust deed. A deed of trust given as a mortgage is distinguished from other deeds of trust in that the former is conditional and defeasible as is a mortgage, whereas the latter are indefeasible and unconditional. The important distinction between a trust deed given as a mortgage and a mortgage as such is that in the former case the conveyance is to a third person while in the latter it is directly to the creditor. Moreover the trust deed with power of sale may be foreclosed by the trustee according to the powers given in the deed and without authority of court. A simple mortgage can be foreclosed only under decree of court.[153]

The formal parts of a mortgage are the description of the parties, the recital of consideration, the description of the premises, and a definition of the estate conveyed.

The condition or defeasance clause is most important. It is an integral part of a legal mortgage but not so of a trust deed, and therefore its insertion in a trust deed which is to be used as a mortgage instrument should be definitely verified by the mortgagor. The defeasance clause has no particular form but it is

[151] A civil lawyer is permitted membership on the Diocesan Council of Administration.—C. 1520, §1; Coronata, *Institutiones*, II, 474.

[152] Jones, *Mortgages*, I, 62.

[153] Jones, *op. cit.*, 66, 67.

essential that it be some equivalent of: "Upon the payment of the debt or performance of the duty named, then this deed (or conveyance) shall be void." It should moreover describe the debt, the interest, the rate of interest before and after default; contain the covenant to pay the debt, the time of payments, stipulations concerning default, possible acceleration at maturity, the payment of taxes, insurance and attorneys' fees.[154]

The solemnities accompanying the contract include the seal, signature, witnesses, delivery and acceptance, date, and recordation.[155] In states where the required use of seals has not been abolished, a corporation cannot make a valid mortgage except through the instrument's being under the corporate seal. In some states, authority of court is required in order that a religious corporation may mortgage its real estate.[156] But this is a result only of an express or clearly implied prohibition to mortgage passed by the Legislature.[157]

Laws govern also the construction and effect of a mortgage. Certain principles can be stated as the general rule:

1. The law of the State where the mortgaged property is situated determines its construction.[158]
2. The law in force at the time of the execution of the mortgage determines its execution and performance.
3. A mortgage is subject, and is construed according, to all the laws existing in the State where it is executed.
4. Because a mortgagor has the advantage of making his own selection of words and terms in drawing up the contract, it is construed most strongly against him whenever the language is equivocal or ambiguous.
5. The intention of the parties is gathered from the mortgage instrument and governs as long as it is legally enforceable. The sole duty of construction is to determine what was meant by the language of the instrument.
6. The document is to be constructed as a whole, with a fair

---

[154] For further information on these points, consult Jones, *op. cit.*, 68–97.

[155] Cf. Jones, *op. cit.*, 105–132.

[156] Jones, *op. cit.*, 199.

[157] Zollmann, *American Church Law* (St. Paul: West Publishing Co., 1933), p. 176.

[158] 41 C. J. 292.

consideration of all the terms and provisions contained therein.[159]

The rights and duties of the mortgagor and mortgagee should be clearly stated in the mortgage contract. Since State statutes control these in many instances, consultation of them is necessary. "Frequently the legislatures have changed the common law and it is essential that the controlling statutes be consulted to ascertain the true status of the law relating to the:

(a) Validity of the mortgage;
(b) Personal liability of the mortgagor;
(c) Form and method of foreclosure;
(d) Propriety of a deficiency decree;
(e) Fixing of the time and manner of sale on foreclosure;
(f) Possibility of an 'upset price';
(g) Redemption of the property;
(h) Scope and operation of mortgage moratorium legislation, etc." [160]

Laws and judicial decisions govern also (1) the liability of the mortgagor (a) in general; (b) for deficiency; and (c) when signing in a representative capacity, i.e., as agent or trustee; [161]

---

[159] Numbers 1–6.—Jones, *Mortgages*, I, 139–142.

[160] Kearney, *Church Mortgages Memorandum re the Liability Created by Mortgages on Church Property* (Notre Dame, Indiana: University of Notre Dame, 1939), p. 1. Hereafter cited *Memorandum.*

[161] Sec. 12, Uniform Trusts Act: "The addition of the word 'trustee' or the words 'as trustee' after the signature of a trustee to a contract shall be deemed *prima facie* evidence of an intent to exclude the trustee from personal liability."

Sec. 20, Uniform Negotiable Instruments Law: "Where the instrument contains or a person adds to his signature words indicating that he signs for or on behalf of a principal, or in a representative capacity, he is not liable on the instrument if he was duly authorized; but the mere addition of words describing him as agent, or as filling a representative character, without disclosing his principal, does not exempt him from personal liability."

Cases holding representative personally liable: *Schuling v. Ervin,* 185 Iowa 1, 169 N. W. 686 (1918), criticized adversely in 28 Yale L. J. 613; *Schumacher v. Dolan,* 154 Iowa 207, 134 N. W. 624 (1912); *Catlett v. Hawthorne,* 157 Va. 372, 161 S. E. 46 (1931); *Burress v. Banks,* 50 Ga. App. 561, 179 S. E. 139 (1935). Cases wherein representative was absolved from personal liability: *Chelsea Exchange Bank v. First United Presbyterian Church,* 89 Misc. Rep. 616, 152 N. Y. Supp. 201 (1915); *George D.*

(2) the liability of trust property to satisfy a mortgage debt; (3) the liability of one trust to satisfy the debts of another trust; (4) the liability of the local Ordinary in various cases depending on the tenure of parochial or diocesan property in fee simple, as a corporation sole, or a corporation aggregate.

A summary of the more important state laws of the several states, taken from Martindale-Hubbell Law Digest [162] is herewith presented to show particularly the extreme variance of state laws regarding mortgages.

Most states require the *execution* of a mortgage to be in the form of a deed.[163] A warranty deed is required in Vermont, but is only customary in Connecticut, and is permissible in New Hampshire. Rhode Island requires an absolute deed. The trust deed is used throughout the country with varying degrees of frequency. Thus it might be used exclusively,[164] generally,[165] frequently,[166] or merely tolerated.[167] The use of a trust deed is restricted to bond issues in Massachusetts and Washington, and to corporation mortgages in Maryland, Vermont, and Maine. Delaware permits the trust deed only where the sum is substantial and *all* the assets of the corporation are mortgaged. Wisconsin recognizes no trust deed to correspond to those of other States and the term is used to designate large mortgages or indentures given to a trustee or mortgagee as security for a bond

---

Harter Bank v. Schrembs, 55 Ohio App. 116, 9 N. E. 2d 154 (1936); *Hawthorne v. Austin Organ Co.,* 71 F. 2d 945 (1934), cert. den. in *Austin Organ Co. v. Hawthorne,* 293 U. S. 623, 55 Sup. Ct. 237, 79 L. Ed. 710, commented upon in 21 Va. L. Rev. 706, and 48 Harv. L. Rev. 674; *American Trust Co. v. Canevin,* 184 F. 657, 107 C. C. A. 543 (1911); *Wilson v. Clinton Chapel African Methodist Episcopal Zion Church,* 138 Tenn. 348, 198 S. W. 244 (1917); *G. C. Riordan & Co. v. Thornsbury,* 178 Ky. 324, 198 S. W. 920 (1917)—as cited in Kearney, *op. cit.,* pp. 2–9, additional references on page 9.

[162] *Martindale-Hubbell Law Dictionary* (74. ed., 2 vols., Summitt, N. J.: Martindale Hubbell, Inc., 1942). Vol. II, *Digests.*

[163] Ala., Ariz., Ark., Conn., Id., Ill., Ind., Ia., Ky., Me., Md., Minn., Mont., N. M., N. Y., N. Dak., Okla., Oreg., R. I., S. C., S. Dak., Tex., Vt., Va., Wash., W. Va., Wy.

[164] D. C., Tenn., Tex.

[165] Cal., Ill., Kan., Mo., Nev., N. M., Va., W. Va.

[166] Mont., and with a public trustee in Col.

[167] Ky., N. J., R. I., S. Dak., Wy.

issue, the documents being in fact mortgages and are recorded and foreclosed as such. A loan deed, which passes title, is used in Georgia.

In New York a bond customarily accompanies a mortgage and the latter is collateral for payment of the bond, though a mortgage alone can be given and then no liability *in personam* is contracted unless specifically stated in the mortgage. Louisiana has the Conventional, Judicial and Legal mortgages, of which the Conventional is the type corresponding to those used in other states.[168] Massachusetts requires an absolute conveyance but with a condition subsequent and the grant of power of sale on default. In Arkansas any instrument showing on its face an intent that the land referred to therein shall secure a debt is considered a mortgage.

Many states have a *statutory short form* which provides a legally recognized mortgage but its use is not obligatory.[169] California has a Code form, though other forms with separate notes may be used.

Provisions in the mortgage instrument for *attorneys' fees* in case of foreclosure are considered void in some states,[170] but are legal in others.[171] Michigan and Minnesota have regulated by statute the fees which are in proportion to the amount of the mortgage debt.

Practically all the States require the *recordation* of a mortgage either in order to be valid in itself [172] or, in relation to third persons, that it might become a lien,[173] or become effective,[174] or to constitute notice.[175] Some states require the recordation in order

---

[168] Roman Law knew of these three kinds of mortgages, but only the Conventional was considered in the Roman Law section of this dissertation.

[169] Cal., Ill., Mass., Miss., Nev., N. Dak., Wash., Wis., Wy., Okla., R. I., N. Y., Minn.

[170] Ky., S. Dak., Utah.

[171] Mont., Cal., in which latter the court can nevertheless fix fees without regard to the stipulations in the mortgage.

[172] Del., Ala.

[173] Ark.

[174] Col., La., Mo., N. M., N. Car., Tenn., Utah, Wis. Against third persons having no knowledge—Mass.

[175] Ga., R. I. To constitute constructive notice—N. J.

to affect subsequent purchasers or encumbrancers in good faith [176] without notice; [177] or to be valid against innocent purchasers in good faith recording their conveyances first; [178] or to be valid against creditors and subsequent purchasers without notice,[179] in good faith.[180] Some states require it for validity against purchasers for valuable consideration without notice; [181] or against subsequent purchasers and mortgagees in good faith for valuable consideration whose deed or mortgage is first recorded; [182] or against subsequent *bona fide* purchasers [183] for value; [184] or against simply subsequent purchasers for value and lien creditors.[185] In other states the recordation simply operates as notice to subsequent purchasers or encumbrancers.[186] Some states demand that a mortgage be recorded just as a deed must be.[187]

The recording takes place in different offices of the city or county where the mortgaged land lies, depending on the state laws and customs. Thus it might be with the County Recorder,[188] the Circuit Clerk,[189] the Clerk of the Superior Court,[190] the Recorder of Deeds,[191] the Clerk of the County Court,[192] the Recorder of Mortgages,[193] the Clerk of the County Circuit Court,[194] the Register of Deeds,[195] the Clerk of the Chancery Court,[196] the

---

[176] N. Dak.

[177] Cal., Mont., N. Y.

[178] Mich., Minn.

[179] Fla., Ill.

[180] Ky., Neb.

[181] Miss. Against both purchasers and creditors of this type—W. Va.

[182] Nev.

[183] Ohio, Oreg.

[184] Wy.

[185] Va.

[186] Okla., S. Dak.

[187] Ind., Ia., Kan., Me., Md., S. C.

[188] Ariz., Cal.

[189] Ark.

[190] Ga.

[191] Ill.

[192] Ky.

[193] La.

[194] Md.

[195] Mich., Minn., Neb., N. H., Wy.

[196] Miss.

County Clerk,[197] the Recorder of Conveyances,[198] or the Clerk of the Town.[199]

The *cost of recording* varies in every state and at times in different counties or cities within the same state. The cost is computed either on the value of the mortgage [200] or more frequently on the length of the instrument recorded.

Mortgages are *released* as of record in many ways, some states having optional methods. The legally acknowledged method depends on the laws in force. The most common ways are by the mortgagee recording it on the record of the mortgage,[201] by a duly acknowledged and recorded instrument of satisfaction,[202] or by a separate release deed.[203] Other methods of release are by filing a quit-claim deed,[204] or filing a certificate,[205] or by delivery of a duly acknowledged deed of trust.[206] Georgia requires that the original mortgage together with an order from the mortgagee be presented to the Superior Court upon which the Clerk writes "satisfied" across the face of the record. Some states require the mortgagor to record the receipt endorsed on the mortgage.[207] Releases through Courts are also known in Connecticut, where the Superior Court decree is handed down after seventeen years of pacific possession, and in Delaware and Virginia through a rule of court sixty days after payment.

The *foreclosure* of a mortgage is usually by action at law,[208]

---

[197] Mont., Oreg.

[198] Oreg.

[199] Vt. It is supposed that the States not listed would follow the laws for the recording of deeds.

[200] Ex. gr., N. Y.

[201] Ala., Ariz., Ark., Cal., Col., Id., Ia., Ill., Ind., Kan., Ky., Me., Md., Miss., Mass., Minn., Mo., Neb., Nev., N. M., N. Car., Ohio, Oreg., Pa., S. Dak., Tenn., Utah, Vt., Va., Wash., Wy.

[202] Ark., Cal., Ind., Ia., Kan., Mass., Mich., Minn., Nev., N. H., N. Y., Okla., Tex., Utah, Wash., W. Va. Some places in New York require the presentation of the original mortgage also.

[203] Ark., Ill., Ky., Me., Mass., Mo., N. Dak., Tenn., Vt., Wy.

[204] Conn., Me., Tenn.

[205] Id., S. Dak.

[206] Ariz., Col.

[207] Kan., Md., Mich.

[208] Ala., Ariz., Col., Conn., Del., Ga., Id., Ind., La., Minn., Neb., Nev., N. H., N. J., N. M., N. Y., N. Car., N. Dak., Ohio, S. C., S. Dak., Tex. By action at law for possession—Me.

or under power of sale in the mortgage[209] or trust deed.[210] Some states allow an action in equity.[211] Connecticut retains the outdated execution of ejectment proceedings, while the equally old-fashioned concept of mortgage is witnessed in Maine, Rhode Island, Massachusetts, New Hampshire, and Pennsylvania by their permitting possession to be taken in various ways. Pennsylvania also allows entering judgment on the bond.

Some states have passed *moratorium acts* affecting foreclosure sales. The moratorium is available through petition to the courts.[212] The mortgages affected vary as to the date of their execution[213] or foreclosure. The termination of the moratorium is likewise determined in some states.[214] The applicability of the moratorium to mortgages on church rectories is doubtful in Ohio.

In some states no provisions have been made by law for *redemption* after foreclosure.[215] In others redemption after foreclosure sale might be allowed within six months,[216] nine months,[217] one year,[218] eighteen months,[219] or two years.[220] In

---

209 Ala., Ark., Ill., Md., Mass., Mich., Minn., Mont., N. Y., N. Car., R. I., S. Dak. Only when the power of sale is given to the Bank of North Dakota—N. Dak. Only when the power of sale is exercised by proceedings in equity—Cal.

210 Miss., Mo., Okla., Tenn.

211 Ark., Fla., Mich., N. J., Tenn., Conn., Ga., Ia., Ky., Me., Mont., Okla., Oreg., R. I.

212 Cal., Ia., Minn., Mont., Ohio, S. Dak. There are limitations on foreclosure actions, deficiency judgments and actions on bonds prior to July 1, 1943—N. Y.

213 E. g., Mortgages entered prior to April 18, 1933—Minn.; prior to February 1, 1935—Cal.

214 E. g., July 1, 1943—Cal.; March 1, 1943—Mont., S. Dak.

215 Miss., N. Y., Tex., Wis.

216 Ariz., Col., Utah., Wy. If less than one-third price in a purchase-money mortgage—Kan. Six months after entry of judgment—N. J.; after sale by Court decree—Mich.

217 N. M.

218 Ark., Cal., Ia., Id., Ill., Minn., Mont., Nev., N. Dak., Oreg., S. Dak., Wash. More than one year if the mortgage was executed after June 30, 1931—Ind. In trust mortgages—Me. Subject to extension or restriction by Chancery Court—Vt. After mortgagee's acquiring possession—Me. After attempted recovery of judgment—Mass. If no court proceedings and prop-

some states the time is set by the Court in equity proceedings.[221] In others there is no period of grace after the day set for redemption in strict foreclosure,[222] or after the foreclosure sale itself.[223] Ohio permits no redemption after the confirmation of a sale.

The usual *interest* chargeable in redemption proceedings is six per cent,[224] although in some states it is higher, reaching ten per cent in a few.[225]

A *deficiency judgment* is possible in twenty-nine states,[226] though even in some of these it is not allowed on a purchase-money mortgage.[227] In most all of the states permitting a deficiency judgment there are certain circumstances wherein, or periods of time after which, it is not obtainable.[228]

In conclusion it can be recommended that after the observance of the canons and the adherence to the civil laws, to which latter purpose an expert civil lawyer should be consulted, an attempt should be made wherever possible to limit liability in a mortgage contract to the particular property which is to secure the debt; and where this is not possible, to insert an express statement in the mortgage limiting the possibility of satisfaction to the property of only the one ecclesiastical corporation, and expressly ex-

---

erty is bought by creditor or his heir—Mo. After sale through power of sale in the mortgage—Mich.

219 Kan.

220 Ala., Tenn.

221 E. g., Conn., Va.

222 Conn., Md.

223 Conn., Del., Fla., La., Mass., Neb., Pa., S. C. When the sale is the result of court proceedings—Mo., N. Car., Okla. When sale is the result of power of sale in a deed of trust—Okla., W. Va. When sale is the result of power of sale in the mortgage—R. I.

224 Minn., N. Dak., Tenn., Utah, Ill.

225 Ark., Oreg., Wy.

226 Ala., Ark., Cal., Conn., Fla., Ga., Id., Ill., Ind., Ia., Ky., La., Md., Mich., Minn., Mont., Nev., N. J., N. Y., N. Car., Ohio, Okla., Oreg., Pa., S. C., S. Dak., Tex., Wash., Wy.

227 Cal., N. Car., Oreg., S. Dak.

228 E. g., When sale brings the amount of the judicial decree on foreclosure—Ark. When power of sale was in a mortgage or deed of trust executed after September 19, 1939—Cal. Ninety days after foreclosure—N. Y.

cluding any other property held in trust or in any other manner by the mortgagor. Personal liability of administrators, local Ordinaries and religious superiors executing the mortgage should likewise be excluded by the use of appropriate terms.[229]

[229] Cf. Kearney, *op. cit.*, p. 15.

CHAPTER IX

Mortgages and Canon 2347

That the Church has the *right* to inflict penalties on administrators of ecclesiastical property for contracting mortgages without observing the laws of the Code is patent. Since it is a society that is juridically perfect, it reserves to itself the coercive power to punish the transgressors of its laws, regardless of the fact that at certain times or in regard to certain infractions it does not exercise this power.[1] Whether or not any enactments appear in the Code witnessing the exercise of this coercive power relative to illegal mortgages is the purpose of this chapter.

Immediately prior to the Code an *ipso facto* excommunication was incurred when the *Beneplacitum Apostolicum* was not obtained for a mortgage. This censure was inflicted in virtue of the Constitution *Apostolicae Sedis* (1869), which punished alienators according to the set form of the Constitution *Ambitiosae* (1467). Therefore the penalties for illegal mortgages were interpreted from March 1, 1467, until May 19, 1918, according to the Constitution *Ambitiosae.*[2]

Since the promulgation of the Code, much confusion has existed among the commentators thereof in this point at issue, and, it seems, quite unnecessarily. The source of the trouble seems to be the opening words of canon 2347, which reads:

> Firma nullitate actus et obligatione, etiam per censuram urgenda, restituendi bona illegitime acquisita ac

[1] Cf. C. 2214, §1; Chelodi, *Ius Poenale et Ordo Procedendi in Iudiciis Criminalibus iuxta Codicem Iuris Canonici* (ed. 4, recognita et aucta a Vigilio Dalpiaz, Tridenti: Liberia Moderna Editrice A. Ardesi, 1935), pp. 1, 2. Hereafter cited *Ius Poenale.*

[2] Cf. Cappello, *Tractatus Canonico-Moralis De Censuris iuxta Codicem Iuris Canonici* (ed. altera, Taurinorum Augustae: Marietti, 1925), pp. 351, 357, 358 (hereafter cited: *De Censuris*); cf. also text of *Ambitiosae, supra,* Chapter III, p. 37; also *supra,* pp. 61–64.

> reparandi damna forte illata, qui bona ecclesiastica alienare praesumpserit aut in iis alienandis consensum praebere contra praescripta can. 534, §1, et can. 1532:

All the remainder of the canon merely lists separate penalties depending on the *amount* alienated. It can be immediately seen that the whole question of penalties for illegal mortgaging depends on the interpretation of the word *alienare* as used in the portion of the canon just quoted.

One school of thought would have the penalties applicable to mortgages. It includes such reputable authors as Augustine,[3] Blat,[4] Cerato,[5] Cipollini,[6] Fanfani,[7] Pruemmer,[8] Sole,[9] Vermeersch-Creusen,[10] and Vromant.[11] Ordinarily one would be hesitant in contesting the opinion of such an imposing array of authorities. But the more common opinion, upheld by commentators equally esteemed and even more numerous, seems more in accord with the history of the penalties for mortgages and with the proper interpretation of the present law. The view that the canon does not apply to illegal mortgages is supported by Ayrinhac, Beste, Cappello, Cavigioli, Chelodi, Cocchi, Coronata, Ferreres, Ojetti, Pistocchi, Sabetti-Barrett, Teodori, and Wernz-Vidal.[12]

Certainly the extrinsic authority of these two opinions is sufficient to establish a positive and objective doubt of law in the matter, in which case this alone would cause the contract of mortgage to be excluded from the penalties of the canon.[13] But it seems that a greater certainty of the absence of any infraction of canon 2347 by illegal mortgages can be reached. Prior to the

---

[3] *Practical Commentary,* VIII, 393; III, 183, 184; VI, 593.

[4] *Commentarium Textus Codicis Iuris Canonici* (5 vols. in 7, Romae: Collegio Angelico, 1924), Vol. V, 244. Hereafter cited *Commentarium.*

[5] *Censurae Vigentes,* p. 78.

[6] *De Censuris Latae Sententiae iuxta Codicem Iuris Canonici* (Taurini: Marietti, 1925), pp. 187, 188. Hereafter cited *De Censuris.*

[7] *De Iure Parochorum,* p. 204.

[8] *Manuale Iuris Canonici,* pp. 543–545.

[9] *De Delictis et Poenis* (Romae, 1920), p. 310.

[10] *Epitome,* III, 337, 338.

[11] *De Bonis Ecclesiae Temporalibus,* p. 320.

[12] Cf. *infra* for text references.

[13] "Leges . . . in dubio iuris non urgent;"—C. 15; "Contra eum, qui legem dicere potuit apertius, est interpretatio facienda."—R. J. 57 in VI°.

Code it was held by some authors that no penalties were incurred unless the possession of property was transferred [14] and *dominium* along with it.[15] This may have been a correct interpretation of "alienation" but the Constitution *Ambitiosae* extended its penalties to mortgages as such.[16] The Code no longer refers to the Constitution *Ambitiosae,* but speaks explicitly only of alienation and thereby changes the law of the Constitution *Apostolicae Sedis* and its reference to those who "alienated according to the form of the Constitution *Ambitiosae.*" [17] In speaking explicitly only of alienation the present canon of the Code refers to canons 534, §1 and 1532, which formally deal also with alienation, and does not refer to canon 1533 which requires the formalities of alienation strictly so called for other contracts which can impair the condition of the Church. Canons 1530–1532 therefore, in virtue of the terminology of canon 1533, are directed toward alienation in the proper sense of the word, and by canon 1533 these formalities are extended to alienation in the wide sense of the word, particularly loans, mortgages, leases, and renting.[18] Rather than extend the penalties of canon 2347 to contracts which are alienation only in the wide sense of the term, there is every reason to restrict the penalties to those acts only which are alienation in the strict sense.[19]

In the strict sense of the word mortgage is not alienation. Having seen that this was held even before the Code it remains to be shown that this is still a common opinion. The strict interpretation of the word alienation still requires the transfer of *domi-*

---

[14] Merlinus, *De Pignoribus,* lib. II, tit. II, q. 85, n. 15; cf. also *supra,* p. 94.

[15] "Non tamen vera est alienatio, nisi per quam transfertur dominium. Et per hoc in statutis odiosis, et poenalibus, ubi debemus restringere interpretationem."—Redoanus, *De Alienationibus,* Q. II, cap. VI, n. 6.

[16] Cf. text *supra,* p. 37; Chelodi, *Ius Poenale,* p. 109, note 3; Cavigioli, *De Censuris Latae Sententiae quae in Codice Iuris Canonici Continentur Commentariolum* (Torino, 1918), p. 145, note 1. Hereafter cited *De Censuris.*

[17] Cf. *supra,* p. 64 for text; also Cappello, *De Censuris,* p. 351.

[18] Cf. Ayrinhac-Lydon, *Penal Legislation,* p. 235.

[19] "Leges, quae poenam statuunt . . . strictae subsunt interpretationi."—C. 19; "Poena lege statuta non incurritur, nisi delictum fuerit in suo genere perfectum secundum proprietatem verborum legis."—C. 2228; "In poenis benignior est interpretatio facienda."—C. 2219, §1; Cappello, *op. cit.,* p. 357.

nium, or ownership, of property. Referring to the application of canon 2347 to alienation, this is the *explicit* opinion of Cappello,[20] Cavigioli,[21] Chelodi,[22] Sabetti-Barrett,[23] Teodori,[24] Vernz-Vidal,[25] Pistocchi,[26] Coronata,[27] Cocchi,[28] and Beste.[29] This critical explanation of alienation is not a new one. It was a fundamental idea in Roman law,[30] and was carried over into the Church law for many centuries with an explicit statement of the proposition.[31] It has always been the basis for distinguishing between a strict and lenient, or wide, meaning of alienation,[32] and the interpretation of the penal laws today demands the preference of the strict meaning of words to any other so long as the strict meaning is

---

[20] "Igitur censura incurritur ob solam alienationem stricte sumptam. Alienare autem est transferre dominium: proinde, vendere, donare, permutare, in solutionem dare, in emphyteusim concedere; non autem commodare, locare, pecuniam mutuo dare, hypothecae subdere, oblata vel relicta Ecclesiae repudiare, in re dubia transigere. In iure antiquo non omnia haec excludebantur, v. g. locatio et hypotheca, cum latior esset textus legis; unde nihil ex antiqua disciplina ac veterum DD opinione erui potest contra traditam doctrinam."—*De Censuris,* pp. 357, 358.

[21] "Alienatio, quam haec censura percellit, non concipitur nisi translatio dominii: "—*De Censuris,* p. 145.

[22] "Alienare est dominium transferre: "—*Ius Poenale,* p. 109.

[23] "Alienatio designat omnia pacta quibus dominium transfertur; "—*Compendium Theologiae Moralis* (ed. 6, post Codicem, New York, Cincinnati: Frederick Pustet Co., Inc., 1929), p. 1037.

[24] ". . . quoad effectus poenales alienatio stricte sensu sumenda est, prout significat solam et veram dominii translationem; "—*Consultationes Iuris Canonici,* I (1934), p. 321.

[25] *Ius Canonicum,* Tom. VII, 505, and Tom. IV, Vol. 2, 233, note (170).

[26] *De Bonis,* p. 381, note (2).

[27] "Alienatio hic, quia in poenalibus versamur, stricto sensu intelligenda est seu pro contractibus quibus dominium bonorum transfertur."—*Institutiones,* VI, 450.

[28] "Ad delictum patrandum requiritur ut alienatio perfecta sit; perficitur autem statim, cum . . . dominium rei de se censeri debet translatum . . ."—*Commentarium,* V, 295.

[29] Pp. 953 and 744.

[30] Cf. D. (5. 23), 1; N. (7. 1), text, *supra,* p. 28.

[31] "Alienationis autem verbum contineat conditionem, donationem, permutationem et emphyteoseos perpetuum contractum."—From the canon *Nulli,* cf. *supra,* p. 34.

[32] Cf. Chapter VII, *supra,* pp. 75-77. Hence the authors quoted there implicitly hold that canon 2347 does not apply to mortgage.

a proper signification of the word.[33] In view of which it seems practically certain that the correct interpretation of the law is that supporting the observance of the strict sense of the meaning of alienation in canon 2347 as the loss of *dominium*.

One difficulty yet remains. In the title theory States the legal title to the property is transferred by a mortgage. Does this mean that in these States a mortgage would assume the nature of alienation in the strict sense? It seems the answer must be in the negative. The conveyance in a mortgage is an altogether different legal concept than the transfer of *dominium*. *Dominium* is a legal relationship between a person and a thing which vests in the owner the fullest control and the widest rights and powers which are conceded to anyone with respect to the thing owned, namely, its use, possession, enjoyment, alienation, fruits and the like. These rights and powers can be divested by the owner in favor of others so that his ownership becomes a valueless thing, but none the less he still remains owner (*dominus*), though naked of any of the advantages of ownership.[34] This concept of *dominium* is quite different from the concept of holding the legal title as security for a loan. Even in the so-called title theory States the mortgagor is treated as owner at law and in equity in any case arising between either party to the mortgage and a third person, while the technical common law doctrine of title is reserved to cases arising between the mortgagor and mortgagee.[35] "It ought to be perfectly clear to anyone having any real understanding of what the mortgage relation is and has been since the latter part of the seventeenth century that it does not involve the transfer of any beneficial interest in the mortgaged property other than the right of security." [36] The absence of the transfer of the rights and powers peculiar to *dominium* should therefore make it certain that the conditional transfer of title is not similar to the transfer of *dominium*. Hence the penalties of canon 2347 incurred for the transfer of *dominium* (alienation) without the

[33] Cf. Roberti, *De Delictis et Poenis* (Vol. I, pars I–II, impressio altera emendata, Romae: Apud Custodiam Librariam Pontificii Instituti Utriusque Iuris, —), p. 81.

[34] Cf. Leage, *Roman Private Law*, p. 142.

[35] Walsh, *On Mortgages*, p. 26.

[36] *Op. cit.*, p. 95.

proper consent are not incurred even in title theory States by contracting a mortgage without the proper consent.[37]

There is no desire on the part of the writer to remove all possible sanctions from the law for the administrator who illegally mortgages the property in his charge, but only to show conclusively that canon 2347 does not apply to mortgages, and that in virtue of this canon no penalties can be inflicted on, or incurred by, such an administrator. Without in any way suggesting that each and every infraction of the laws for mortgaging be punished, it might be pointed out that the local Ordinary who is charged with the supervision of the ecclesiastical property within his diocese [38] can, if circumstances demand, see to it that any loss to the Church be compensated,[39] and can, if necessary, proceed to the removal of the administrator even if he is a pastor.[40]

The authors do not comment on the application of the penalties of canon 2347 to the foreclosure at default. The kind of foreclosure in almost universal use in the United States is by formal action in equity or statutory proceeding to sell the mortgaged property.[41] Since the Church would in a sale of this kind lose the *dominium* over the property, it seems that whether the mortgage was entered with or without permission it is a new act of alienation in the strict sense and would as a separate act follow the procedural and penal laws of alienation.

---

[37] Without considering this difficulty Ayrinhac-Lydon (*Penal Legislation*, p. 235) and Beste (p. 744) hold that mortgaging is not subject to the penalties.

Ojetti's view, namely, that the penalties are incurred only upon delivery (*traditio*) of the object, would make it impossible for the question to arise. —*Synopsis*, p. 17; cf. also Ferreres, *Institutiones Canonicae*, p. 216.

[38] C. 1519, §1.

[39] C. 1476, §2.

[40] C. 1476, §2; C. 2147, §2, 5°; C. 2157, §1; cf. also Connor, *The Administrative Removal of Pastors*, The Catholic University of America Canon Law Studies, No. 104 (Washington, D. C.: The Catholic University of America, 1937), pp. 77–79.

[41] Cf. Walsh, *On Mortgages*, p. 278. In Maine, Massachusetts, New Hampshire and Rhode Island statutes provide for foreclosure by entry made without opposition by the mortgagor and possession thereunder for three years.—Rev. St. Me. (1916), c. 95, §3; Gen. Laws R. I. (1923), c. 302, §§3, 4; Gen. Laws Mass. (1921), c. 244, §§1, 2; Pub. St. N. H. (1901), c. 139, §14 (one year), as in Walsh, *op. cit.*, p. 277.

CONCLUSIONS

FROM the foregoing study the following conclusions have been reached:

1. Though mortgaging of Church property was originally merely forbidden in Roman law, it was later made to appear as a form of alienation in Church law by being inserted in the canon *Nulli*. (Cf. pp. 33, 60.)

2. It was most probably Burchard of Worms who changed the inscription of the canon *Nulli* to make it appear as having an ecclesiastical origin. Gregory IX incorporated the false title in his Decretals. (Cf. pp. 34, 35.)

3. The most common opinion before the Code held that the concept of alienation must go no further than to include Special mortgages. (Cf. pp. 45–49.)

4. Before the Code the canonical penalties did not apply even to Special mortgages as such. (Cf. p. 63.)

5. After the Roman Empire fell it took many centuries for the peoples and the systems of law to revive the advantageous contract of mortgaging without transfer of possession. (Cf. pp. 65, 68, 71.)

6. By Code law any real estate of the Church can be mortgaged. (Cf. pp. 20–24.)

7. The textual examination of canon 1533 must extend the concept of alienation to the transfer of a *jus ad rem* (Cf. p. 89) and hence to a General mortgage (Cf. p. 103) when the stable capital may be subjected to satisfy the debt. (Cf. pp. 89, 103.)

8. Even if the term *hypotheca* mentioned in canon 1538 did not include a General mortgage, the phrase *aere alieno contrahendo* in the same canon would include it. (Cf. p. 101.)

9. Construction mortgages and purchase money mortgages can be allowed without the solemnities of alienation when in the former the plot of ground on which the building is to be erected has been acquired for that purpose, the initial payment comes from non-stable capital and the amortization and interest are paid from current revenue, and when in the latter the initial payment

for the property comes from non-stable capital and the amortization and interest payments come from current revenue. (Cf. pp. 112–113.)

10. The solemnities of, and penalties for, alienation are applicable to foreclosure sales at default. (Cf. pp. 113, 159.)

11. Even Special mortgages (much less General) do not fall under any of the penalties of canon 2347. (Cf. p. 158.)

12. It is impossible to use canon 81 to grant permission for a mortgage (Cf. p. 137), but it can be used to dispense with the permission required, i.e., to dispense from canon 1530, §1, 3° (Cf. p. 139); and it is advisable to dispense when the *Beneplacitum Apostolicum* cannot be obtained in order to protect the validity of the mortgage. (Cf. pp. 139–141.)

13. A mortgage which is entered after the obtaining of permission merely to contract a debt is invalid. (Cf. p. 123.)

14. The General mortgage as understood by canonists does not exist in American law (Cf. p. 93), but it is comparable to an unsecured note (Cf. p. 98) and an unsecured bond. (Cf. p. 103.)

15. Canon 19 cannot be used to protect the rights of administrators of Church property. (Cf. p. 83.)

16. A mortgage ought not to be placed on the property of one ecclesiastical corporation to assist the financial condition of another apart from compliance with the solemnities of alienation. (Cf. pp. 94–95.)

17. Canon 1538, by ordering the Superior to *hear* the interested parties, relieves from the necessity of obtaining their consent as is required for other alienations by canon 1532, §3. (Cf. pp. 124–127.)

BIBLIOGRAPHY

SOURCES

Acta Apostolicae Sedis, Commentarium Officiale, Romae, 1909–

Acta et Decreta Concilii Plenarii Baltimorensis Tertii, A. D. MDCCCLXXXIV, Baltimorae: Typis Joannis Murphy et Sociorum, 1886.

Acta et Decreta Sacrorum Conciliorum Recentiorum, Collectio Lacensis, 7 vols., Friburgi Brisgoviae, 1870–1890.

Acta Sanctae Sedis, 41 vols., Romae, 1865–1908.

Appendix ad Concilium Plenarium Americae Latinae Romae celebratum anno Domini MDCCCXCIX, additis Recentioribus Documentis, Romae, 1910.

Bizzarri, A., *Collectanea in Usum Secretariae Sacrae Congregationis Episcoporum et Regularium,* Romae, 1885.

Bullarum Diplomatum et Privilegiorum Sanctorum Romanorum Pontificum Taurinensis Editio, 24 vols. et Appendix, Augustae Taurinorum, Neapoli, 1857–1872.

Canones et Decreta Concilii Tridentini ex editione Romana A. MDCCCXXXIV repetiti, Editio Neapolitana, Neapoli, 1859.

Code of Hammurabi, the King of Babylon about 2250 B. C., The, Robert Francis Harper, Chicago, 1904.

Codex Iuris Canonici Pii X Pontificis Maximi iussu digestus Benedicti Papae XV auctoritate promulgatus, Praefatione, Fontium annotatione et Indice Analytico-Alphabetico ab Emo. Petro Card. Gasparri Auctus, Romae: Typis Polyglottis Vaticanis, 1917. Reimpressio, 1934.

Codicis Iuris Canonici Fontes cura Emi. Petri Card. Gasparri editi, 9 vols., Romae (postea Civitate Vaticana): Typis Polyglottis Vaticanis, 1923–1939. (Vols. VII–IX ed. cura et studio Emi. Iustiniani Serédi.)

Collectanea S. Congregationis de Propaganda Fide, 2 vols., Romae: Typographia Polyglotta S. C. de Propaganda Fide, 1907.

Concilii Plenarii Baltimorensis II., in Ecclesia Metropolitana Baltimorensi, a die VII. ad diem XXI. Octobris, A. D. MDCCCLXVI., Habiti, et a Sede Apostolica Recogniti, Acta et Decreta, Baltimorae: John Murphy, 1868.

Corpus Iuris Canonici, ed. Lipsien. 2. post Aemilii Ludovici Richteri curas instruxit Aemilius Friedberg, 2 vols., Lipsiae: Ex Officina Bernhardi Tauchnitz, 1879–1881. Editio anastatice repetita, Lipsiae: Tauchnitz, 1922.

Corpus Iuris Civilis, 3 vols., Berolini, 1928–1929. *Institutiones,* quas recognovit P. Krueger; *Digesta,* quae recognovit et retractavit P. Krueger; *Codex Iustinianus,* quem recognovit et retractavit P. Krueger; *Novellae,* quas recognovit R. Schoell, et absolvit G. Kroll.

Decisiones Sacrae Rotae Romanae in Tractatu de Pignoribus, et Hypothecis Mercurialis Merlini relatae et ab eodem collectae, Venetiis, 1649.

HARDOUIN, JEAN, *Acta Conciliorum et Epistolae Decretales ac Constitutiones Summorum Pontificum,* 12 vols., Parisiis, 1715.

KIRCH, CONRADUS, *Enchiridion Fontium Historiae Ecclesiasticae Antiquae,* 4 ed., Friburgi Brisgoviae: Herder & Co., 1923.

Liber Sextus Decretalium D. Bonifacii Papae VIII suae integritati una cum Clementinis et Extravagantibus, earumque glossis restitutus, Romae: in Aedibus Populi Romani, 1582.

MANSI, JOANNES, *Sacrorum Conciliorum Nova et Amplissima Collectio,* 53 vols. in 60, Parisiis, Lipsiae-Arnhem, 1901–1927.

Monumenta Germaniae Historica, Legum Sectio II, Capitularia Regum Francorum, Tom. I, ed. Alfredus Boretius, Hannoverae, 1883.

————, *Legum Sectio III, Concilia,* Tom. I, *Concilia Aevi Merovingici,* recensivit Fredericus Maassen, Hannoverae, 1893.

PALLOTTINI, SALVATOR, *Collectio Omnium Conclusionum et Resolutionum Quae in causis propositis apud Sacram Congregationem Cardinalium S. Concilii Tridentini Interpretum Prodierunt ab eius institutione anno MDLXIV ad annum MDCCCLX, distinctis titulis alphabetico ordine per materias digesta,* 18 vols., Romae, 1868–1895.

Synodus Dioecesana Bellevillensis Quinta, 1939.

REFERENCE WORKS

AICHNER, SIMON, *Compendium Juris Ecclesiastici ad Usum Cleri,* ed. 6, Brixinae, 1887.

ALCIATI, ANDREAS, *De Iustiniani Novellis, Authentica,* Lugduni, 1549.

ARREGUI, A., *Summarium Theologiae Moralis,* 3. ed., Bilbao, 1919.

AUGUSTINE, CHARLES, *A Commentary on the New Code of Canon Law,* 8 vols., St. Louis: Herder & Co., 1925–1938. Vol. I, 6. ed., 1931; Vol. II, 6. ed., 1936; Vol. III, 5. ed., 1938; Vol. IV, 3. ed., 1925; Vol. V, 5. ed., 1935; Vol. VI, 3. ed., 1931; Vol. VII, 3. ed., 1930; Vol. VIII, 3. ed., 1931.

AYRINHAC, H. A., *Administrative Legislation in the New Code of Canon Law,* London-New York-Toronto: Longmans, Green and Co., 1930.

————, *Penal Legislation in the New Code of Canon Law,* revised by Lydon, P. J., New York, Cincinnati, Chicago, San Francisco: Benziger Brothers, 1936.

BARBOSSA, AUGUSTINUS, *Pastoralis Sollicitudinis, sive De Officio et Potestate Episcopi tripartita descriptio,* Lugduni, 1656.

BARRACLOUGH, GEOFFREY, *Mediaeval Germany 911–1250, Essays by German Historians,* Studies in Mediaeval History, No. II, Oxford: Basil Blackwell and Mott, Ltd., 1938.

BASTIEN, PIERRE, *Directoire Canonique,* 4. ed., Paris: Bloud et Gay, 1933.

BASTNAGEL, CLEMENT V., *The Appointment of Parochial Adjutants and Assistants,* The Catholic University of America Canon Law Studies, No. 58, Washington, D. C.: The Catholic University of America, 1930.

BAYS, ALFRED, *Cases and Materials on Business Law,* 4. ed., National Casebook Series, Chicago: Callaghan and Company, 1939.

BERUTTI, C., *Institutiones Iuris Canonici,* Vol. I, *Normae Generales,* Taurin-Romae: Marietti, 1936.

BESTE, U., *Introductio in Codicem,* Collegeville, Minnesota: St. John's Abbey Press, 1938.

BLAT, ALBERTUS, *Commentarium Textus Codicis Iuris Canonici,* 5 vols. in 7, Romae: Collegio Angelico, 1921–1938, Vol. V, 1924.

BONACINA, MARINUS, *Opera Omnia,* 3 vols. *et Tractationes Variae* in 1, Lugduni, 1639.

BOUIX, DOMINICUS, *Tractatus de Jure Regularium,* 2 vols., Parisiis, 1857.

BOUSCAREN, T. LINCOLN, *The Canon Law Digest,* 2 vols., and Supplement, 1941, Milwaukee: Bruce, 1934–1941.

Bouvier's Law Dictionary, New York: The Banks Law Publishing Co., 1928.

BRISSAUD, JEAN, and HOWELL, RAPELJE, *A History of French Private Law,* The Continental Legal History Series, No. 3, Boston, 1912.

BROWN, BRENDAN, *The Canonical Juristic Personality with Special Reference to Its Status in the United States of America,* The Catholic University of America Canon Law Studies, No. 39, Washington, D. C.: The Catholic University of America, 1927.

BUCKLAND, W. W., *Elementary Principles of the Roman Private Law,* Cambridge, 1912.

BUCKLER, W. H., *The Origin and History of Contract in Roman Law Down to the End of the Republican Period,* London, 1895.

BURDICK, WILLIAM L., *The Principles of Roman Law and Their Relation to Modern Law,* Rochester: The Lawyers Co-operative Publishing Co., 1938.

CAPPELLO, FELIX, *Tractatus Canonico-Moralis De Censuris iuxta Codicem Iuris Canonici,* ed. altera, Taurinorum Augustae: Marietti, 1925.

CAVIGIOLI, G., *De Censuris Latae Sententiae quae in Codice Iuris Canonici Continentur Commentariolum,* Torino, 1918.

CENSIUS, LUDOVICUS, *Tractatus de Censibus, cum Sacrae Rotae Romanae Decisionibus Recentissimis,* ed. novissima, Lugduni, 1730.

CERATO, PROSDOCIMUS, *Censurae Vigentes Ipso Facto A Codice Iuris Canonici Excerptae,* ed. 2., Patavii, 1921.

CHELODI, I., *Ius Poenale et Ordo Procedendi in Iudiciis Criminalibus iuxta Codicem Iuris Canonici,* ed. 4. recognita et aucta a Vigilio Dalpiaz, Tridenti: Liberia Moderna Editrice A. Ardesi, 1935.

CICOGNANI, AMLETO GIOVANNI, *Canon Law,* 2. ed., authorized English version by J. O'Hara and F. Brennan, Philadelphia: Dolphin Press, 1935.

CIPOLLINI, A., *De Censuris Latae Sententiae iuxta Codicem Iuris Canonici,* Taurini: Marietti, 1925.

CLEARY, JOSEPH F., *Canonical Limitations on the Alienation of Church Property,* The Catholic University of America Canon Law Studies, No. 100, Washington, D. C.: The Catholic University of America, 1936.

CLERCQ, CARLO DE, *La Législation Religieuse Franque de Clovis à Charle-*

magne, Étude sur les Actes de Conciles et les Capitulaires les Statuts Diocésains et les Règles Monastiques (507–814), Université de Louvain, Recueil de travaux publiés par les Membres des Conférences d'Histoire et de Philologiae, 2e série, 38e fascicule, Louvain: Bureaux du Recueil, Bibliothèque de l'Université, 1936.

CLEVELAND, FREDERICK A., HALL, HENRY B., *Funds and Their Uses,* New York: D. Appleton and Company, 1922.

COCCHI, GUIDUS, *Commentarium in Codicem Iuris Canonici,* 8 vols., Taurinorum Augustae: Marietti, 1931–1940. Vol. I, 5. ed., 1938; Vol. II, 4. ed., 1937; Vol. III, 3. ed., 1931; Vol. IV, 3. ed., 1932; Vol. V, 3. ed., 1932; Vol. VI, 3. ed., 1933; Vol. VII, 3. ed., 1940; Vol. VIII, 4. ed., 1938.

CONNOLLY, N. P., *The Canonical Erection of Parishes,* The Catholic University of America Canon Law Studies, No. 114, Washington, D. C.: The Catholic University of America, 1938.

CONNOR, MAURICE, *The Administrative Removal of Pastors,* The Catholic University of America Canon Law Studies, No. 104, Washington, D. C.: The Catholic University of America, 1937.

CONRAT, M., *Die Lex Romana Canonice Compta,* Amsterdam, 1904.

CORONATA, MATTHAEUS CONTE A, *Institutiones Iuris Canonici,* 5 vols., Taurini Romae: Marietti, 1933–1939. Vols. I et II, 2. ed., 1939; Vol. III, 1933; Vol. IV, 1935; Vol. V, 1936.

CREUSEN, J.-GARESCHE, EDWARD F.-ELLIS, ADAM C., *Religious Men and Women in the Code,* 3. English ed., Milwaukee: Bruce, 1940.

DE MEESTER, A., *Juris Canonici et Juris Canonico-Civilis Compendium,* nova ed., Tom. III, pars prima, Brugis: Desclée, de Brouwer et Sii, 1926.

DOHENY, WILLIAM J., *Church Property: Modes of Acquisition,* The Catholic University of America Canon Law Studies, No. 41, Washington, D. C.: The Catholic University of America, 1927.

————, *Practical Problems in Church Finance,* Milwaukee: The Bruce Publishing Company, 1941.

DU CANGE, CAROLUS DUFRESNE, *Glossarium ad Scriptores Mediae et Infimae Latinitatis,* 6 vols., Parisiis, 1733.

ENGEL, L., *Collegium Universi Iuris Canonici* (ed. 9, cui adjectae sunt annotationes Caspari Barthel), 3 vols., Beneventi, 1760.

FAGNANUS, PROSPER, *Jus Canonicum seu Commentaria Absolutissima in Quinque Libros Decretalium,* 5 vols., Romae, 1661.

FANFANI, LUDOVICUS, *De Iure Parochorum,* ed. altera, Taurini-Romae: Marietti, 1936.

FERRARIS, F. LUCIUS, *Prompta Bibliotheca, Canonica, Juridica, Moralis Theologica necnon Ascetica, Polemica, Rubricistica, Historica,* ed. Migne, 8 vols., Parisiis, 1860–1863.

FERRERES, J., *Institutiones Canonicae,* Barcinone, 1918.

FOURNIER, PAUL, and LE BRAS, GABRIEL, *Histoire des Collections Canoniques en Occident depuis les Fausses Décrétales jusqu'au Décret de*

Gratien, Tom. I: *De la Réforme Carolingienne à la Réforme Grégorienne,* Paris: Recueil Sirey, 1931.

FROMMELT, H. A., *Church Property and its Management,* New York, Milwaukee, Chicago: The Bruce Publishing Company, 1936.

GUTIERREZ, J., *Opera Omnia Civilia, Canonica et Criminalia, Decisionibus S. Rot. Roman. Recentissimis necnon Repertorio Generali,* 16 vols., Coloniae, 1730–1731.

GONZALEZ-TELLEZ, EMMANUEL, *Commentaria Perpetua in Singulos Textus Quinque Librorum Decretalium Gregorii IX,* 5 vols., Maceratae, 1761.

HAENEL, G., *Iuliani Epitome Latina Novellarum Iustiniani,* Lipsiae, 1873.

HANNAN, JEROME D., *The Canon Law of Wills,* The Catholic University of America Canon Law Studies, No. 86, Washington, D. C.: The Catholic University of America, 1934.

HEFELE, C., and LECLERCQ, H., *Histoire des Conciles,* 10 vols. in 19, Paris: Letouzey et Ané, 1907–1938.

HERGENROETHER, P., *Lehrbuch des katholischen Kirchenrechts,* Freiburg im Breisgau, 1888.

HESTON, EDWARD L., *The Alienation of Church Property in the United States,* The Catholic University of America Canon Law Studies, No. 132, Washington, D. C.: The Catholic University of America Press, 1941.

HOAGLAND, HENRY E., *Corporation Finance,* New York: McGraw-Hill Book Company, Inc., 1933.

HOLLWECK, JOSEPH, *Die kirchlichen Strafgesetze,* Mainz, 1899.

HOSTIENSIS, CARDINALIS (Henricus de Segusio), *Commentaria in Quinque Decretalium Libros,* 5 vols. in 3, Venetiis, 1581.

JONES, LEONARD A., *A Treatise on the Law of Mortgages of Real Property,* 8. ed., 4 vols., Indianapolis: The Bobbs-Merrill Company, 1928.

KEARNEY, JAMES J., *Church Mortgages Memorandum re the Liability Created by Mortgages Upon Church Property,* Notre Dame, Indiana: University of Notre Dame, 1939.

KENT, JAMES, *Commentaries on American Law,* ed. 11 by George Comstock, 4 vols., Boston, 1867.

LANCELOTTUS, IOANNES PAULUS, *Institutiones Iuris Canonici, quibus Ius Pontificium Singulari Methodo Libros Quatuor Comprehenditur,* 4 vols. in 1, Lugduni, 1579.

LEAGE, R. W., *Roman Private Law founded on the 'Institutes' of Gaius and Justinian,* 2. ed. by C. H. Ziegler, London: MacMillian and Co., Ltd., 1937.

LEGA, MICHAEL, *Praelectiones in Textum Iuris Canonici de Iudiciis Ecclesiasticis,* 4 vols., Romae, 1896–1902.

LESNE, EMILE, *Histoire de la Propriété Ecclésiastique en France,* Vol. I, *Époques Romaine et Mérovingienne,* Lille, 1910. Vol. III, *L'inventaire de la Propriété. Églises et trésors des Églises du Commencement du VIII*[e] *a la fin du XI*[e] *Siècle.* Lille: Facultés Catholiques, 1936.

LOWRIE, WALTER, *The Church and its Organization in Primitive and*

Catholic Times, and Interpretation of Rudolph Sohm's Kirchenrecht (the Primitive Age), London, 1904.

MACERATEN, MARIUS ANTONIUS, *Variae Practicabilium Rerum Resolutiones in Tres Libros Digestae*, Papiae, 1606.

MAINE, HENRY SUMNER, *Ancient Law, its Connection with the Early History of Society, and its Relation to Modern Ideas*, New York, 1875.

MAKEE, CH., *Institutiones Juris Ecclesiastici tum Publici tum Privati*, Parisiis, 1897.

Martindale-Hubbell Law Dictionary, 74. ed., 2 vols., Summitt, N. J.: Martindale Hubbell, Inc., 1942.

MCMANUS, JAMES EDWARD, *The Administration of Temporal Goods in Religious Institutes*, The Catholic University of America Canon Law Studies, No. 109, Washington, D. C.: The Catholic University of America, 1937.

MEIER, CARL ANTHONY, *Penal Administrative Procedure Against Negligent Pastors*, The Catholic University of America Canon Law Studies, No. 140, Washington, D. C.: The Catholic University of America Press, 1941.

MERLINUS, MERCURIALIS, *De Pignoribus et Hypothecis, Tractatus Absolutissimus*, Venetiis, 1649.

MIASKEWICZ, F. S., *Supplied Jurisdiction According to Canon 209*, The Catholic University of America Canon Law Studies, No. 122, Washington, D. C.: The Catholic University of America Press, 1940.

MICHIELS, G., *Normae Generales Juris Canonici*, 2 vols., Lublin-Polonia: Universitas Catholica, 1929.

MIGNE, JACQUES PAUL, *Patrologiae Cursus Completus, Series Latina*, 221 vols., Parisiis, 1844–1855.

MONTGOMERY, ROBERT H., *Financial Handbook*, New York: The Ronald Press Co., 1927.

OJETTI, BENEDICT, *Synopsis Rerum Moralium et Iuris Pontificii*, Romae, 1899.

PAPIENSIS, BERNARDUS, *Summa Decretalium*, ed. Ern. Laspeyres, Ratisbonae, 1860.

PAULY, AUGUST F., *Real Encyclopaedie der classischen Altertumswissenschaft: Neue Bearbeitung, unter Mitwirkung zahlreicher Fachgenossen*, herausgegeben von Wissowa, Kroll und Mittelhaus, 38 vols., and 6 supplements in 56, Stuttgart, 1914.

PIRHING, ERNRICUS, *Jus Canonicum Nova Methodo Explicatum*, 5 vols. in 4, Dillingae, 1674–1678.

PETRA, VINCENTIUS, *Commentaria ad Constitutiones Apostolicas*, 5 vols. in 2, Venetiis, 1729.

PICHLER, VITUS, *Candidatus Jurisprudentiae Sacrae, seu Juris Canonici, secundum Gregorii Papae IX. Decretalium Titulos explicati*, 5 vols., Augustani, 1723.

PISTOCCHI, MARIUS, *De Bonis Ecclesiae Temporalibus*, Taurini: Marietti, 1932.

POLLOCK, FREDERICK, and MAITLAND, FREDERIC, *History of English Law before the time of Edward I*, 2 vols., Cambridge, 1895.

PRUEMMER, DOMINICUS, *Manuale Iuris Canonici in Usum Scholarum*, 5. ed., Friburgi Brisgoviae: Herder & Co., 1927.

RAUS, JOANNES B., *Institutiones Canonicae juxta Novum Codicem Juris*, 2. ed., Lugduni, Parisiis: Vite, 1931.

R. DE M., *Institutiones Juris Canonici Publici et Privati*, Vol. II, Parisiis, 1853.

REDOANUS, GULIELMUS, *De Alienationibus Rerum Ecclesiarum*, Placentiae, 1589.

REIFFENSTUEL, ANACLETUS, *Jus Canonicum Universum*, 4 vols., Romae, 1833.

REILLY, EDWARD M., *The General Norms of Dispensation*, The Catholic University of America Canon Law Studies, No. 119, Washington, D. C.: The Catholic University of America Press, 1939.

ROBERTI, F., *De Delictis et Poenis*, Vol. 1, pars I–II, impressio altera emendata, Romae: Apud Custodiam Librariam Pontificii Instituti Utriusque Iuris, ——.

Ruling Case Law, ed. by William M. McKinney and Burdett A. Rich, 38 vols., Rochester, Northport, San Francisco, 1914–1931.

SÀ, EMANUEL, *Aphorismi Confessariorum ex variis Doctorum Sententiis Collecti*, ed. novissima, Lugduni, 1669.

SABETTI, ALOYSIUS, and BARRETT, TIMOTHEUS, *Compendium Theologiae Moralis*, ed. 6. post Codicem, New York, Cincinnati: Frederick Pustet Co., Inc., 1929.

SABINI, FABIANUS DE MONTE S., *Tractatus de Emptione et Venditione eorumque omnium quae ad eandem Materiam Pertinent*, Venetiis, 1575.

SANTI, FRANCISCUS, *Praelectiones Juris Canonici*, 2 vols., Ratisbonae, Neo Eboraci, Cincinnati, 1886.

SCHAEFER, TIMOTHEUS, *Compendium de Religiosis ad normam Codicis Iuris Canonici*, 3. ed., Roma: S.A.L.E.R., 1940.

SCHMALZGRUEBER, FRANCISCUS, *Jus Ecclesiasticum Universum*, 5 vols. in 12, Romae, 1843–1845.

SCHMIDT, JOHN ROGG, *The Principles of Authentic Interpretation in Canon 17 in the Code of Canon Law*, The Catholic University of America Canon Law Studies, No. 141, Washington, D. C.: The Catholic University of America Press, 1941.

SCHMIER, P. FRANCISCUS, *Jurisprudentia Canonico-Civilis, seu Jus Canonicum Universum, juxta Quinque Libros Decretalium*, 5 vols. in 2, Venetiis, 1745.

SCHULTE, FREDERIC DE, and FOURNIER, MARCEL, *Histoire du Droit et des Institutions de L'Allemagne*, Paris, 1882.

SCHULTE, J. F. RITTER VON, *Lehrbuch des katholischen Kirchenrechts*, Giessen, 1873.

SHERMAN, C. P., *Roman Law in the Modern World*, 3. ed., 3 vols., New Haven, 1922.

SOHM, RUDOLPH, and LEDLIE, J. C., *The Institutes of the History and Systems of Roman Law,* 3. ed., Oxford, 1907.

SOLE, J., *De Delictis et Poenis,* Romae, 1920.

THESAURUS, CAROLUS ANTONIUS, *De Poenis Ecclesiasticis seu Canonicis Latae Sententiae a Iure Communi, et Constitutionibus Apostolicis Decretisque Sacrarum Congregationum,* Romae, 1640.

THOMPSON, JAMES WESTFALL, and JOHNSON, EDGAR NATHANIEL, *An Introduction to Medieval Europe 300–1500,* New York: W. W. Norton & Company, Inc., 1937.

TIFFANY, HERBERT THORNDIKE, *A Treatise on the Modern Law of Real Property and other Interests in Land,* 2 vols. in 1, Chicago, 1912.

TURRICELLIUS, IOANNES BAPTISTA, *De Rebus Ecclesiae non Alienandis ex Sententia Sacrae Romanae Rotae Tractatus,* Ferrariae, 1674.

VAN HOVE, A., *Commentarium Lovaniense in Codicem Iuris Canonici,* 1 vol. in 5 toms., Mechliniae-Romae: H. Dessain, 1928–1939. Tom. I, *Prolegomena,* 1928; Tom. II, *De Legibus Ecclesiasticis,* 1930; Tom. V, *De Privilegiis, De Dispensationibus,* 1939.

VERMEERSCH, ARTHURUS, and CREUSEN, IOSEPHUS, *Epitome Iuris Canonici,* 3 vols., Mechliniae-Romae: H. Dessain, 1934–1937. Vol. I, 6. ed., 1937; Vol. II, 5. ed., 1934; Vol. III, 5. ed., 1936.

VROMANT, G., *De Bonis Ecclesiae Temporalibus,* Louvain: Desbarax, 1927.

WALSH, WILLIAM F., *A Treatise on Mortgages,* National Textbook Series, Chicago: Callaghan and Co., 1934.

WANENMACHER, FRANCIS, *Canonical Evidence in Marriage Cases* (a revised and augmented form of *The Evidence in Ecclesiastical Procedure Affecting the Marriage Bond,* The Catholic University of America Canon Law Studies, No. 9, Washington, D. C., 1920), Philadelphia, Pa.: Dolphin Press, 1935.

WERNZ, FRANCISCUS X., *Ius Decretalium,* 2. ed., 6 vols., Romae, 1908–1913.

WERNZ, F., and VIDAL, P., *Ius Canonicum,* 7 toms. in 8 vols., Romae: Apud Aedes Universitatis Gregorianiae, 1927–1938. Tom. IV, pars II, 1935; Tom. VII, 1937.

WOYWOD, S., *A Practical Commentary on the Code of Canon Law,* 3. ed., 2 vols., New York: Wagner, 1929.

ZITELLI-NATALI, ZEPHYRINUS, *Apparatus Iuris Ecclesiastici,* Romae, 1886.

ZOLLMANN, CARL, *American Church Law,* St. Paul: West Publishing Co., 1933.

PERIODICALS

Archiv für katholisches Kirchenrechts, Innsbruck, 1857–1861; Mainz, 1862—

Analecta Juris Pontificii, Romae, 1855–1868; Paris, 1869–1891.

Australasian Catholic Record, The, Manly, 1923—

Consultationes Iuris Canonici, Romae, 1934—

Commentarium pro Religiosis, Romae, 1920–1934.

Commentarium pro Religiosis et Missionariis, Romae, 1935—

Ecclesiastical Review, The (originally *The American Ecclesiastical Review)*, Philadelphia, 1889—

Homiletic and Pastoral Review, The, New York, 1900—

Jurist, The, Washington, D. C., 1941—

Jus Pontificium, Romae, 1921—

Theological Studies, New York, 1940—

Periodica de Re Canonica et Morali utili praesertim Religiosis et Missionariis, Bruges, 1905—

ARTICLES

DOHENY, W. J., "Church Finance and Problems of Alienation,"—*The Jurist,* I (1941), 97–107.

ELLIS, A., "Some Canonical Terms Dealing With Temporalities—Bona Temporalia,"—*Theological Studies,* I (1940), 171–174.

GRASHOF, OTTO, "Die Gesetze der Roemischen Kaiser ueber die Veraeusserung des kirchlichen Vermoegens,"—*AKKR,* XXXVI (1876), 203–214.

HANNAN, J. D., "Refinancing a Mortgage,"—*The Jurist,* II (1942), 57–58.

HESTON, EDWARD L., "The Element of Stable Capital in Temporal Administration,"—*The Jurist,* II (1942), 120–133.

STUTZ, ULRICH, "The Proprietary Church as an Element of Mediaeval Germanic Ecclesiastical Law," (a translation of "Die Eigenkirche als Element des mittelalterlichgermanischen Kirchenrechts," the inaugural lecture in the University of Basel, delivered on 23 October, 1894. Berlin, 1895)—Studies in Mediaeval History, No. II (1938), 35–70. Cf. "Barraclough," *supra.*

WOYWOD, S., "Laws of the Code on the Temporal Goods of the Church,"—*The Homiletic and Pastoral Review,* XXX (1929), 42–51.

————, "The Law of Contracts Concerning Ecclesiastical Goods,"—*The Homiletic and Pastoral Review,* XXX (1929), 269–277.

ABBREVIATIONS

AAS—Acta Apostolicae Sedis.
ACR—Australasian Catholic Record.
AER—American Ecclesiastical Review.
AKKR—Archiv für katholisches Kirchenrecht.
ASS—Acta Sanctae Sedis.
Bull. Rom. Taur.—Bullarum Diplomatum . . . Romanorum Pontificum Taurinensis Editio.
C.—Codex (Iustinianus); Canon.
C. J.—Corpus Juris.
Coll. Lac.—Collectio Lacensis.
Coll. S. C. EE. RR.—Collectanea S. C. Episcoporum et Regularium.
Coll. S. C. P. F.—Collectanea S. C. de Propaganda Fide.
CpR—Commentarium pro Religiosis et Missionariis.
D.—Digesta (Iustiniana).
Ferraris—*Prompta Bibliotheca,* etc.
Fontes—Codicis Iuris Canonici Fontes cura . . . Gasparri editi.
Hardouin—*Acta Conciliorum,* etc.
I.—Institutiones (Iustinianae).
Kent. Comm.—*Commentaries on American Law,* James Kent.
Mansi—*Sacrorum Conciliorum Nova et Amplissima Collectio.*
MGH—Monumenta Germaniae Historica.
MPL—Migne, *Patrologia, Series Latina.*
N.—Novellae (Iustinianae).
Periodica—Periodica de Re Canonica et Morali, etc.
R. C. L.—*Ruling Case Law.*
R. J.—Regula Juris.
S. C. C.—Sacra Congregatio Concilii.
S. C. Ep. et Reg.—Sacra Congregatio Episcoporum et Regularium.

BIOGRAPHICAL NOTE

Joseph Bernard Stenger was born November 16, 1908, in Belleville, Illinois. He attended St. Peter's Cathedral parochial school of that city for his elementary education. After completing his high school course, a year of Junior College work and a year of philosophical studies at Quincy College, Quincy, Illinois, he entered Kenrick Seminary, St. Louis, Missouri, in September, 1928, and was ordained to the priesthood on June 10, 1933, at St. Peter's Cathedral, Belleville, Illinois, by the Most Reverend Henry Althoff, D.D., Bishop of Belleville. He entered The Catholic University of America in September, 1939, to pursue a graduate course of studies in the School of Canon Law. From this institution he received the degrees of the Baccalaureate in Canon Law in June, 1940, and of the Licentiate in Canon Law in June, 1941.

ALPHABETICAL INDEX

CANON LAW STUDIES

1. Freriks, Rev. Celestine A., C.PP.S., J.C.D., Religious Congregations in Their External Relations, 121 pp., 1916.
2. Galliher, Rev. Daniel M., O.P., J.C.D., Canonical Elections, 117 pp., 1917.
3. Borowski, Rev. Aurelius L., O.F.M., J.C.D., De Confraternitatibus Ecclesiasticis, 136 pp., 1918.
4. Castillo, Rev. Cayo, J.C.D., Disertacion Historico-Canonica sobre la Potestad del Cabildo en Sede Vacante o Impedida del Vicario Capitular, 99 pp., 1919 (1918).
5. Kubelbeck, Rev. William J., S.T.B., J.C.D., The Sacred Penitentiaria and Its Relations to Faculties of Ordinaries and Priests, 129 pp., 1918.
6. Petrovits, Rev. Joseph J. C., S.T.D., J.C.D., The New Church Law on Matrimony, X-461 pp., 1919.
7. Hickey, Rev. John J., S.T.B., J.C.D., Irregularities and Simple Impediments in the New Code of Canon Law, 100 pp., 1920.
8. Klekotka, Rev. Peter J., S.T.B., J.C.D., Diocesan Consultors, 179 pp., 1920.
9. Wanenmacher, Rev. Francis, J.C.D., The Evidence in Ecclesiastical Procedure Affecting the Marriage Bond, 1920 (Printed 1935).
10. Golden, Rev. Henry Francis, J.C.D., Parochial Benefices in the New Code, IV-119 pp., 1921 (Printed 1925).
11. Koudelka, Rev. Charles J., J.C.D., Pastors, Their Rights and Duties According to the New Code of Canon Law, 211 pp., 1921.
12. Melo, Rev. Antonius, O.F.M., J.C.D., De Exemptione Regularium, X-188 pp., 1921.
13. Schaaf, Rev. Valentine Theodore, O.F.M., S.T.B., J.C.D., The Cloister, X-180 pp., 1921.
14. Burke, Rev. Thomas Joseph, S.T.D., J.C.D., Competence in Ecclesiastical Tribunals, IV-117 pp., 1922.
15. Leech, Rev. George Leo, J.C.D., A Comparative Study of the Constitution, "Apostolicae Sedis" and the "Codex Juris Canonici," 179 pp., 1922.
16. Motry, Rev. Hubert Louis, S.T.D., J.C.D., Diocesan Faculties According to the Code of Canon Law, II-167 pp., 1922.
17. Murphy, Rev. George Lawrence, J.C.D., Delinquencies and Penalties in the Administration and Reception of the Sacrament, IV-121 pp., 1923.
18. O'Reilly, Rev. John Anthony, S.T.B., J.C.D., Ecclesiastical Sepulture in the New Code of Canon Law, II-129 pp., 1923.

19. Michalicka, Rev. Wenceslas Cyrill, O.S.B., J.C.D., Judicial Procedure in Dismissal of Clerical Exempt Religious, 107 pp., 1923.
20. Dargin, Rev. Edward Vincent, S.T.B., J.C.D., Reserved Cases According to the Code of Canon Law, IV–103 pp., 124.
21. Godfrey, Rev. John A., S.T.B., J.C.D., The Right of Patronage According to the Code of Canon Law, 153 pp., 1924.
22. Hagedorn, Rev. Francis Edward, J.C.D., General Legislation on Indulgences, II–154 pp., 1924.
23. King, Rev. James Ignatius, J.C.D., The Administration of the Sacraments to Dying Non-Catholics, V–141 pp., 1924.
24. Winslow, Rev. Francis Joseph, A.F.M., J.C.D., Vicars and Prefects Apostolic, IV–149 pp., 1924.
25. Correa, Rev. Jose Servelion, S.T.D., J.C.D., La Potestad Legislativa de la Iglesia Catolica, IV–127 pp., 1925.
26. Dugan, Rev. Henry Francis, A.M., J.C.D., The Judiciary Department of the Diocesan Curia, 87 pp., 1925.
27. Keller, Rev. Charles Frederick, S.T.B., J.C.D., Mass Stipends, 167 pp., 1925.
28. Paschang, Rev. John Linus, J.C.D., The Sacramentals According to the Code of Canon Law, 129 pp., 1925.
29. Pointek, Rev. Cyrillus, O.F.M., S.T.B., J.C.D., De Indulto Exclaustrationis necnon Saecularizationis, XIII–289 pp., 1925.
30. Kearney, Rev. Richard Joseph, S.T.B., J.C.D., Sponsors at Baptism According to the Code of Canon Law, IV–127 pp., 1925.
31. Bartlett, Rev. Chester Joseph, A.M., LL.B., J.C.D., The Tenure of Parochial Property in the United States of America, V–108 pp., 1926.
32. Kilker, Rev. Adrian Jerome, J.C.D., Extreme Unction, V–425 pp., 1926.
33. McCormick, Rev. Robert Emmett, J.C.D., Confessors of Religious, VIII–266 pp., 1926.
34. Miller, Rev. Newton Thomas, J.C.D., Founded Masses According to the Code of Canon Law, VII–93 pp., 1926.
35. Roelker, Rev. Edward G., S.T.D., J.C.D., Principles of Privilege According to the Code of Canon Law, XI–166 pp., 1926.
36. Bakalarczyk, Rev. Richardus, M.I.C., J.U.D., De Novitiatu, VIII–208 pp., 1927.
37. Pizzuti, Rev. Lawrence, O.F.M., J.U.L., De Parochis Religiosis, 1927. (Not printed.)
38. Bliley, Rev. Nicholas Martin, O.S.B., J.C.D., Altars According to the Code of Canon Law, XIX–132 pp., 1927.
39. Brown, Mr. Brendan Francis, A.B., LL.M., J.U.D., The Canonical Juristic Personality with Special Reference to Its Status in the United States of America, V–212 pp., 1927.
40. Cavanaugh, Rev. William Thomas, C.P., J.U.D., The Reservation of the Blessed Sacrament, VIII–101 pp., 1927.

41. Doheny, Rev. William J., C.S.C., A.B., J.U.D., Church Property: Modes of Acquisition, X–118 pp., 1927.
42. Feldhaus, Rev. Aloysius H., C.PP.S., J.C.D., Oratories, IX–141 pp., 1927.
43. Kelly, Rev. James Patrick, A.B., J.C.D., The Jurisdiction of the Simple Confessor, X–208 pp., 1927.
44. Neuberger, Rev. Nicholas J., J.C.D., Canon 6 or the Relation of the Codex Juris Canonici to the Preceding Legislation, V–95 pp., 1927.
45. O'Keefe, Rev. Gerald Michael, J.C.D., Matrimonial Dispensations, Powers of Bishops, Priests and Confessors, VIII–232 pp., 1927.
46. Quigley, Rev. Joseph, A.M., A.B., J.C.B., Condemned Societies, 139 pp., 1927.
47. Zaplotnik, Rev. Johannes Leo, J.C.D., De Vicariis Foraneis, X–142 pp., 1927.
48. Duskie, Rev. John Aloysius, A.B., J.C.D., The Canonical Status of the Orientals in the United States, VIII–196 pp., 1928.
49. Hyland, Rev. Francis Edward, J.C.D., Excommunication, Its Nature, Historical Development and Effects, VIII–181 pp., 1928.
50. Reinmann, Rev. Gerald Joseph, O.M.C., J.C.D., The Third Order Secular of Saint Francis, 201 pp., 1928.
51. Schenk, Rev. Francis J., J.C.D., The Matrimonial Impediments of Mixed Religion and Disparity of Cult, XVI–318 pp., 1929.
52. Coady, Rev. John Joseph, S.T.D., J.U.D., A.M., The Appointment of Pastors, VII–150 pp., 1929.
53. Kay, Rev. Thomas Henry, J.C.D., Competence in Matrimonial Procedure, VIII–164 pp., 1929.
54. Turner, Rev. Sidney Joseph, C.P., J.U.D., The Vow of Poverty, XLIX–217 pp., 1929.
55. Kearney, Rev. Raymond A., A.B., S.T.D., J.C.D., The Principles of Delegation, VII–149 pp., 1929.
56. Conran, Rev. Edward James, A.B., J.C.D., The Interdict, V–163 pp., 1930.
57. O'Neil, Rev. William H., J.C.D., Papal Rescripts of Favor, VII–218 pp., 1930.
58. Bastnagel, Rev. Clement Vincent, J.U.D., The Appointment of Parochial Adjutants and Assistants, XV–257 pp., 1930.
59. Ferry, Rev. William A., A.B., J.C.D., Stole Fees, V–135 pp., 1930.
60. Costello, Rev. John Michael, A.B., J.C.D., Domicile and Quasi-domicile, VII–201 pp., 1930.
61. Kremer, Rev. Michael Nicholas, A.B., S.T.B., J.C.D., Church Support in the United States, VI–1930.
62. Angulo, Rev. Luis, C.M., J.C.D., Legislation de la Inglesia sobre la intencion en la application de la Santa Misa, VII–104 pp., 1931.
63. Frey, Rev. Wolfgang Norbert, O.S.B., A.B., J.C.D., The Act of Religious Profession, VIII–174 pp., 1931.
64. Roberts, Rev. James Brendan, A.B., J.C.D., The Banns of Marriage, XIV–140 pp., 1931.

65. Ryder, Rev. Raymond Aloysius, A.B., J.C.D., Simony, IX–151 pp., 1931.
66. Campagna, Rev. Angelo, Ph.D., J.U.D., Il Vicario Generale del Vescovo, VII–205 pp., 1931.
67. Cox, Rev. Joseph Godfrey, A.B., J.C.D., The Administration of Seminaries, VI–124 pp., 1931.
68. Gregory, Rev. Donald J., J.U.D., The Pauline Privilege, XV–165 pp., 1931.
69. Donohue, Rev. John F., J.C.D., The Impediment of Crime, VII–110 pp., 1931.
70. Dooley, Rev. Eugene A., O.M.I., J.C.D., Church Law on Sacred Relics, IX–143 pp., 1931.
71. Orth, Rev. Raymond Clement, O.M.C., J.C.D., The Approbation of Religious Institutes, 171 pp., 1931.
72. Pernicone, Rev. Joseph M., A.B., J.C.D., The Ecclesiastical Prohibition of Books, XII–267 pp., 1932.
73. Clinton, Rev. Connell, A.B., J.C.D., The Paschal Precept, IX–108 pp., 1932.
74. Donnelly, Rev. Francis B., A.M., S.T.L., J.C.D., The Diocesan Synod, VIII–125 pp., 1932.
75. Torrente, Rev. Camilo, C.M.F., J.C.D., Las Processiones Sagradas, V–145 pp., 1932.
76. Murphy, Rev. Edwin J., C.PP.S., J.C.D., Suspension Ex Informata Conscientia, XI–122 pp., 1932.
77. Mackenzie, Rev. Eric F., A.M., S.T.L., J.C.D., The Delict of Heresy in Its Commission, Penalization, Absolution, VII–124 pp., 1932.
78. Lyons, Rev. Avitus E., S.T.B., J.C.D., The Collegiate Tribunal of First Instance, XI–147 pp., 1932.
79. Connolly, Rev. Thomas A., J.C.D., Appeals, XI–195 pp., 1932.
80. Sangmeister, Rev. Joseph V., A.B., J.C.D., Force and Fear as Precluding Matrimonial Consent, V–211 pp., 1932.
81. Jaeger, Rev. Leo A., A.B., J.C.D., The Administration of Vacant and Quasi-vacant Episcopal Sees in the United States, IX–229 pp., 1932.
82. Rimlinger, Rev. Herbert T., J.C.D., Error Invalidating Matrimonial Consent, VII–79 pp., 1932.
83. Barrett, Rev. John, D.M., S.S., J.C.D., A Comparative Study of the Third Plenary Council of Baltimore and the Code, IX–221 pp., 1932.
84. Carberry, Rev. John J., Ph.D., S.T.D., J.C.D., The Juridical Form of Marriage, X–177 pp., 1934.
85. Dolan, Rev. John L., A.B., J.C.D., The Defensor Vinculi, XII–157 pp., 1934.
86. Hannan, Rev. Jerome D., A.M., S.T.D., LL.B., J.C.D., The Canon Law of Wills, IX–517 pp., 1934.
87. Lemieux, Rev. Delisle A., A.M., J.C.D., The Sentence in Ecclesiastical Procedure, IX–131 pp., 1934.
88. O'Rourke, Rev. James J., A.B., J.C.D., Parish Registers, VII–109 pp., 1934.

89. Timlin, Rev. Bartholomew, O.F.M., A.M., J.C.D., Conditional Matrimonial Consent, X–381 pp., 1934.
90. Wahl, Rev. Francis X., A.B., J.C.D., The Matrimonial Impediments of Consanguinity and Affinity, VI–125 pp., 1934.
91. White, Rev. Robert J., A.B., LL.B., S.T.B., J.C.D., Canonical Ante-Nuptial Promises and the Civil Law, VI–152 pp., 1934.
92. Herrera, Rev. Antonio Parra, O.C.D., J.C.D., Legislation Ecclesiastica sobra el Ayuno y la Abstinencia, XI–191 pp., 1935.
93. Kennedy, Rev. Edwin J., J.C.D., The Special Matrimonial Process in Cases of Evident Nullity, X–165 pp., 1935.
94. Manning, Rev. John J., A.B., J.C.D., Presumption of Law in Matrimonial Procedure, XI–111 pp., 1935.
95. Moeder, Rev. John M., J.C.D., The Proper Bishop for Ordination and Dismissorial Letters, VII–135 pp., 1935.
96. O'Mara, Rev. William A., A.B., J.C.D., Canonical Causes for Matrimonial Dispensations, IX–155 pp., 1935.
97. Reilly, Rev. Peter, J.C.D., Residence of Pastors, IX–81 pp., 1935.
98. Smith, Rev. Mariner T., O.P., S.T.L., J.C.D., The Penal Law for Religious, VII–169 pp., 1935.
99. Whalen, Rev. Donald W., A.M., J.C.D., The Value of Testimonial Evidence in Matrimonial Procedure, XII–297 pp., 1935.
100. Cleary, Rev. Joseph F., J.C.D., Canonical Limitations on the Alienation of Church Property, VIII–141 pp., 1936.
101. Glynn, Rev. John C., J.C.D., The Promoter of Justice, XX–337 pp., 1936.
102. Brennan, Rev. James H., S.S., A.M., S.T.B., J.C.D., The Simple Convalidation of Marriage, VI–135 pp., 1937.
103. Brunini, Rev. Joseph Bernard, J.C.D., The Clerical Obligations of Canons 139 and 142, X–121 pp., 1937.
104. Connor, Rev. Maurice, A.B., J.C.D., The Administrative Removal of Pastors, VIII–159 pp., 1937.
105. Guilfoyle, Rev. Merlin Joseph, J.C.D., Custom, XI–144 pp., 1937.
106. Hughes, Rev. James Austin, A.B., A.M., J.C.D., Witnesses in Criminal Trials of Clerics, IX–140 pp., 1937.
107. Jansen, Rev. Raymond J., A.B., S.T.L., J.C.D., Canonical Provisions for Catechetical Instruction, VII–153 pp., 1937.
108. Kealy, Rev. John James, A.B., J.C.D., The Introductory Libellus in Church Court Procedure, XI–121 pp., 1937.
109. McManus, Rev. James Edward, C.SS.R., J.C.D., The Administration of Temporal Goods in Religious Institutes, XVI–196 pp., 1937.
110. Moriarity, Rev. Eugene James, J.C.D., Oaths in Ecclesiastical Courts, X–115 pp., 1937.
111. Rainer, Rev. Eligius George, C.SS.R., J.C.D., Suspension of Clerics, XVII–249 pp., 1937.
112. Reilly, Rev. Thomas F., C.SS.R., J.C.D., Visitation of Religious, VI–195 pp., 1938.

113. Moriarty, Rev. Francis E., C.SS.R., J.C.D., The Extraordinary Absolution from Censures, XV–334 pp., 1938.

114. Connolly, Rev. Nicholas P., J.C.D., The Canonical Erection of Parishes, X–132 pp., 1938.

115. Donovan, Rev. James Joseph, J.C.D., The Pastor's Obligation in Prenuptial Investigation, XII–322 pp., 1938.

116. Harrigan, Rev. Robert J., M.A., S.T.B., J.C.D., The Radical Sanation of Invalid Marriages, VIII–208 pp., 1938.

117. Boffa, Rev. Conrad Humbert, J.C.D., Canonical Provisions for Catholic Schools, X–211 pp., 1939.

118. Parsons, Rev. Anscar John, O.M. Cap., J.C.D., Canonical Elections, XII–236 pp., 1939.

119. Reilly, Rev. Edward Michael, A.B., J.C.D., The General Norms of Dispensation, X–156 pp., 1939.

120. Ryan, Rev. Gerald Aloysius, A.B., J.C.D., Principles of Episcopal Jurisdiction, XII–172 pp., 1939.

121. Burton, Rev. Francis James, C.S.C., A.B., J.C.D., A Commentary on Canon 1125, X–222 pp., 1940.

122. Miaskiewicz, Rev. Francis Sigismund, J.C.D., Supplied Jurisdiction According to Canon 209, XII–340 pp., 1940.

123. Rice, Rev. Patrick William, A.B., J.C.D., Proof of Death in Prenuptial Investigation, VIII–156 pp., 1940.

124. Anglin, Rev. Thomas Francis, M.S., J.C.D., The Eucharistic Fast, VIII–183 pp., 1941.

125. Coleman, Rev. John Jerome, J.C.L., The Minister of Confirmation, VI–153 pp., 1941.

126. Downs, Rev. John Emmanuel, A.B., J.C.D., The Concept of Clerical Immunity, XI–163 pp., 1941.

127. Esswein, Rev. Anthony Albert, J.C.D., Extrajudicial Penal Powers of Ecclesiastical Superiors, X–144 pp., 1941.

128. Farrel, Rev. Benjamin Francis, M.A., S.T.L., J.C.D., The Rights and Duties of the Local Ordinary Regarding Congregations of Women Religious of Pontifical Approval, V–195 pp., 1941.

129. Feeney, Rev. Thomas John, A.B., S.T.L., J.C.D., Restitutio in Integrum, VI–169 pp., 1941.

130. Findlay, Rev. Stephen William, O.S.B., A.B., J.C.D., Canonical Norms Governing the Deposition and Degradation of Clerics, XVII–279 pp., 1941.

131. Goodwine, Rev. John, A.B., S.T.L., J.C.L., The Right of the Church to Acquire Property, VIII–119 pp., 1941.

132. Heston, Rev. Edward Louis, C.S.C., Ph.D., S.T.D., J.C.D., The Alienation of Church Property in the United States, XII–222 pp., 1941.

133. Hogan, Rev. James John, S.T.L., J.C.D., Judicial Advocates and Procurators, VIII–200 pp., 1941.

134. Kealy, Rev. Thomas M., A.B., Litt. B., J.C.D., Dowry of Women Religious, IX–152 pp., 1941.

135. Keene, Rev. Michael James, O.S.B., J.C.D., Religious Ordinaries and Canon 198, 1941.
136. Kerin, Rev. Charles A., S.S., M.A., S.T.B., J.C.D., The Privation of Christian Burial, XVI–279 pp., 1941.
137. Louis, Rev. William Francis, M.A., J.C.D., Diocesan Archives, X–109 pp., 1941.
138. McDevitt, Rev. Gilbert Joseph, A.B., J.C.D., Legitimacy and Legitimation, X–247 pp., 1941.
139. McDonough, Rev. Thomas Joseph, A.B., J.C.D., Apostolic Administrators, X–217 pp., 1941.
140. Meier, Rev. Carl Anthony, A.B., J.C.D., Penal Administrative Procedure Against Negligent Pastors, XI–240 pp., 1941.
141. Schmidt, Rev. John Rogg, A.B., J.C.D., The Principles of Authentic Interpretation in Canon 17 of the Code of Canon Law, XII–331 pp., 1941.
142. Slafkosky, Rev. Andrew Leonard, A.B., J.C.D., The Canonical Episcopal Visitation of the Diocese, X–197 pp., 1941.
143. Swoboda, Rev. Innocent Robert, O.F.M., J.C.D., Ignorance in Relation to the Imputability of Delicts, IX–271 pp., 1941.
144. Dubé, Rev. Arthur Joseph, A.B., J.C.D., The General Principles for the Reckoning of Time in Canon Law, VIII–299 pp., 1941.
145. McBride, Rev. James T., A.B., J.C.D., Incardination and Excardination of Seculars, XX–585 pp., 1941.
146. Król, Rev. John J., J.C.L., The Defendant in Contentious Trials.
147. Comyns, Rev. Joseph J., C.SS.R., J.C.L., The Papal and Episcopal Administration of Church Property.
148. Barry, Rev. Garrett Francis, O.M.I., J.C.L., Violation of the Cloister.
149. Bolduc, Rev. Gatien, C.S.V., A.B., S.T.L., J.C.L., Les études dans les religions cléricales.
150. Boyle, Rev. David John, M.A., J.C.L., The Juridic Effects of Moral Certitude on Pre-Nuptial Guarantees.
151. Canavan, Rev. Walter Joseph, M.A., Litt.D., J.C.L., Profession of Faith.
152. Desrochers, Rev. Bruno, A.B., Ph.L., S.T.B., J.C.L., Le Premier Concile Plénier de Québec et le Code de Droit Canonique.
153. Dillon, Rev. Robert Edward, A.B., J.C.L., Common Law Marriage.
154. Dodwell, Rev. Edward John, Ph.D., S.T.B., J.C.L., The Time and Place for the Celebration of Marriage.
155. Donnellan, Rev. Thomas Andrew, A.B., J.C.L., The Obligation of the Missa pro Populo.
156. Eltz, Rev. Louis Anthony, A.B., J.C.L., Co-operation in Crime.
157. Gass, Rev. Sylvester Francis, M.A., J.C.L., Ecclesiastical Pensions.
158. Guiniven, Rev. John Joseph, C.SS.R., J.C.L., The Precept of Hearing Mass on Sundays and Holy Days of Obligation.
159. Gulczynski, Rev. John Theophilus, J.C.L., The Desecration and Violation of Churches.

160. Hammill, Rev. John Leo, M.A., J.C.L., The Obligations of the Traveler According to Canon 14.
161. Haydt, Rev. John Joseph, A.B., J.C.L., Reserved Benefices.
162. Huser, Rev. Roger John, O.F.M., A.B., J.C.L., The Crime of Abortion in Canon Law.
163. Kearney, Rev. Francis Patrick, A.B., S.T.L., J.C.L., The Principles of Canon 1127.
164. Linahen, Rev. Leo James, S.T.L., J.C.L., De Absolutione Complicis in Peccato Turpi.
165. McCloskey, Rev. Joseph Aloysius, A.B., J.C.L., The Subject of Ecclesiastical Law according to Canon 12.
166. O'Neill, Rev. Francis Joseph, C.SS.R., J.C.L., The Dismissal of Religious in Temporary Vows.
167. Prince, Rev. John Edward, A.B., S.T.B., J.C.L., The Diocesan Chancellor.
168. Riesner, Rev. Albert Joseph, C.SS.R., J.C.L., Apostates and Fugitives from Religious Institutes.
169. Stenger, Rev. Joseph Bernard, J.C.L., The Mortgaging of Church Property.
170. Waldron, Rev. Joseph Francis, A.B., J.C.L., The Minister of Baptism.
171. Willett, Rev. Robert Albert, J.C.L., The Probative Value of Documents in Ecclesiastical Trials.
172. Woeber, Rev. Edward Martin, M.A., J.C.L., The Interpellations.

www.ingramcontent.com/pod-product-compliance
Lightning Source LLC
LaVergne TN
LVHW050233080826
844660LV00012B/522

* 9 7 8 0 8 1 3 2 2 3 5 8 2 *